The impulse behind the making of this book was the editors' desire to offer some critical appreciation of a literary genre that has often been read, praised, edited, and studied but seldom examined as a work of art. Naturally, they hoped that their exploratory efforts will tempt others to deal further with the problems raised here.

To think of Cicero or of the younger Pliny is to be reminded that the familiar letter has a long history, but with the eighteenth century the genre came into its own. In an atmosphere more leisurely than ours, the growth of an efficient postal service and the stimulus of a prose tradition conducive to informality, to say nothing of the examples of classical and Continental models and other sources of inspiration, contributed to the development of a form that flourished at a time when literature was especially sensitive to social influences. Indeed correspondents were aware of the kinship between good letters and good conversation, knowing, too, that spontaneity and seeming artlessness may be the creation of a highly sophisticated art.

Variety in letters may result from the circumstances in which the authors write. "We should do well to remember," Herbert Davis declares in an introductory paper, "that they were written in many different moods for various purposes. Letters could be used to threaten or cajole, to deceive as well as to tell the truth; and the authors were perhaps above all inclined to indulge in letter-writing in order to divert and amuse one another, and to provide entertainment and fun."

THE FAMILIAR LETTER
IN THE EIGHTEENTH CENTURY

The Familiar Letter in the Eighteenth Century

Edited by

Howard Anderson
Philip B. Daghlian
Irvin Ehrenpreis

University of Kansas Press
Lawrence, 1966

Preface

This book is an outgrowth of a conference on eighteenth-century letter-writers held at Indiana University in April, 1964, when the papers by Professors Davis, Free, Halsband, and Zirker were originally delivered. Under the devoted guidance of Professor Irvin Ehrenpreis (whose initials are not subscribed to this preface) the idea of inviting additional essays developed into the present volume.

Since each contributor has quoted from the best available text of his author's letters, and since editorial practices vary, the reader will encounter unusual spellings and punctuation in quotations. What he reads is an accurate transcript of an authentic text.

Specific acknowledgments occur in notes to individual essays, but we wish to express thanks to the University of Toronto Press and to *PMLA* for permission to reprint here the papers by Professors Davis and Halsband respectively. We also thank the McGraw-Hill Book Company and the Editorial Committee of the Yale Boswell for permission to print the quotations in Professor Reiberg's essay.

We are grateful to Mrs. David Brower and the Joint Office of Research, Contracts, and Grants at Indiana University, the one for preparing the index, and the other for supplying a grant in aid to make her labors possible. We have a particular debt to Clyde K. Hyder and his assistants of the University of Kansas Press, whose meticulous editing has made this book decidedly superior to the version originally submitted.

Bloomington, Indiana   H.A.
June, 1966   P.B.D.

Contents

THE CORRESPONDENCE OF
THE AUGUSTANS

HERBERT DAVIS

IT IS ONLY as the result of the intensive search for papers
and documents which has been going on for the last fifty years
that the full extent and variety of the private correspondence
of the Augustans have been revealed; and when we look at the
most recent editions of their correspondence we find that many
of the letters written by them or addressed to them are still
missing and have probably been lost. Nevertheless we can now
observe the characteristics of this art of letter-writing as practised by the eminent men of the age, poets and wits and
churchmen and politicians, and by the varied circle of their
friends and patrons and acquaintances—ministers and courtiers, duchesses who could not spell, bluestockings and learned
citizens'-wives, country gentlemen and parsons. We can more-
over read many of these letters, printed from the original autographs, exactly as they came into the hands of their first recipients, unrevised and uncorrected; we can read such replies as
are available; we can compare letters sent out to very different
sorts of correspondents on the same dates, sometimes with
echoes or repetitions, sometimes with modifications or even
contradictions. We can obtain from the whole correspondence
of a writer's lifetime a many-faceted vision of his personality as
its different surfaces are presented to those around him, first

1

somewhat veiled, to those of an older generation, then shining more brilliantly in the midst of a larger circle of contemporaries, and later glowing with a softer radiance as these give way to a younger generation offering homage or seeking patronage.

For a biographer there can hardly be any documents more reliable, more valuable, and more essential than the whole corpus of a writer's correspondence, once the full texts are available; if it is properly used, not to afford carefully selected illustrations for some preconceived judgment, but to provide in its entirety the detailed evidence of many different witnesses to check our hasty impressions and to prevent us from misinterpreting things that were said in a certain way for a particular person at a particular moment. It is this which gives its unique character to the personal letter, and distinguishes it from other forms of familiar writing. A letter has an address and a date; it is written for a certain recipient, and may often be concerned with matters of a particular time. If it is one of a series of letters to the same correspondent, it may be affected by a sort of momentum given by their previous interchange. Its style is conditioned by these facts, and also by many other considerations present in the mind of the writer as he begins to write.

There was always the danger, perhaps greater for Pope than for the others, of being disturbed by the consciousness that anything he wrote might be preserved for a witness against him. And this I believe is liable too often to spoil the quality of his letters. It was this that disturbed Dr. Johnson and led him in his Life of Pope to the utterance of that magnificent warning about the temptations that beset a man when he sits down to write a personal letter to a friend: "There is indeed no transaction which offers stronger temptation to fallacy and sophistication than epistolary intercourse. A friendly letter is a calm and deliberate performance in the cool of leisure, in the stillness of solitude, and surely no man sits down to depreciate by design his own character."

2

Arbuthnot and Gay are less often affected. They do not write carelessly, but always their principal concern is with the person they are addressing. It is wise to remember, when we read Arbuthnot's letters to Swift, that the two men share the same delight in irony. They address one another in a way they know very well each will understand. Apart from this there is an extreme directness and sincerity between them; there can be no doubt of the complete understanding they maintained during their five and twenty years' acquaintance. Arbuthnot seems to have been a person valued by his friends without any reservations at all. He was enjoyed as a delightful companion and respected as a man of character and integrity. Perhaps as a mere amateur in letters, with an unchallenged reputation in his own profession, he never aroused any feelings of jealousy. He could write with a rare warmth and depth of affection, as in his reply to Swift's letter of farewell at the time of the death of Queen Anne: "Dear Freind the last sentence of your letter quite kills me: never repeat that melancholy tender word that you will endeavour to forgett me. I am sure I never can forgett yow, till I meett with, (what is impossible) another whose conversation I can so much delight in as Dr Swifts & yet that is the smallest thing I ought to value you for. That hearty sincere freindship That plain and open ingenuity in all your commerce, is what I am sure I can never find in another alas. I shall want often, a faithfull monitor one that would vindicate me behind my back & tell me my faults to my face. god knows I write this with tears in my eyes."[1] It is very different from the tone of the letter which Ford took to Swift in Dublin in the summer of 1716 where Pope plays upon the idea that a friend in Ireland is like a friend in another world, "whom (popishly speaking) I believe constantly well-disposed towards me, and ready to do me all the good he can. . . . A protestant divine cannot take it amiss that I treat him in the same manner with my patron Saint" (II, 211). Swift of course does not miss the chance to make good use of such an opening: "You are an ill Catholick, or a worse Geographer, for I can assure you, Ireland is not Paradise, and I appeal even to any Spanish divine, whether addresses were ever made to a friend in Hell, or Purgatory." He lives in fact in an obscure scene of which Pope would know nothing, and so has nothing to write about—except a Quaker poet in Dublin, and the thought that had come to him that Gay might try a set of Quaker-pastorals. This form of ridicule, he feels, is not exhausted and he tosses off another suggestion, which may have led to *The Beggar's Opera:* "Or what think you of a Newgate pastoral, among the whores and thieves there?" (II, 214-215).

Gay, in his letters to Swift, takes upon him the duty of sending news and gossip about his friends; he says little about himself, except perhaps to promise that he is following Swift's advice to revise his work and finish it as well as he can. He writes always without pretensions and without malice or guile. Only we may feel sometimes when he is writing to Swift that he allows himself little asides which he knows will be rightly understood and relished. Swift is always admonishing him about the care of his money, and hopes he will soon be rich enough to have some little place of his own, either in town or in the country. He replies that he is afraid of getting into debt: "I cannot bear to pawn five pounds worth of my liberty to a Taylor or a Butcher; I grant you this is not having the true spirit of modern Nobility, but tis hard to cure the prejudice of education." As to more writing, he hesitates from fear of incurring the displeasure of his superiors—"for I cannot for my life think so well of them as they themselves think they deserve" (III, 384-385).

The best of these letters between Pope and Swift and Arbuthnot and Gay are those which follow Swift's memorable visit to London in 1726, when he left behind the manuscript of *Gulliver's Travels* to be printed. His visit had renewed his ties with his old friends; and the correspondence that followed has inevitably the quality of a conversation that is being continued after having gone on merrily all through the months they had spent together. We even find Swift reminding them that when they were together he could never get in a word, because of the stream of talk from Pope and Gay. This sounds a little unlikely, but it gives him an excuse to have his say now that he has a pen in hand. He had provided them with plenty to talk about, and they are joined by others of his acquaintance, all in their several ways under the spell of the creator of Lemuel Gulliver. He complains that he could not understand their strange talk at all until a bookseller happened to send him a book of Travels, two volumes of 700 pages, which he was forced to read through in order to be able to interpret a few lines in their letters. These letters began to arrive in November 1726 and were soon followed by others from Mrs. Howard, the Earl of Peterborough, and Lady Bolingbroke; and there was talk of others, either lost or intercepted. He was delighted to hear from Peterborough, who had described the "strange distempers [that] rage in this nation," said to have been "brought about by the black Art, and by the spells of a notorious, scribbling Magitian, . . . [who had appeared] in severall shapes—att one time a Drappier, att another a Wapping Surgeon, sometimes a Nardac, sometimes a Reverend Divine" (III, 191-192). And Mrs. Howard, who had signed herself "Sieve Yahoo" in her letter of November 17, received a suitable reply from the Dean, from Dublin and dated November 27, and also an acknowledgment from Lemuel Gulliver, written from Newark on the next day, asking her to reconcile him "to the Maids of Honour whom they say I have most grievously offended" and begging leave "to lay the crown of Lilliput at your feet, as a small acknowledgment of your favours to my book & person" (III, 190). Only Bolingbroke, according to Gay, was inclined to "blame the book as a design of evil consequence to depreciate human nature." But he too wrote to Swift early in 1727, warning him not to break his engagement with them to spend the next summer between Dawley and Twickenham: "What matter if you are deaf, what matter if you cannot hear what we say? you are not dumb, & we shall hear you, and that is enough" (III, 200).

Shortly after this Pope wrote to report that their joint *Miscellanies* were printed off (though the two volumes did not appear until June) and speaks of them in terms which might well be used to describe their correspondence: "I am prodigiously pleas'd with this joint-volume, in which methinks we look like friends, side by side, serious and merry by turns, conversing interchangeably, and walking down hand in hand to posterity; not in the stiff forms of learned Authors, flattering each other, and setting the rest of mankind at nought: but in a free, un-important, natural, easy manner; diverting others just as we diverted our selves" (III, 201). That was certainly the kind of impression he wished to give when he arranged some twelve years later to gather together a selection of letters written by them and their friends between the years 1714 and 1738. This selection has since been added to in some rather striking ways, and we are now provided with a great variety of splendid examples of the varied purposes and methods of the epistolary art of the Augustans.

First, there are the letters to Swift from a group of ladies, like Lady Elizabeth Germaine, Lady Carteret and her mother Lady Worsley, Mrs. Howard (later the Countess of Suffolk), the Duchess of Queensberry, Martha Blount, and Esther Vanhomrigh, which give us an opportunity of comparing the quality of their writing with that of their correspondents, the poets and men of letters. We may hesitate to treat as a mere compliment Swift's own remark about the excellence of Esther Vanhomrigh's letters—"which I never look into without wondering how a Brat who cannot read, can possibly write so well" (II, 335-336). She can put things to him so shrewdly: "Tell me did those curcumstances crowd on you or did you recolect them only to make me happy?" She can write in a way that could not but have rent his heart: "With the utmost distress and confusion I behold my self the cause of uneasie reflections to you yet I can not comfort you but here declair that tis not in the power of arte time or accident to lessen the unexpressible passion which I have for — — . . . don't flatter your self that separation will ever change my sentiments for I find my self unquiet in the midst of silence and my heart is at once pierced with sorrow and love" (II, 363). Even set down awkwardly in print with their curious spellings and entire absence of punctuation, the letters fully justify Swift's astonishment and explain the hold this fascinating and passionate creature continued through so many years to have upon him. His replies to her are often awkward and sometimes difficult by reason of his restraint and his fear of giving himself away; but when she complains of his puzzling her with difficult writing, he only threatens to give her more of it.

There is no difficult writing in his letters to Lady Elizabeth Germaine or Mrs. Howard, who perhaps more than any of even his closest friends allowed themselves to amuse him in the same terms which he used to them. If he begins a letter to Mrs. Howard (14 August 1727): "I wish I were a young Lord, and you were unmarryed. I should make you the best husband in the world," she immediately replies: "I did desire you to write me a love letter but I never did desire You to talk of marrying me." And she finishes by giving him orders in the very manner in which he always delighted to demand obedience from the ladies. After giving him that advice which was to cause so much trouble between them later on—not to leave England until she had seen him—she insists that he should let her make a courtier of him: "I have been a Slave twenty years without ever receiving a reason for any one thing I ever was oblig'd to do. and I have now a mind to take the pleasure once in my life of absolute power which I expect you to give me in obeying all my orders without one question why I have given them" (III, 230, 231).

There is nothing quite like this short exchange of letters between them in August 1727—the answers returned almost immediately, the same strokes played on both sides until the short game is finished. The easy terms in which this exchange of letters had been carried on must be remembered when it is resumed three years later. Some of his friends felt that he was

fully refers to as "Dirty Patty," whom he had seen so often when he was staying with Pope during his last visit to Twickenham. And to all this Swift answers very meekly: "She was the onely Girl I coquetted in the whole half year that I lived with Mr. Pope. . . . She was a neighbor's child, a good Catholick, an honest Girl, and a tolerable Courtier at Richmond. I deny she was dirty, but a little careless, and sometimes wore a ragged gown, when she and I took long walks" (IV, 79). And then he turns to thank her for the escritoire she had sent him —the work of her own hands—and indulges in his usual ironies and graceful compliment.

An exchange with the Duchess of Queensberry, who had never met him, and only began a correspondence with him through their friend Gay, reminds us of another point we should bear in mind when we are considering the truthfulness of statements that we may find in letters and the weight of authority that such statements should be given. Swift admits that in a letter to Pope he had mentioned good qualities which she seemed to have; but after all he had never even had a glimpse of her since she was a girl, and her letters might be "false copies of her mind." She quickly tosses this back to him, as if their letters were a pleasant conversation: "I denie I am touchy, yet am going to seem so again by assuring you my letters are never false copies of my mind, . . . tho I will not take upon me to declare my way of thinking to be eternally the same Yett whatever I write is at that instant true" (IV, 141). We must allow for imperfect copies of what is in the mind of the writer, and recognize also that views and opinions, however emphatically stated, may possibly be only "at that instant true."

Such forms of the epistolary art as these—sometimes including the sort of irony which Swift claimed to have introduced among his friends—are naturally limited for use among a group of people who through conversation have become familiar with one another's habits of mind and play of humor; they assume a considerable freedom and ease and informality. But the epistolary art must also provide very different forms from these, such as are required between strangers, or on more formal occasions. One which was much in use at this period was the letter of solicitation, written to a patron to obtain a place for oneself or for a friend; and equally necessary, a form which the patron might use in his reply. In Swift's correspondence there are some excellent examples, from the early letter of Sir William Temple recommending his young secretary Swift for a place with Sir Robert Southwell, to the many letters written by the Dean of St. Patrick's on behalf of his friends to various Lord Lieutenants from Carteret to Chesterfield. Hidden beneath the necessary formality are a variety of different tones, nicely calculated to fit the tastes of the recipient. With Carteret he is on such friendly terms, and has such respect for his integrity and his intelligence, that he can risk using all his powers of humor and raillery. With Chesterfield he is more cautious, permitting himself only a slight touch of playfulness, so that his irony is not too obvious; and the interchange of letters shows that there is a possibility of an adequate understanding between them, and a sort of courtier-like elegance is maintained. He adopts a different manner—"a style very different from what I use to my friends with titles"—in asking the Duke of Chandos to present to Ireland the ancient records relating to that kingdom which were in his possession; and Swift is very angry when all his civilities and compliments on the fame of the Duke's generosity meet with no response.

There is one other kind of letter at which we might expect Swift, with his powers of satire and invective, to excel—the letter in which the intention is to hurt an opponent or to hurl defiance at an enemy. And he is likely to be at his best when he is addressing his immediate superiors the bishops and archbishops—whenever they have been so ill-advised as to try to assume an authority over him which he refuses to recognize. For in his letters as in his pamphlets he is stirred to exert all his powers, most of all perhaps when he is faced by petty tyranny or authority claiming to assert itself against the laws of God

11

and man. On two occasions Bishop Evans at his visitation of St. Patrick's refused to admit the Dean's proxy, and made personal reflections on the Dean for his absence. On the first occasion Swift was content to remind the Bishop that he had not deserved such treatment, since he had been more than ordinarily officious in his respects to him from the time of his first coming over, though he had nothing to hope or fear from his Lordship. But the second time he took full advantage of the opportunity to express his utter and complete defiance, and to let the Bishop know plainly that in any circumstances he would avoid being present at his visitation: "And by the grace of God, I am still determined to absent myself on the like occasions, as far as I can possibly be dispensed with by any law, while your Lordship is in that diocese and I a member of it" (II, 389). This may seem a very trivial matter, a foolish squabble over ecclesiastical authority; and it was not very different when some years later, while Swift was away on his last visit to England, the Archbishop of Dublin adjourned his visitation until a proxy should be provided for the Dean. But here was a demand for which there was no justification whatever: "It is a thing wholly new and unheard of, let the consequences be what they will, I shall never comply with it. . . . My proceeding shall be only upon one maxim: Never to yield to an oppression, to justify which no precedent can be produced." And an archbishop must be taught to know the difference between servitude and proper obedience: "My Lord, I have lived, and by the grace of God will die, an enemy to servitude and slavery of all kinds: And I believe, at the same time, that persons of such a disposition will be the most ready to pay obedience wherever it is due" (III, 210). This kind of letter is equally conditioned by the character of the person to whom it is addressed. It takes on something of the form of a duel in which the writer is entirely concerned with the necessity of discovering his opponent's weakness, and using this to triumph over him; while at the same time he shows his own perfect mastery and skill.

These letters were first printed by Deane Swift twenty years and more after Swift's death, and the manuscripts have still not been discovered; they were presumably printed from drafts or copies found among Swift's papers. We may be sure that he would have had no objection to appearing before posterity, not merely as Pope would have shown him in the company of a few friends, exchanging pleasantries and compliments, but also as he was in his more formal letters, bargaining with governors and members of the House of Lords on behalf of his friends or in the interests of Ireland, or facing his accusers and defying those who tried to use their authority to break his proud spirit.

Finally, then, in the face of all that heap of letters which survives from the eighteenth century, we should do well to remember that they were written in many different moods and for various purposes. Letters could be used to threaten or cajole, to deceive as well as to tell the truth; and the authors were perhaps above all inclined to indulge in letter-writing in order to divert and amuse one another, to provide entertainment and fun. They were not intentionally setting down records or bringing together the information which we may be looking for to solve our problems, whether we are concerned with historical facts, with the interpretation of works of art, with the understanding of the mind of genius, or with the ordinary complexities of human behavior. It was an art which they naturally looked upon as a continuation of the art of conversation; which for a generation that liked to imagine itself Augustan was the very mark of polite society, possible only among civilized men and women—an art which at its best should be the triumph of wit and humor and imagination.

Oxford University

Jonathan Swift

"NATURE AND FRIENDSHIP": THE PERSONAL LETTERS OF JONATHAN SWIFT

Oliver W. Ferguson

In his biography of Swift, John Boyle, Earl of Orrery, deplored "that license which of late has too much prevailed of publishing epistolary correspondences." What disturbed the Earl was not so much the invasion of privacy itself as the effect such an invasion might come to have on the practice of letter-writing. The fashion of publishing personal letters would, he feared, "tend to restrain that unsuspicious openness, which is the principal delight of writing to our friends." This "unsuspicious openness" Orrery found abundantly displayed in Swift's letters. "I have often heard Swift say," he recalled, " 'When I sit down to write a letter, I never lean upon my elbow, till I have finished it.' "[1] The reminiscence is probably genuine; Swift expressed himself similarly on more than one occasion. In answer to a joint epistle from some of his English friends, he replied to a criticism from Bolingbroke that an earlier letter had been indifferently written: "Is it imagined that I must be always leaning upon one hand while I am writing with the other, always upon the *qui vive* and the slip-slop, instead of an honest plain letter . . . ?" Given the casual syntax of this sentence and the extraordinarily compressed phrase, "upon the *qui vive* and the slip-slop" (which makes sense only with some help from the reader), one is tempted to guess that

14

Swift here defended his epistolary naturalness with an exaggerated indifference. "May I never think again," he continued, "if I think three seconds whenever I write to the best or the worst of you."[2] And some ten years later, he affirmed to Pope his belief that "we neither of us ever leaned our head upon our left hand to study what we should write next ..." (V, 227).

But if Orrery's memory did not play him false, his perceptiveness did (a fact which should surprise no one familiar with his biography of Swift). He supposed that Swift's letters were as uncalculated as they sounded, that Swift "never studied for particular phrases, or polished paragraphs" (p. 176). There are, to be sure, throughout Swift's extensive correspondence, letters that are as close to genuine spontaneity as it is possible for a written communication to be. A great many of the letters to Stella are of this sort, as are even more of those to Charles Ford.[3] These instances notwithstanding, Swift often leaned upon his elbow, sometimes for the most trifling of letters. Here are two excerpts from the *Journal to Stella*:

I . . . came home early, and now am got into bed, for you must always write to your MDs in bed, that's a maxim. Mr. White and Mr. Red, Write to MD when abed; Mr. Black and Mr. Brown, Write to MD when you're down; Mr. Oak and Mr. Willow, Write to MD on your pillow.—What's this? faith I smell fire; what can it be; this house has a thousand s – – ks in it. I think to leave it on Thursday, and lodge over the way. Faith I must rise, and look at my chimney, for the smell grows stronger, stay—I have been up, and in my room, and found all safe, only a mouse within the fender to warm himself, which I could not catch. I smelt nothing there, but now in my bed-chamber I smell it again; I believe I have singed the woolen curtain, and that's all, though I cannot smoak it. Presto's plaguy silly to-night; an't he? Yes, and so he be. Aye, but if I should wake and see fire. Well; I'll venture; so good night, &c. (I, 139)

Lord treasurer has had an ugly return of his gravel. 'Tis good for us to live in gravel pits, but not for gravel pits to live in us: a man in this case should leave no stone unturned. Lord treasurer's sickness, the queen's gout, the forwarding the Peace, occasion putting off the parliament a fortnight longer. My head has had no ill returns. I had good walking to-day in the city, and take all opportunities of it on purpose for my health; but I can't walk in the Park, because that is only for walking sake, and loses time, so I mix it with business: I wish MD walked half as much as Presto. If I was with you, I'd make you walk; I would walk behind or before you, and you should have masks on, and be tucked up like any thing, and Stella is naturally a stout walker, and carries herself firm, methinks I see her strut, and step clever over a kennel; and Dingley would do well enough, if her petticoats were pinned up; but she is so embroiled, and so fearful, and then Stella scolds, and Dingley stumbles, and is so daggled. Have you got the whale-bone petticoats amongst you yet? I hate them; a woman here may hide a moderate gallant under them. Pshaw, what's all this I'm saying? methinks I am talking to MD face to face. (II, 408-409)

These passages are perfect in their air of spontaneity—the first with its vivid sense of immediacy; the second with its helter-skelter organization, held together by the unassailable logic of random association. The naturalness is genuine, but it is not unstudied. Swift certainly did not *polish* these paragraphs; he probably did not study very long for any particular phrases. What he did study was the particular attitude he struck in each, and the tone appropriate to that attitude.

I chose these examples from the *Journal to Stella* (and they are by no means untypical) because this collection of letters reveals Swift in not only his most casual but also his most personal epistolary vein. The letters which Swift wrote to Esther Johnson and Rebecca Dingley were intended for their eyes alone; yet even here Swift frequently leaned—if lightly—upon his elbow. The point is obvious: for Swift, writing a letter was a literary activity. He almost certainly wrote no personal letters that were really intended for publication. The epistles of Voiture and Cicero had entertained him, but he did not choose to follow their example in his own correspondence: "They cease to be letters," he observed to Pope, "when they become a *jeu d'esprit*" (V, 251; IV, 126). Yet we should expect Swift to take pains when he writes to Pope or Bolingbroke or Gay (whether he anticipates eventual publication or not); and we should not be surprised to find even in his letters to less challenging correspondents the signs of art.

The effectiveness of a given letter does not necessarily depend on whether Swift has concealed his art. A letter to Vanessa, written shortly after he had reluctantly left England to become Dean of St. Patrick's, scarcely shows its art—but the art is there, shaping the matter of Swift's discontent so lightly that it succeeds in partially relieving the bitter expression of his feelings:

At my first coming I thought I should have died with discontent, and was horribly melancholy while they were installing me; but it begins to wear off, and change to dulness. My river walk is extremely pretty, and my canal in great beauty, and I see trout playing in it.

I know not anything in Dublin, but Mr. Ford is very kind, and writes to me constantly what passes among you. I find you are likewise a good politician. . . . But I am now fitter to look after willows, and to cut hedges, than to meddle with affairs of state. I must order one of the workmen to drive those cows out of my island, and make up the ditch again; a work much more proper for a country vicar, than driving out factions, and fencing against them. . . .

How does Davila go on? Johnny Clark is chosen portreeve of our town of Trim, and we shall have the assizes there next week, and fine doings, and I must go and borrow a horse to meet the judges, and Joe Beaumont, and all the boys that can get horses will go too. Mr. Warburton has but a thin school. Mr. Percival has built up the other side of his house, but people whisper that it is but scurvily built. Mr. Steers is come to live in Mr. Melthorp's house, and it is thought the widow Melthorp will remove to Dublin. Nay, if you do not like this sort of news, I have no better, so go to your Dukes and Duchesses, and leave me to Goodman Bomford, and Patrick Dollan of Clondoogan.[4]

In contrast, the art of the following excerpt is apparent. Swift is writing to a friend, Mrs. John Pratt, thanking her for her gift of a fire screen, decorated with maps of the world painted on it:

17

Mrs. Fitzmaurice did the unkindest thing she could imagine. She sends an open note by a servant, for she was too much a prude to write me a letter, desiring that the Dean of St. Patrick's should inquire for one Howard, master of a ship, who had brought over a screen to him, the said Dean, from Mrs. Pratt. Away I ran to the Custom House, where they told me the ship was expected every day; but the god of winds, in confederacy with Mrs. Fitzmaurice to tease me, kept the ship at least a month longer, and left me miserable in a state of impatience, between hope and fear, worse than a lady who is in pain that her clothes will not be ready against the birth-day. I will not move your good nature, by representing how many restless nights and days I have passed, with what dreams my sleep hath been disturbed, where I sometimes saw the ship sinking, my screen floating in the sea, and the mermaids struggling which of them should get it for her own apartment. At last Mr. Medlycott . . . gave me notice of its safe arrival . . . and . . . sent my screen to the Deanery, where it was immediately opened, on Tuesday the 16th instant, three minutes seven seconds after four o'clock in the afternoon, the day being fair, but somewhat windy, the sun in Aries, and the moon within thirty-nine hours eight seconds and a half of being full; all which I had, by consulting Ptolemy, found to be fortunate incidents, prognosticating that, with due care, my screen will escape the mops of the housemaid, and the greasy hands of the footmen.

Swift was fond of affecting this style in his letters. The art of this passage, with its exaggerated drama and its pseudo-respect for minutiae, is reminiscent of that of much of the *Journal to Stella*. The letter continues:

At the opening the screen just after dinner, some company of both sexes were present. The ladies were full of malice, and the men of envy, while I remained very affectedly calm. But all agreed, that nothing showed a better judgement, than to know how to make a proper present, and that no present could be more judiciously chosen; for no man in this kingdom wanted a screen so much as myself, and besides, since I had left the world, it was very kind to send the world to me. . . . I know it is as hard to give thanks as to take them, therefore I shall say no more, than that I receive your acceptable present, just as I am sure you desire I should. Though I cannot sit under my own vine, or my own fig-tree, yet I will sit under my own screen, and bless the giver; but I cannot promise it will add one jot to the love or esteem I have for you, because it is impossible for me to be more than I have always been, and shall ever continue, Madam,

Your most obedient and obliged servant. (III, 231-233)

There are times when the art fails either to convince or to delight. An example is the letter of proposal (one hesitates to call it a love letter) to Jane Waring, the first (and least important) of Swift's serious romantic attachments. From the letter, it is clear that Swift had already suggested marriage to "Varina" (he customarily addressed her by this latinized version of her surname) but that she was reluctant to accept his offer. "Madam," Swift begins, "Impatience is the most inseparable quality of a lover, and indeed of every person who is in pursuit of a design whereon he conceives his greatest happiness or misery to depend." With great care and patience, Swift then expands the theme of a lover's impatience into a miniature essay. He urges his suit with equal deliberation and follows with a description of the joys of marriage which is unpersuasive in the extreme. At only one point does the letter flare briefly to life, as Swift exclaims, "I am a villain if I have not been poring this half hour over the paper merely for want of something to say to you" (I, 15-20).

The question of sincerity is not, I think, pertinent in determining what is wrong here; and as a matter of fact, I see no reason to doubt that Swift was being any less sincere in this letter than in the stillborn odes (to Temple, to Sancroft, to William III) he had written shortly before this time. The letter fails, not because it is insincere or because it is rhetorical but because the rhetoric is of the expected kind, lavished on the expected topics, pitched at the expected level. Much of the letter could have been printed verbatim in one of the formularies so popular in the eighteenth century—ready at hand for the impatient, ardent, and inarticulate lover to copy out and send to his own Varina. The letter to Mrs. Pratt, on the other hand, would have been the most unhelpful of models in the same handbook; the student could no more apply it to his individual needs than he could apply to his own problems of composition Swift's definition of style: "Proper words in proper places."

Some others of the letters, like the one to Varina, fail to come off, but the number is remarkably small. In reading the six-volume *Correspondence,* the *Letters to Ford,* and the two volumes of the *Journal to Stella,* one is impressed by how successfully Swift passes the severe test of having the most personal of his writings subjected to a critical examination.

The letters make excellent reading. Swift's friends might well have applied to them the witty compliment he once made to Lord Bathurst: "When I receive a letter from you, I summon a few very particular friends, who have a good taste, and invite them to it, as I would do if you had sent me a haunch of venison" (V, 253). One can single out for special praise their wit and clarity, their conciseness, their force. But the outstanding quality is their air of complete assurance. Whether Swift is writing to a curate or an archbishop, whether he is soliciting a favor from a man in power or correcting Stella's spelling, whether he is praising the virtues of a friend or telling the villainies of a knave, the letter is exactly and inevitably right. This ability to communicate his supreme confidence in his power to put proper words in proper places is the abiding characteristic of Swift's prose; and it is the one constant point of resemblance between the letters and the formal literary works.

In this connection it should be noted that Swift's epistolary pamphlets do not, as a class, stand in any special relation to his correspondence. His productions in this genre are fairly numerous and include such varied examples as *A Letter to a Young Lady, on her Marriage* (a public letter to a real person), *A Letter to a Young Gentleman, Lately enter'd into Holy Orders* (a public letter to a fictitious person), and *The Drapier's Letters* (a series of pseudonymous public letters variously addressed to Irish individuals and classes). All are tracts of instruction or propaganda. Most have nothing of the epistolary about them beyond a salutation and a complimentary close. Naturally, they occasionally contain attitudes or stylistic features found in Swift's personal letters but in no greater degree than might a pamphlet not written in epistolary form. For example, the Drapier's narrative skill is sometimes like Swift's. Replying to Walpole's threat to force the Irish to swallow Wood's halfpence in fireballs, the Drapier is reminded of "the known Story of a *Scotch* Man, who receiving Sentence of Death, with all the Circumstances of *Hanging, Beheading, Quartering, Embowelling,* and the like; cried out, *What need all this* COOKERY?"[5] This anecdote would not seem out of place in one of Swift's letters; it is altogether in his manner. But, then, Swift's anecdotal manner is like that of the "Author" of *A Tale of a Tub,* whose story of the fat man in Leicester Fields Sheridan called a classic of its kind.[6]

So it is with the *Letter to a Young Gentleman* and the *Letter to a Young Lady,* instructional pamphlets, respectively, on the proper conduct for a clergyman and a wife. The *Letter to a Young Gentleman* no more resembles Swift's personal letters than does his *Project for the Advancement of Religion,* a tract addressed to the Countess of Berkeley. Rather, the resemblance is between the *Letter* and the *Project;* several passages from the latter would be perfectly appropriate—in style as well as content—in the *Letter to a Young Gentleman.*[7] *A Letter to a Young Lady* is reminiscent of the notorious letter to Varina in which Swift stipulated the conditions she must agree to if she wished to become his wife. In each letter—the public and the private—Swift enjoins the lady in question to improve her mind and suffer herself to be guided by her husband; in each he pays particular attention to the "tender" subject of personal cleanliness; in each he is strikingly lacking in warmth. In fact, the public letter, *because* it is less personal, does not have the chilling tone of the letter to Varina. That the two are so similar is evidence not that the *Letter to a Young Lady* is—despite its having been written for publication—a genuinely personal letter, but that Swift had, when he wrote the letter to Varina, effectively rid himself of his earlier passion for her.[8]

It is more instructive to see how a trait common to Swift's prose is differently employed in the epistolary pamphlets. Swift's letters are rich in pertinent, easily managed allusions. The Drapier, too, is aware of the rhetorical effectiveness of allusion, but his technique is different from Swift's. In the third *Letter* he describes his inability to fight William Wood with material supplied him by more learned men: "I was in the Case of *David,* who *could not move in the Armour of* Saul; and therefore I rather chose to attack this *uncircumcised Philistine* (*Wood* I mean) *with a Sling and a Stone*" (*Works,* X, 48). The sixth *Letter* is not written by "M.B." Its author is the Dean of St. Patrick's, writing to Lord Chancellor Midleton in the Drapier's defense. As the Dean of St. Patrick's, Swift is more sophisticated in his allusive technique than is the simple Drapier: ". . . if Authority shall think fit to forbid all Writings, or Discourses upon this Subject . . . I will obey as it becomes me; only when I am in Danger of bursting, I will go and whisper among the Reeds . . . these few Words, BEWARE OF WOOD'S HALF-PENCE" (X, 114-115). This *Letter*—like those written by "M.B."—was intended for public consumption, but it was admittedly from the pen of Swift (it was signed "J.S., Deanry House"). It resembles in style and tone, therefore, many of Swift's formal private letters. Hence the Dean's allusion to Midas is in a manner quite unlike that of the Drapier's to David and Goliath.

All of the epistolary pamphlets are public performances and thus have little relevance to a study of Swift's personal letters. There is, however, at least one *private* performance in the *Correspondence* which bears a strong resemblance to one of Swift's pamphlets. This is a letter to an Irish squire named Robert Percival; its interest for us here does not lie in determining whether or not it was intended for publication but in recognizing it as an authentic personal letter that is at the same time a highly polished literary creation. Swift had been a friend of Percival's father and had given the elder Percival advice on his son's education. The letter, however, is anything but amicable; it is the climax of a quarrel between Swift and the young squire over the payment of tithes:

Sir,

Seeing your frank on the outside, and your address in the same hand, it was obvious who was the writer, and before I opened it, a worthy friend being with me, I told him the contents of the difference between us . . . [Swift then summarizes the details of the controversy]. I told my friend, that . . . I expected nothing from you that became a gentleman; that I had expostulated this scurvy matter very gently with you; that I conceived this letter was an answer; that from the prerogative of a good estate . . . and the practice of lording over a few Irish wretches, and from the natural want of better thinking, I was sure your answer would be extremely rude and stupid, full of very bad language in all senses; that a bear in a wilderness will as soon fix on a philosopher as on a cottager, and a man wholly void of education, judgement, or distinction of persons, has no regard, in his insolence, but to the passion of fear; and how heartily I wished that, to make you show your humility, your quarrel had rather been with a captain of dragoons than the Dean of St. Patrick's. All this happened before my opening your letter; which being read, my friend told me, I was an ill guesser; that you affirmed you despised me only as a clergyman, by your own confession; and that you had reason, because clergymen pretend to learning, wherein you value yourself as what you are an utter stranger to.

. . . You are wholly out of my danger: the weapons I use will do you no hurt, and to that which would keep nicer men in awe, you are insensible. A needle against a stone wall can make no impression. Your faculty lies in making bargains: stick to that. . . . One thing I desire you will be set right in: I do not despise all squires. It is true, I despise the bulk of them. But pray take notice, that a squire must have some merit before I shall honour him with my contempt; for I do not despise a fly, a maggot, or a mite. If you send me an answer to this, I shall not read it, but open it before company, and in their presence burn it; for no other reason but the detestation of bad spelling, no grammar, and that pertness which proceeds from ignorance and an invincible want of taste.

I have ordered a copy of this letter to be taken, with an intention to print it as a mark of my esteem for you, which, however, perhaps I shall not pursue, for I could willingly excuse our two names from standing in the same paper, since I am confident you have as little desire of fame as I have to give it you. (IV, 118-120)

This letter was obviously written with as much attention to its rhetorical effect as were any of Swift's pamphlets. The pace is slow, but deliberate rather than leisurely. The predominant sentence pattern is periodic, with frequent inversions and parenthetical elements. For all its formality, however, the letter never lapses into the stately emptiness of the letter to Varina quoted earlier—the sharp diction, the specific, concrete images, the unbroken tone of contempt insure against that danger. Swift did not make good his threat to publish the letter. Indeed, I read the threat as a gesture that serves the important rhetorical function of allowing Swift to deny Percival his one chance for fame. I am likewise skeptical about the "worthy friend," whose presence is suspiciously convenient; real or imagined, he is put to excellent rhetorical use.

The most striking thing about this letter—more so, even, than the sustained intensity of tone—is its strategy, of which the convenient friend and the unfulfilled threat are subordinate parts. Swift evaluates the character of his antagonist and focuses his attack on the assertion that Percival is without shame and hence is attack-proof. Every jibe—at Percival's ignorance, his boorishness, his insignificance—appears to glance harmlessly off the stone wall of his insensitivity. Swift establishes and amplifies this assertion with such thoroughgoing singlemindedness that we almost believe it; we almost accept the assertion as fact. It is only when we consider the paradox that if the assertion is indeed fact the letter loses its point, that we appreciate the superb example of hyperbole which Swift has contrived. Among his pamphlets there is one which employs the same strategy. This is *A Short Character of the Earl of Wharton,* written twenty years earlier. Here, too, Swift feigns an inability to damage his victim because of Wharton's indifference to reputation—and in the very assertion subjects him to corrosive, humiliating invective: "He is without the Sense of Shame or Glory, as some Men are without the Sense of Smelling; and, therefore, a good Name to him is no more than a precious Ointment would be to these" (*Works,* III, 178).

Throughout the *Correspondence* there are other letters which, although they do not bear so close a resemblance to one of the pamphlets as does the letter to Percival, do none the less have affinities with Swift's public writings.

A device which Swift was extremely fond of using—in letters, in conversation, and in published works—was raillery. This, as he defined it, was "to say something that at first appeared a Reproach, or Reflection; but, by some Turn of Wit unexpected and surprising, ended always in a Compliment, and to the Advantage of the Person it was addressed to" (*Works,* IV, 91). Swift's friend and biographer Patrick Delany thought that he employed raillery so frequently because of "his detestation of flattery, [so] that he made even his praise as like abuse as he could possibly make it."[9] This was doubtless an added appeal, but Swift was primarily attracted to the device because of its wit. He called it "the *finest* Part of Conversation," and in one of his poems praised Voiture for his dexterity in using it:

> Voiture in various Lights displays
> That Irony which turns to Praise,
> His Genius first found out the Rule
> For an obliging Ridicule:
> He flatters with peculiar Air
> The Brave, the Witty, and the Fair;
> And Fools would fancy he intends
> A Satyr where he most commends.[10]

These lines are especially pertinent, because if Voiture did not teach Swift the art of raillery, he did afford a striking example of its effectiveness in the familiar letter.

Swift's public compliments in this vein are well known. The tributes to Pope, Gay, Arbuthnot, Bolingbroke, and Pulteney in "Verses on the Death of Dr. Swift" are exercises in the art in miniature; and the supreme example is the *Dedication to Lord Somers,* in *A Tale of a Tub.* A letter written to the Earl of Halifax contains a railing passage distinctly reminiscent of this *Dedication:* ". . . I must inform you to your great mortification, that your Lordship is universally admired by this tasteless people [the Irish]. But not to humble you too much, I find it is for no other reason, than that for which women are so fond of those they call the wits, merely for their reputation" (I, 175-176).

Swift often worked variations on the device. A favorite one was afforded by the letter of thanks. He writes to Thomas Tickell:

Your whole behaviour, with relation to myself, ever since I had the honour to be known to you, hath tended maliciously to hinder me from writing, or speaking anything that could deserve to be read or heard. I can no sooner hint my desire of a favour to a friend, but you immediately grant it, on purpose to load me, so as to put it out of my power to express my gratitude; and against your conscience you put compliments upon the letter I write, where the subject is only to beg a favour, on purpose to make me write worse, or not at all, for the future. I remember some faint strokes of this unjust proceeding in myself, when I had a little credit in the world, but in no comparison with yours, which have filled up the measure of iniquity.[11]

Another variation was the letter reproaching an absent friend for writing, because his letter has aroused painful memories. One example among many is this excerpt from a letter to Gay, written from Swift's bitter exile in Ireland: "What can be the design of your letter but malice, to wake me out of a scurvy sleep, which however is better than none? I am towards nine years older since I left you, yet that is the least of my alterations; my business, my diversions, my conversations, are all entirely changed for the worse, and so are my studies and my amusements in writing. Yet, after all, this humdrum way of life might be passable enough, if you would let me alone. I shall not be able to relish my wine, my parsons, my horses, nor my garden, for three months, until the spirit you have raised shall be dispossessed" (III, 148).

Probably the rhetorical device most characteristic of Swift's works is the persona. We could not expect to find the device in his personal letters, but we do find something akin to it in his frequent custom of assuming a role with a correspondent (we have seen examples of it already). The function of the role is different from that of the persona, for the latter is a mask, through which Swift's meaning but never his personality appears, while the epistolary role is an exaggeration of an aspect of Swift's personality. Sometimes the role determines the course of the entire letter, sometimes of a series of letters; sometimes it is used for only a paragraph or so. But whatever its extent, Swift's technique in managing it is much the same: he selects a mood or a condition or an activity and uses it as the focus for a single-faceted self-characterization, which he then develops by means of expository or descriptive or even quasi-narrative detail; the total effect is sharpened by hyperbole.

Here is Swift (in a letter to Bolingbroke) in the role of discarded man of affairs and erstwhile genius past his prime. A reader unaware of the date of this letter—and unfamiliar with Swift in this role—would suppose that it was written toward the end of his life. Actually, it was written shortly before he began serious work on *Gulliver's Travels:*

If you will recollect that I am towards six years older than when I saw you last, and twenty years duller, you will not wonder to find me abound in empty speculations. I can now express in a hundred words, what would formerly have cost me ten. I can write epigrams of fifty distichs, which might be squeezed into one. I have gone the round of all my stories three or four times with the younger people, and begin them again. I give hints how significant a person I have been, and nobody believes me. I pretend to pity them, but am inwardly angry. I lay traps for people to desire I would show them some things I have written, but cannot succeed;

27

and wreak my spite, in condemning the taste of the people and company where I am. But it is with place, as it is with time. If I boast of having been valued three hundred miles off, it is of no more use than if I told how handsome I was when I was young. The worst of it is, that lying is of no use; for the people here will not believe one half of what is true. If I can prevail on anyone to personate a hearer and admirer, you would wonder what a favourite he grows. He is sure to have the first glass out of the bottle, and the best bit I can carve.

As he drops the pose, Swift pays a compliment to Bolingbroke by comparing his own chagrin at being neglected with the exiled nobleman's philosophic acceptance of his forced inactivity: "Why cannot you lend me a shred of your mantle, or why did not you leave a shred of it with me when you were snatched from me?"[12]

It is worth noting that when, more than ten years later, Swift wrote "Verses on the Death of Dr. Swift"—a poem in which he cast himself in the role of the late Jonathan Swift—he used some of the details of this earlier playing of the part: The Dean, one of his "special Friends" observes,

> Plyes you with Stories o'er and o'er,
> He told them fifty Times before.
> How does he fancy we can sit,
> To hear his out-of-fashion'd Wit?
> But he takes up with younger Fokes,
> Who for his Wine will bear his Jokes.[13]

On another occasion—this time in a letter to the Duchess of Queensbury—Swift is the imperious tyrant whose every whim is unquestioned law (a role he frequently assumed in his letters to women). John Gay, the Duchess, and her husband had written Swift to come to England for an extended visit with them. The initial letter from the Duchess provoked this characteristic reply: "I am glad you know your duty; for it has been a known and established rule above twenty years in England, that the first advances have been constantly made me by all ladies who aspired to my acquaintance, and the greater

their quality, the greater were their advances" (IV, 180-181).
And subsequently he wrote her that if he came to Amesbury,
there would be no confusion as to who would be master there:
"Since Mr. Gay affirms that you love to have your own way,
and since I have the same perfection, I will settle that matter
immediately, to prevent those ill consequences he apprehends.
Your Grace shall have your own way in all places except your
own house, and the domains about it. There, and there only, I
expect to have mine, so that you have all the world to reign in,
bating only two or three hundred acres, and two or three
houses in town or country" (IV, 203). The compliment, as
graceful as it is subtle, is a typical adjunct to this role.

One of the most delightful roles that Swift ever adopted
was in a letter to Henrietta Howard (afterwards Countess of
Suffolk). Mrs. Howard suffered from Swift's chronic complaints of deafness and giddiness; and her letter recounting a
recent attack of sickness called forth a reply from the stoical
valetudinarian par excellence. In developing the role, Swift
added two familiar touches: raillery and a pedantic insistence
on highly circumstantial detail:

About two hours before you were born I got my giddiness, by eating a hundred golden pippins at a time at Richmond; and when
you were four years and a quarter old bating two days, having
made a fine seat about twenty miles farther in Surrey, where I used
to read and sleep, there I got my deafness, and these two friends
have visited me, one or other, every year since, and being old
acquaintance, have now thought fit to come together. So much for
the calamities wherein I have the honour to resemble you; and you
see your sufferings are but children in comparison of mine; and
yet, to show my philosophy, I have been as cheerful as Scarron.
You boast that your disorders never made you peevish. Where is
the virtue when all the world was peevish on your account, and so
took the office out of your hands? Whereas I bore the whole load
myself, nobody caring threepence what I suffered, or whether I
were hanged or at ease. I tell you my philosophy is twelve times
greater than yours; for I can call witnesses that I bear half your
pains, beside all my own, which are in themselves ten times greater.
. . . Thus I write by your commands. . . . But, deaf or giddy, heav-

ing or steady, I shall ever be, with the truest respect, Madam. . . .
(III, 413-415)

One of Swift's most celebrated roles, the misanthrope, may
be represented by the well-known letter to Pope, written in
1725, a year before the publication of *Gulliver's Travels*. Pope
had written longingly of the day when the old friends of
Queen Anne's time might be reunited, "to divert ourselves,
and the world too if it pleases" (III, 269). "I like the scheme,"
Swift answered, "of our meeting after distresses and disper-
sions; but the chief end I propose to myself in all my labours
is to vex the world rather than divert it." Warming to his part,
he continues:

. . . when you think of the world give it one lash the more at my
request. I have ever hated all nations, professions, and communi-
ties, and all my love is toward individuals: for instance, I hate the
tribe of lawyers, but I love Counseller Such-a-one, and Judge Such-
a-one: so with physicians—I will not speak of my own trade—sol-
diers, English, Scotch, French, and the rest. But principally I hate
and detest that animal called man, although I heartily love John,
Peter, Thomas, and so forth. This is the system upon which I have
governed myself many years, but do not tell, and so I shall go on
till I have done with them. I have got materials toward a treatise,
proving the falsity of that definition *animal rationale,* and to show
it would be only *rationis capax.* Upon this great foundation of
misanthropy, though not in Timon's manner, the whole building
of my Travels is erected; and I never will have peace of mind till
all honest men are of my opinion. By consequence you are to
embrace it immediately, and procure that all who deserve my
esteem may do so too. (III, 276-277)

This passage is a hyperbolic expression of Swift's serious
view of man—just as the letter to Bolingbroke is the dramatized statement of his frustration at being in Ireland after his
days of glory with the Oxford ministry; just as the letter to
Mrs. Howard is the wry celebration of his wretched health;
just as the flat ultimatums to the Duchess of Queensbury are
a comically heightened expression of the independent attitude
which is an undeniable characteristic of Swift's relations with

women in particular and with any social superior in general. But the pose of misanthropy here is no more genuine than are any of these other poses. Swift is careful to qualify his "misanthropy": it is not in Timon's manner. And there are other indications as to how he wanted the passage to be read. The peremptory tone of his demand that Pope embrace his system *immediately* reminds us of Gulliver, who at the end of his book is himself the supreme example of that pride which he condemns in the Yahoo kind. Swift steps out of his role in the sentence following this one; and he does so with a subtle compliment to Pope: "The matter is so clear that it will admit of no dispute; nay, I will hold a hundred pounds that you and I agree in the point." The *matter,* the substance at the center of the exaggerated role, is perfectly and immediately clear, as Pope—who has Swift's esteem as an honest man—must agree. The *manner,* however, was another thing; and Pope did not misunderstand it. His answer to this part of Swift's letter was pitched at the properly heightened level: "I have fancied, I say, that we should meet like the righteous in the millennium, quite in peace, divested of all our former passions, smiling at all our own designs, and content to enjoy the kingdom of the just in tranquillity. But I find you would rather be employed as an avenging angel of wrath, to break your vial of indignation over the heads of the wretched, pitiful creatures of this world; nay, would make them eat your book, which you have made, I doubt not, as bitter a pill for them as possible."[14]

In his edition of Sir William Temple's letters, Swift expressed his particular admiration for Temple's perceptiveness and tact in suiting the style to the correspondent: "One may discover the Characters of most of those Persons he writes to, from the Stile of his Letters."[15] Within limits, this observation applies to Swift's letters. But of greater interest is the way in which they reveal the steady intelligence and honesty of their author. Swift's own character is the constant behind the shifting moods and various roles in his personal letters. They show the wit and the compelling power that delight and fascinate the reader of *Gulliver's Travels* and *A Tale of a Tub,* but they also show a gentleness and warmth that may surprise the reader who has known Swift only through such public performances. Here is a note to Pope, written under obvious emotional stress, as Swift, on the eve of departing for Ireland, learns that his friend is ill:

I had rather live in forty Irelands than under the frequent disquiets of hearing you are out of order. I always apprehend it most after a great dinner; for the least transgression of yours, if it be only two bits and one sup more than your stint, is a great debauch; for which you certainly pay more than those sots who are carried dead drunk to bed. . . . Pray let me have three lines under any hand or pot-hook that will give me a better account of your health; which concerns me more than others, because I love and esteem you for reasons that most others have little to do with, and would be the same, although you had never touched a pen further than with writing to me.

I am gathering up my luggage, and preparing for my journey. I will endeavour to think of you as little as I can, and when I write to you, I will strive not to think of you. This I intend in return to your kindness; and further, I know nobody has dealt with me so cruelly as you, the consequences of which usage I fear will last as long as my life, for so long shall I be, in spite of my heart,

Entirely yours. (III, 325)

The letters show, too, an acute sense of tact that goes far beyond the adopting of a style to suit the occasion. When the Earl of Oxford was committed to the Tower on charges of treason, Swift's "poor service and attendance" were proffered with precisely the right balance of friendship and gratitude, gentleness and dignity: "It is the first time I ever solicited you in my own behalf, and, if I am refused, I think it will be the first request you ever refused me" (II, 293).

Swift was being partly disingenuous when he wrote to Pope, "I believe my letters have escaped being published, because I writ nothing but nature and friendship, and particular incidents which could make no figure in writing" (V, 251). He knew how eagerly the booksellers in 1735 would have seized the chance to publish his letters (he also knew that some of Pope's letters had already been published—with Pope's connivance—so his assessment of the public interest in his private writings was doubly ironic). When in fact Swift's letters were published (the first collection appeared in 1740), they were valued for that very "nature and friendship" that he mentioned so casually. Orrery is not the only critic who has commended the naturalness in Swift's personal letters. He called it "unsuspicious openness," not recognizing it for what it really was: that "nature" which is the source and end and test of art.

Duke University

SHADOW AND SUBSTANCE:
A DISCUSSION OF POPE'S CORRESPONDENCE

ROSEMARY COWLER

WHETHER OR NOT it was as Swift suggested, that "you have been a writer of Letters almost from your infancy, and by your own confession had Schemes even then of Epistolary fame,"[1] it is literary record that Pope published his correspondence as a significant part of his Works and that his letters did achieve an impressive contemporary reputation. What lies between the rumor of "Schemes" and the fact of history is a fascinating chapter in the annals of letter-writing. Although Pope was eventually to do much to establish letter-writing as a literary mode, in his time letters were still considered private communications and to publish one's own was a breach of taste. For Pope, to preserve appearances was necessary; for him to publish his letters, and as he wanted them published, was equally imperative in an age of unscrupulous printers. As Pope himself described the situation, it called for desperate measures; it was a worthy challenge to his taste and talent for subterfuge:

To state the case fairly in the present situation. A Bookseller advertises his intention to publish your Letters: He openly promises encouragement, or even pecuniary rewards to those who will help him to any; and ingages to insert whatever they shall send: Any scandal is sure of a reception, and any enemy who sends it skreen'd from a discovery. Any domestick or servant, who can snatch a letter from your pocket or cabinet, is encouraged to that vile practise. If the quantity falls short of a volume, any thing else shall be join'd with it (more especially scandal) which the collector can think for his interest, all recommended under your Name: You have not only Theft to fear, but Forgery. Any Bookseller, tho' conscious in what manner they were obtain'd, not caring what may be the consequences to your Fame or Quiet, will sell and disperse them in town and country. The better your Reputation is, the more your Name will cause them to be demanded, and consequently the more you will be injur'd. The injury is of such a nature, as the Law (which does not punish for *Intentions*) cannot prevent; and when done, may punish, but not redress. You are therefore reduc'd, either to enter into a personal treaty with such a man, (which tho' the readiest, is the meanest of all methods) or to take such other measures to suppress them, as are contrary to your Inclinations, or to publish them, as are contrary to your Modesty.[2]

The various publications of Pope's letters were accordingly marked by transactions much too complex to be reviewed here. Whether it was the bizarre maneuvers with Curll that culminated in his being tricked into publishing in 1735 *Mr. Pope's Literary Correspondence for Thirty Years; from 1704 to 1735* or the equally involved but more dubious intrigue several years later that resulted in the publication of Pope's correspondence with Swift, the events attendant on these printings make a remarkable account of dealings and double-dealings often verging on the melodramatic (in the first plot, for example, veiled communications, a mysterious messenger disguised as a clergyman, impoundment by the House of Lords, charges and counter-charges . . .).[3] But the letters did appear, and the necessary "authorized" editions did follow, all to be met by an audience eager for them. As Professor Griffith once commented, "If Pope is not the greatest among English poets, he is the greatest advertiser and publisher among them."[4]

Absorbing as these episodes are—and Pope's horrified Victorian editors found it difficult ever to move far beyond them[5]

—they should not obscure the fact that Pope's active concern for publication has significant literary implications. Historically, of course, it meant a convention broken, a changed popular attitude toward letter-writing and letter-reading; after Pope the way is paved for a Walpole. Equally important, as Pope helped to elevate letter-writing to an art, he also helped to define and emphasize that art. As early as 1712 he was writing to Caryll requesting the return of some of his letters for the "several thoughts which I throw out that way in the freedom of my soul, that may be of use to me in a design I am lately engaged in, which will require so constant a flux of thought and invention, that I can never supply it without some assistance and 'tis not impossible but so many notions, written at different times, may save me a good deal of trouble."[6] He is referring to the set pieces which make up so much of his youthful correspondence. These little dissertations on life and death would lend themselves well to "designs," as Pope had already realized when he addressed some to Steele and had the gratification of seeing them printed in the *Spectator*[7]—where they obviously had been directed, sometimes not too subtly ("If you think me right in my notion of the last words of *Adrian*, be pleas'd to insert it in the *Spectator*, if not, to suppress it"[8]).

Because Pope considered his letters literature, he later treated them to the revisions and modifications to which he subjected all his works. His practice here is consistent with his general editing principles: as Professor Sherburn summarizes it, "Trivialities concerning daily life or finances are omitted; so also are small indecorous remarks, either slightly salacious or profane. Perhaps the most common changes are purely stylistic: the letters are made more concise, the sentences more straightforward, the diction more elegant. There is little change in the sense of any letter except such as is due to omissions."[9] To compare the manuscript of Pope's "Preface" to his 1717 *Works* with the first printed version is to encounter exactly the same type of editing. Since Pope was proud of his letters and proud too of his associations with "worthy" men, he would also occasionally transfer choice letters, or passages from choice letters, from the original recipient to one whom he considered more appropriate, in whose reflected light his words could shine more brightly. (There is an art even to this, and Professor Sherburn cites a fabricated letter to Addison as a "masterpiece in this kind."[10]) But these doctorings, which so outraged his nineteenth-century editors and critics—who saw in them the worst that they were constantly suspecting in Pope —actually represent only twenty-seven letters, less than 1.5 per cent of the total correspondence[11] as it is now available to us in Professor Sherburn's magnificent edition.

If the completeness of that edition (which increases by about one-third the number of letters printed in the Elwin-Courthope edition) provides us the means of a much more objective view of Pope's tamperings, it also, in a sense, complicates a study of Pope's epistolary art. In its inclusiveness the collection covers everything from what Pope would have considered a printable letter (and only about 10 per cent of the present gathering were originally published by him) to the hasty scraps that are the eighteenth-century equivalents of telephone messages. The range is invaluable in giving the reader a sense of Pope's activity as he manages his writings, his estate, and his friendships, but it means that one must distinguish between letters that were merely communications and those that constitute literature.

Ignoring the notes arranging appointments, the terse business chits, and the casual memoranda, one is still left with a vast bulk of letters. But from the most artless to the most artful, from the most playful to the most sententious, from the efforts of 1704 to those of 1744, they almost all have one thing in common—the projection of a man. That this is so is deliberate. To Lady Mary he spoke of "These Shadows of me, my Letters,"[12] or, on another occasion, he wrote, "I can say little to recommend the Letters I am beginning to write to you, but that they will be the most impartial Representations of a free heart, and the truest Copies you ever saw, tho' of a very mean Original."[13] When he was gathering his letters for publication, he commented to Caryll, "Some of my own letters have been returned to me . . . and it makes all together an un-important, indeed, but yet an innocent, history of myself,"[14] a view he acknowledged in the Preface of the quarto edition of the collection: "Had he [speaking in the third person] sate down with a design to draw his own Picture, he could not have done it so truly; for whoever sits for it (whether to himself or another) will inevitably find the features more compos'd, than his appear in these letters."[15]

This personal element in the letters may take us also to the center of Pope's art in letter-writing. His own statements about epistolary style emphasize that familiar letters should be just that, familiar and informal, "artless and natural,"[16] or as he is wont to put it, just "talking upon paper."[17] He makes much of the point: Professor Sherburn in his index to the *Correspondence* cites over thirty such references to it in the letters, and one entire letter is dedicated to the topic:

All the pleasure or use of familiar letters, is to give us the assurance of a friend's welfare; at least 'tis all I know, who am a mortal enemy and despiser of what they call fine letters. . . . Now let me fairly tell you, I don't like your style: 'tis very pretty, therefore I don't like it; and if you writ as well as Voiture, I wou'd not give a farthing for such letters, unless I were to sell 'em to be printed. Methinks I have lost the Mrs. L* I formerly knew, who writ and talk'd like other people, (and sometimes better). . . . You see in short, after what manner you may most agreeably write to me. . . . As I have open'd my mind upon this to you, it may also serve for Mr. H— who will see by it what manner of letters he must expect if he corresponds with me. As I am too seriously yours and his servant to put turns upon you instead of good wishes, so in return I shou'd have nothing but honest plain how d'ye's and pray remember me's; which not being fit to be shown to any body for wit, may be a proof we correspond only for our selves, in meer friendlyness; as doth, God is my witness, Your very, &c.[18]

This studied carelessness seems very much in the spirit of the gentleman-author pose which Pope affects generally in discussing his writings. One sees it in his preface to the 1717 *Works* when he speaks of "Poetry and Criticism being by no means the universal concern of the world, but only the affair of idle men who write in their closets, and of idle men who read there."[19] Or, talking more specifically about his own writings: "I confess it was want of consideration that made me an author; I writ because it amused me; I corrected because it was as pleasant to me to correct as to write; and I publish'd because I was told I might please such as it was a credit to please"[20]— statements that were later to be echoed in the "Epistle to Dr. Arbuthnot." In fact, much that is to be found in the "Preface" is to be found in the letters, as both reflect Pope's understanding of himself as an author and as a man: the early concern for the good man as the correlative of the good poet, the pride in independence of faction or patron, the joy in the fellowship of men of good sense.

The acknowledgment in the "Preface" of Pope's indebtedness to the great writers who preceded him is also relevant. For all of his protestations of an untutored style in the letters, Pope could, and did, say to Spence, "It is idle to say that letters should be written in an easy familiar style: that, like most other general rules, will not hold. The style, in letters as in all other things, should be adapted to the subject.—Many of Voiture's letters on gay subjects, are excellent; and so are Cicero's, and several of Pliny's and Seneca's, on serious subjects."[21] If Pope's familiarity with the classical and Continental models for the genre is not surprising, neither should it be unexpected to find him in his early letters imitating the masters as he evolves his own "Epistolary Style" (a phrase which he uses in a youthful note to Cromwell[22]). His apprenticeship in poetry and criticism ("A Discourse on Pastoral Poetry," for example) reflects a similar dependency—a situation that is nicely illustrated when he sends Cromwell an imitation of a poem by Voiture in one of a series of letters which are equally influenced by Voiture, this time as letter-stylist.[23] Later Pope would renounce what Swift called *jeux d'esprit*[24] and relegate the search for pretty things to "fops and Frenchmen,"[25] but in the first decades of the century he was writing very much in that tradition, with the formidable example of Wycherley to guide him.[26]

Those first letters are what one might expect of a precocious, artistically self-conscious young man exchanging *bons mots* with much older, distinguished correspondents, often, as in the case of Wycherley, relics of a past age. The letters are inevitably mannered, pretentious—and witty. If they are "talking upon paper," it is the conversation of Restoration comedy: "In a word, if a Man be a Coxcomb, Solitude is his best School; and if he be a Fool, it is his best Sanctuary."[27] Future letters will undeniably be very different in style and tone; they will be echoing other voices.

What did happen to Pope the letter-writer is best revealed by him, in a letter to Swift: "This letter (like all mine) will be a Rhapsody; it is many years ago since I wrote as a Wit. How many occurrencies or informations must one omit, if one determin'd to say nothing that one could not say prettily? I lately receiv'd from the widow of one dead correspondent and the father of another, several of my own letters of about fifteen or twenty years old; and it was not unentertaining to my self to observe, how and by what degrees I ceas'd to be a witty writer; as either my experience grew on one hand, or my affection to my correspondents on the other."[28] The comment is particularly interesting because in the last line it focuses on a crucial matter: the two worlds of experience, the artistic and the personal, which in Pope, as in this statement of his, are never very far apart. As the "Preface" to the 1717 *Works* demonstrated, there is early in Pope's career an awareness of the duality; the young man, more eager to be counted among the aristocratic wits than the pedant-scholars, finds an acceptable compromise in the graceful pose of the skilled amateur. If in the early works the writer seems to retire behind the gentleman, in the later ones the poet-satirist seems to submerge the individual.

Without becoming involved in the current discussion over the nature, function, and validity of the concept of the *persona* in Augustan satire,[29] one can still point to something taking place in the man-writer relationship in the letters which inevitably has repercussions on the style. From the first we have seen Pope capable of poses. Writing to Caryll in 1716, he assumes the accents of the somewhat world-weary sophisticate:

Tho' the change of my scene of life, from Windsor Forest to the water-side at Chiswick, be one of the grand Æra's of my days, and may be called a notable period in so inconsiderable a history, yet you can scarce imagine any hero passing from one stage of life and entering upon another, with so much tranquillity and so easy a transition, and so laudable a behaviour as myself. I am become so truly a Citizen of the World (according to Plato's expression) that I look with equal indifference on what I have lost, and on what I have gained. The times and amusements past, are not more a dream to me than those which are present.... To grow indifferent to the World is to grow philosophical or religious (whichsoever of those turns we chance to take), and indeed the world is such a thing as one that thinks pretty much must either laugh at, or be angry with.... So shall we live comfortably with our families, quiet with our neighbours, favoured by our masters, happy with our mistresses.[30]

More and more, though, another tone asserts itself in the letters; it is the voice of the man of probity and reason. One could argue that these are merely the natural cadences of the writer except that Pope so very self-consciously and so very explicitly makes his avowals. His preoccupation with his "image" is inescapable. Sometimes it is just a passing reference,[31] but it can be a formal declaration almost constituting an *apologia,* as when he writes to the Earl of Marchmont:

... I am determined to publish no more in my life time, for many reasons; but principally thro' the Zeal I have to speak the *Whole Truth,* & neither to praise nor dispraise by halves, or with worldly managements. I think fifty an age at which to write no longer for Amusement, but for some Use, and with design to do some good. I never had any uneasy Desire of Fame, or keen Resentment of In-

41

juries, & now both are asleep together: Other Ambition I never had, than to be tolerably thought of by those I esteem'd, and this has been gratify'd beyond my proudest Hopes. I hate no human Creature, & the moment any can repent or reform, I love them sincerely. Public Calamities touch me; but when I read of Past Times, I am somewhat comforted as to the present, upon the Comparison: and at the worst I thank God, that I do not yet live under a Tyranny, nor an Inquisition: that I have thus long enjoyed Independency, Freedom of Body & Mind, have told the world of my Opinions, even on the highest subjects, & of the Greatest Men, pretty freely; that good men have not been ashamed of me; and that my Works have not dy'd before me . . . and if they die soon after, I shall probably not know it, or certainly not be concern'd at it, in the next world. . . .[32]

The Pope who emerges is the man Pope would be and the man he does become; it is the poet who "stooped to Truth, and moralized his song." In an essay on Pope and his grotto, Professor Maynard Mack presents a picture of Pope that is relevant here. He argues that at Twickenham the poet created for himself a necessary world:

To be a great satirist, a man must have, literally and figuratively, a place to stand, an angle of vision. For Pope, the garden and the grotto provided this. They supplied him, in fact as well as fiction, with a rallying point for his personal values and a focus for his conception of himself—as master of a poet's "kingdom," a counter-order to a court and a ministry that set no store by poets, a community bound by ties quite other than those uniting the "pensioners" of St. Stephen, as he sardonically calls the members of Walpole's parliament. In a sense, they supplied him with the materials of a *Selbstentwurf*, nourishing his feelings and imagination in much the same way that at a later time the tower and the swan would do for Yeats.

Further, in Pope's case as in Yeats's, the elements of the self-projection were such that they enabled him, like Antaeus, to re-create his limited personal being by drawing on a larger historical identity. This identity for Pope was that of the virtuous recluse, the Horatian *beatus ille* figure. . . .[33]

Professor Reuben Brower, in his *Alexander Pope: The Poetry of Allusion*, also explores the Horatian influence on Pope, in a chapter significantly entitled the "Horatian Image." Outlining the parallels between the world of Horace's Satires and Epistles and that of the English Augustans, he too comments on the tendency of the age to consider itself in Horatian terms; to re-create in its villas a georgic setting. And he also sees Pope's house at Twickenham as a "symbol of a life and literary career that becomes progressively an *Imitatio Horati*"[34]—an imitation that is particularly appropriate since Horace is above all the poet of friendship.[35] There is no question that Pope imitated; but imitation, emulation—when does it become assimilation? When does the mask become the living features?

That this "conception," "identity," "self-projection"—this "imitation"—actually merged with the flesh-and-blood man can be argued from the letters, both Pope's own and those of his correspondents. When Swift wrote, "As for the other parts of your volume of Letters, my opinion is, that there might be collected from them the best System that ever was wrote for the Conduct of human life, at least to shame all reasonable men out of their Follies and Vices,"[36] he could have paid his friend no higher tribute. His comment on Pope as a satirist—"And I will take my oath that you have more Virtue in an hour, than I in seven years; for you despise the follies and hate the vices of mankind, without the least ill effect on your temper; and with regard to particular men, you are inclin'd always rather to think the better, whereas with me it is always directly contrary"[37]—is in the spirit of Pope's own view of himself in that role.[38] It is a remarkable testimonial, especially when one considers that it has not been long since critics were castigating Pope's satire as the splenetic effusions of a twisted mind in a twisted body.[39] Though such misguided judgments are largely a thing of the past, perhaps not even Pope's champions have been so fully aware, before the Sherburn edition of the correspondence, just how loving and loved he was. As Professor Mack has recognized, "His tone may vary in the letters with the subject or the addressee, but their real substance is almost always the substance of a love letter, if that term may still be used today without sexual or romantic implications. . . . The 'business' of the letters tends to be subsidiary to the sense of being in affectionate communication with someone very dear."[40]

There are not merely words of affection; there are acts of love and charity. The range of Pope's generosity is quite amazing, and not confined to easy gifts of money, though Swift commends him on that score.[41] He writes letters of recommendation and notes of condolence, he advises aspiring poets, he attends to the tangled affairs of his sister and her family—the list is so long that in his index Professor Sherburn cites only a "selection" of examples of his "Good Deeds," an entry which consumes the length of a full column!

Above all, though, one is aware of his giving of himself in friendship. Forced by health, religion, and politics to live outside the main currents of Augustan life, retired to the seclusion of Twickenham in the company of an aging mother, he was inevitably dependent on those whom he loved. And these were often those similarly alienated from normal domestic, social, or political involvements. Swift and Gay are the most obvious examples—and the fellowship of the "three Yahoos,"[42] as they are playfully referred to in the letters, makes one of the most endearing chapters in this epistolary history; but Atterbury and Bolingbroke in literal exile are also noteworthy. And because these friends were so dispersed, in Ireland, on the Continent, throughout England, it is the letters which must carry most of the burden of their long association. Time, however, if not distance, becomes insurmountable and some of the saddest reading in the letters is encountered as Pope and Swift begin to lose companion after companion to death. For Pope it means a second generation of friends, and there will be a number whose "merit has forced me to contract an intimacy with, after I had sworn never to love a man more, since the sorrow it cost me to have loved so many, now dead, banished, or unfortunate."[43] His last will and testament will provide a roster of these new names as well as the remaining old ones, and will serve as testimonial to the strength and vitality of his attachments.

It is characteristic of his preoccupation with his own moral nature that Pope's concern for his friends also goes to the core of their beings, not to their activities. Who else would write to Lady Mary, made famous as a traveler through her letters, and assert: "Nothing that regards the Countries you pass thro' engages so much of my Curiosity or Concern, as what relates purely to yourself. You can make no Discoveries that will be half so valuable to me as those of your own mind, temper, and thoughts . . . ."?[44] If he is not interested in places and happenings in letters from others, he is not likely to bother with them for himself. And indeed the letters offer no chronicle of events, no portfolio of scenes and views, no real history, social or political, of his times. Instead there is the history—as minute and detailed as one of Richardson's character studies—of a man of whom the Earl of Oxford wrote: "You are the Best Poet, the truest Friend, and the Best natured man."[45]

With the interest of the letters so psychological and with Pope so self-aware, there may be some truth in Dr. Johnson's rather critical comment on his style: "Pope may be said to write always with his reputation in his head; Swift perhaps like a man who remembered that he was writing to Pope; but Arbuthnot like one who lets thoughts drop from his pen as they rise into his mind."[46] In speaking of "reputation," Dr. Johnson no doubt had in mind Pope's public image as an important literary figure, and consequently his remark would have most bearing on those letters which Pope meant to publish and which he prepared for issuance. In these assuredly Pope did have an eye to his audience. But even in the other letters one can argue that there is a concern for reputation, if of another kind, and that this concern over a personal image made those letters equally self-conscious. Perhaps this is the reason that Pope's correspondence does not have quite the same spontaneity as Swift's or Gay's or the immediacy of Lady Mary's (it is revealing to read Lady Mary's forthright, sardonic reply to a very sentimental account by Pope of the death of two young lovers struck by lightning as they took refuge under a hayrick[47]).

Whatever the motivation for the style, the letters are surprisingly varied, with the tone changing for the recipient and the occasion. His letters to the nobility, Lord Bathurst, for example, are usually more formal than those addressed to an old fellow-rambler like Gay, and his mood with ladies is almost always courtly. But it is the occasion that generally sets the spirit. He can be high-styled on the event of Atterbury's departure into exile, or he can be merely high-toned and ironic when he is answering one of Aaron Hill's tedious and demanding tomes. He can be very sad as he watches his mother slipping into the infirmities of extreme old age; touching as he writes to Swift, also growing feeble (one letter opens, "It is a perfect trouble to me to write to you, and your kind letter left for me at Mr. Gay's affected me so much, that it made me like a girl"[48]); or he can be marvelously funny as he contemplates Lady Kneller and her bulk. He can be jocular as he affects a Biblical tone ("There was a Man in the Land of Twitnam, called Pope"[49]), amusing as he discusses Madame Dacier's attack on his Homeric translation, and gay, especially when writing to Scriblerians. Or he can be reserved and restrained, as when he writes to Richard Savage when the latter has been behaving in an exasperating fashion. And his reply to Beau Nash's request for an inscription for the Prince of Wales is worthy of Dr. Johnson: "You say words cannot express the gratitude you feel for the favour of his R. H. and yet you would have me express what you feel, and in a few words. I own myself unequal to the task; for even, granting it possible to express an inexpressible idea, I am the worst person you could have pitched upon for this purpose, who have received so few favours from the great myself, that I am utterly unacquainted with what kind of thanks they like best."[50]

Perhaps most unexpected of all, he can be playful: talking about money ("I find subscribing much superior to writing, and there are a sort of little epigrams I more especially delight in, after the manner of rondeaus, which begin and end all in the same words; viz, Received—and A: Pope"[51]) or pin money ("O Pin-money! dear, desirable Pin-money! in thee are included all the blessings of woman! In thee are comprised fine clothes, fine lodgings, fine operas, fine masquerades, fine fellows"[52]); naming Mrs. Howard's calf ("All Knights Errants Palfreys were distinguish'd by lofty names: we see no reason why a Pastoral Lady's sheep and calves should want names of the softer sound; we have therefore given her the name of Caesar's wife, Calfurnia"[53]); planning to save a tree, in the highest legal fashion ("That whereas a Certain Tree lying, being, & standing in or on the Grounds of your Lordship, at or before or on one side or the other of a Certain Edifice . . ."[54]); or just throwing out random comments ("Do you keep my Memory fresh, [in the Pickle of good French wine]"[55]) . Above all, Pope can joke about himself and his infirmities; there is, as an example, an evening at Bath: "My Lady Cox, the first night I lay there, mixed my electuary, Lady Codrington pounded sulphur, Mrs. Bridget Bethel ordered broth. Lady Cox marched first up-stairs with the physic in a gallipot; Lady Codrington next, with the vial of oyle; Mrs. Bridget third, with pills; the fourth sister, with spoons and tea-cups. It would have rejoiced the ghost of Dr. Woodward to have beheld this procession. . . ."[56] Shortly six months before his death, he can write to Jonathan Richardson, "We may take a Cup of Sack together, & chatter like two Parrots, which are (at least) more reputable & manlike Animals than the Grasshoppers, to which Homer likens old men."[57] There are two even later comments, perhaps more wry than humorous and certainly very moving as they trace his failing health. One is from January: "Yes, I would see you as long as I can see you, & then shut my eyes upon the world, as a thing worth seeing no longer. If your charity would take up a small Bird that is half dead of the frost, and set it a chirping for half an hour, I'll jump into my Cage, & put myself into your hands to morrow, at any hour you send.

Two horses will be enough to draw me, (& so would two Dogs if you had them), but even the fly upon the chariot wheel required some bigger animal than itself, to set it a going";[58] the last, from February: "I live like an Insect, in hope of reviving with the Spring, and above all, my favorite Project would be to keep myself alive till you could come this way, & try if we can get up the hill together, instead of going down."[59]

If Pope's letters were shadows, as he named them to Lady Mary, then the figure behind them is perhaps fuller, of more substance than might once have been granted.

Lake Forest College

M. Wortley Montagu

LADY MARY WORTLEY MONTAGU
AS LETTER-WRITER

ROBERT HALSBAND

LADY MARY WORTLEY MONTAGU owes her cumbersome
name to a father whose peerage gave her the courtesy title, and
to a husband who sometimes called himself Wortley but usually Wortley Montagu. In her own day there were other Lady
Marys, but her intellectual prominence and connection with
Alexander Pope and his circle earned for her the equivocal
distinction of being recognized in print as *the* Lady Mary.
Merely notorious during her lifetime, she became famous the
year after her death when her Turkish Embassy Letters were
published in 1763. Here at last was visible proof of her wide-
ranging intellect, her cosmopolitan culture, her incisive wit.
"What fire, what ease, what knowledge of Europe and Asia!"
Edward Gibbon exclaimed after reading them. Voltaire reviewed them enthusiastically: they were not only for her own
country but for all nations that wished to be instructed. To-
bias Smollett announced to England that they were unequaled
by letter-writers of any sex, age, or nation. These, the Embassy
Letters, were the only ones Lady Mary deliberately prepared
for publication.

Exactly forty years after they were published, her grandson
was blackmailed into authorizing an edition of her letters that
—even with its fantastically bad editing—shows the full range

of her art, for it includes the vivacious letters of her girlhood, the grave correspondence of her courtship, the brilliant social gossip of her letters to her sister, and the largest and most varied group, those to her daughter. The successive editions of 1837 and 1861 further clarified and expanded this *œuvre*. My new edition of her letters contains the complete and accurate text of her previously known correspondences (with the addition of four important new ones), totaling almost nine hundred letters, and confirming Lady Mary's stature as one of the great eighteenth-century letter-writers.

Although the informal letter is a very individual type of literary expression—pitched, as it is, to the delicate equilibrium of the writer, the occasion, and the recipient—it still has its models; and eighteenth-century practitioners were aware of them. In her library Lady Mary had only one of the classical writers—Cicero; but she had almost all the seventeenth-century French ones—Guez de Balzac, Voiture, Bussy-Rabutin, and (most important) Madame de Sévigné. For Madame de Sévigné's letters are closest in character to her own; and Horace Walpole, who idolized the Frenchwoman, considered that Lady Mary's letters to her sister were almost as good in wit and style. Of all the letter-writers Lady Mary owned, the only one she discussed was Madame de Sévigné. This was her opinion late in life: "How many readers and admirers has Madame de Sévigné, who only gives us, in a lively manner and fashionable phrases, mean sentiments, vulgar prejudices, and endless repetitions! Sometimes the tittle-tattle of a fine lady, sometimes that of an old nurse, always tittle-tattle; yet so well gilt over by airy expressions and a flowing style. . . ." It is surprising, in a way, to find Lady Mary so severe. Her opinion was different when she first read them some thirty years before: "The last pleasure that fell in my way was Madame Sévigné's letters; very pretty they are, but I assert, without the least vanity, that mine will be full as entertaining forty years hence." Could it be that a sense of rivalry changed her opinion?

The variety in Lady Mary's correspondence is astonishing: effusive and pert letters when writing to girlhood friends; sober and energetic ones to her husband about household and political affairs; courtly and somewhat stuffy, to the sedate Countess of Oxford, and with an admixture of spicy gossip to the more sophisticated Lady Pomfret; affectionate and urbane, in two still unpublished correspondences, one with the Earl of Bute's brother and the other with a Venetian lady; and near the end of her life, the strenuously clever letters to Sir James Steuart, the political economist. All these are apart from five major groups of letters which illustrate some aspects of her art as letter-writer.

The courtship correspondence between Lady Mary and Wortley is one of the most extensive prenuptial negotiations on record. Extending over two-and-a-half years, it includes about seventy letters from her to him and about sixty from him to her. Judged by its immediate fruits, it was a success, for the pair eloped and married; but judged by its ultimate result, it was a sad failure: in spite of its laborious analyses of their temperaments and tastes, they were thoroughly unsuited to each other. Their marriage dwindled into a formal arrangement, and during the last twenty years of their lives they lived on opposite sides of Europe. Perhaps Lady Mary's cleverness, her subtlety and rhetorical effectiveness proved self-defeating—she won her lover but lost her chance for wedded happiness.

Her very first letter to Wortley sets the tone: it is plain and unadorned, saved from flatness by its crisp clarity. "You distrust me," she complains (referring to their conversations). "I can neither be easy nor loved where I am distrusted, nor do I believe your passion for me is what you pretend it; at least I'm sure, was I in love I could not talk as you do. . . . I don't enjoin you to burn this letter. I know you will. 'Tis the first I ever writ to one of your sex and shall be the last. You must never expect another. I resolve against all correspondence of this kind. My resolutions are seldom made and never broken." Her prose, like her pose, was cleverly pitched to appeal to the hard-headed M.P. and coal tycoon (who died one of England's richest and stingiest millionaires).

Of course, the correspondence has no formal design beyond its inherent pattern of a beginning, a long middle (interrupted by several breaks), and an end. But its subject-matter is far from epic. The main themes are: financial—Lady Mary's dowry and Wortley's settlement; their meeting at friends' houses and social functions; their future life together (love, solitude, and economy) ; his jealousy and her denials; her father's choice of a husband and her possible defiance; and plans for their elopement. One can perhaps invent a musical structure, as themes are announced, developed, varied, modulated, fragmented, set off by sub-themes, recapitulated *ad libitum,* and finally resolved in a triumphant coda before a country parson.

Lady Mary is a virtuoso in manipulating these themes. "I am incapable of art," she writes in an early letter, "and 'tis because I will not be capable of it. Could I deceive one minute, I should never regain my own good opinion, and who could bear to live with one they despised?" Another trait she emphasizes is her freedom from emotion. "If you expect passion," she writes, "I am utterly unacquainted with any. It may be a fault of my temper. . . . I have no notion of a transport of anger, love, or any other. I here tell you the plain state of my heart. . . ." She wore her humility with becoming grace: "I have not the usual pride of my sex. I can bear being told I am in the wrong, but tell it me gently. Perhaps I have been indiscreet; I came young into the hurry of the world."

Her arsenal of rhetorical weapons included one that can be called "negative suggestion"—as when she writes, "I have neither folly nor vanity enough to suppose you would think of running away with me." She later reinforces that suggestion with a rare literary allusion: that not since the romantic tales of Mademoiselle de Scudéry has any heroine sacrificed a dowry by eloping. She unceasingly pursues her epistolary campaign with vigorous prose, using such pungent phrases as "Let us both be at liberty till the parson puts an end to it," and with such concrete details as "I shall come to you with only a nightgown and petticoat, and that is all you will get with me."

For a romantic courtship the correspondence is terribly earthbound, as one can see when comparing it with Dorothy Osborne's courtship letters. Lady Mary rarely relaxes from her pose of sensible reasonableness—it is, in the main, a correspondence of plain thinking, plain dealing, and plain writing. Only toward the end of the courtship does she betray emotion. "My family is resolved to dispose of me where I hate. I have made all the opposition in my power; perhaps I have carried that opposition too far. . . . I am compelled to submit.—I was born to be unhappy, and I must fulfil the course of my destiny—" But then, as though remembering her claim of being without passion: "You see, Sir, the esteem I have for you. I have ventured to tell you the whole secret of my heart." Another of the late-courtship letters begins: "I tremble for what we are doing.—Are you sure you will love me for ever?—Shall we never repent? I fear and I hope." But it concludes: "You shall hear from me again tomorrow, not to contradict, but to give some directions. My resolution is taken—Love me and use me well." She starts with trembling doubts and questions; she ends with firm commands.

Her literary allusions are sparse: several references to the *Tatler* and *Spectator* papers, a few to Steele's plays, to Dryden, to Aesop's fables, and occasional phrases from the Book of Common Prayer. Wortley, an intimate friend of Addison and of Steele, knew of her wide reading—but this would not have served her purpose. As it was, he suspected her of being too clever. Far better for her to use such proverbial notions as: "Our aunts and grandmothers always tell us men are a sort of animals, that if ever they are constant 'tis only where they are ill used. 'Twas a kind of paradox I could never believe. Experience has taught me the truth of it." Or such homely philosophy as: "Happiness is the natural design of all the world, and every thing we see done, is meant in order to attain it. My imagination places it in friendship."

When Lytton Strachey read this correspondence in 1907, in its truncated form, he thought them "strange love-letters" of the "deepest interest." It is not difficult to see why.

About twenty-five years after the termination of the courtship by marriage, Lady Mary was again involved in a love affair—but this time of a most astonishing kind, with Francesco Algarotti, the Italian savant and writer. Its progress can be followed in her letters to him, thirty-two in all, which have never been printed. In 1736 Algarotti, a handsome young man in his twenties, opportunistic and sexually ambivalent, came to England to make his fortune. When Lady Mary met him, she was almost instantly ignited with love. After he left, she pursued him with her letters, and in 1738 proposed retiring with him to Italy. A year later she abandoned home, husband, and friends to hasten to Venice. But instead of joining her, Algarotti found a richer opportunity in Berlin. When they finally met, almost two years later, her dream of a romantic idyll was decisively shattered. Then, after an interruption of fifteen years, they resumed their friendship, but in a spirit of intellectual camaraderie. As she jotted in her Commonplace Book, he was by then *hors d'œuvre*.

As "literary documents" these love-letters are remarkable for their emotional abandon and extravagance. Even though their literary origins may have been the French romances and letter-writers of the seventeenth century, Lady Mary needed no models; the frantic pulsation clearly came from her own heart. If in her courtship letters, plain feelings engendered plain prose, in these, extravagant feelings bloomed as extravagant prose. "What has become of that philosophical indifference that made the glory and tranquillity of my former days?" she asks (in French). "My feelings are too ardent; I could not possibly explain them or hide them." In another letter—still early in her infatuation—"How timid one is when one loves!" —and she concludes that letter with: "I am torn by a thousand conflicting feelings that concern you very little. . . . All that is certain is that I shall love you all my life in spite of your whims and my reason." In another (still in French), "You must believe that you possess in me the most perfect friend and the most passionate lover."

To express this intense emotion she usually wrote in French, though Algarotti could read English, for she found in that language a freedom from her customary inhibitions. (We can observe the same quality of relaxation and intimacy in Swift's French letters to Vanessa.) Besides French prose, she frequently fell into "the extravagancies of poetry, which indeed are only fit to attempt the expressing my thoughts of you or to you." In one letter, after complaining of winter weather and a tormenting toothache, she tells Algarotti that she looks forward to the spring when he and the sun shall return:

> You, lovely youth, shall my Apollo prove;
> Adorn my verse, and tune my soul to love.

In another effusion—borrowed from Dryden—she assures him she would prefer him to any man as great as the first Caesar and as young as the second. No hyperbole is too elevated—or grotesque—and her reading in Restoration heroic tragedy no doubt helped her. One short letter combines three main devices: French prose that stalks on tiptoe, a comparison from a literary classic, and a volley of heroic couplets. She is about to enter Italy on her way to their rendezvous: "Here I am at the feet of the Alps, and tomorrow I take the step which is to lead me into Italy. I recommend myself to you in all perils like Don Quixote to his Dulcinea, and I have an imagination no less inflamed than his"—and so on, ending with the three soulful couplets.

Her use of literary characters as symbolic of her own state of mind reinforces her generally high-flown style. (In her courtship letters to Wortley, the few she cited were generally satiric; and she never erupted into verse.) In the letter just quoted she calls herself Don Quixote to Algarotti's Dulcinea (the inversion of sexual roles is appropriate for him at least); her other character-identifications are classical: she is Dido, the "soul-racked" Queen of Carthage, bemoaning the departure of her little Aeneas; or she is the Penelope of his absence; or she prepares to leave London to meet him in the Elysian Fields—on the Grand Canal.

Besides this serious imagery, she frequently uses religious wit, of the kind affected by the *libertins* and seventeenth-century poets. She is thus able to lighten her declarations of love, and to appeal to Algarotti's *esprit*. "The Enthusiasm you have infected me with is as violent as ever," she tells him (two years after they had met); she meant Enthusiasm in its religious sense, though modulated upwards from a low Dissenting key. When she waits for him to call on her, she compares herself to the martyrs who have been canonized for suffering less; the Blessed Virgin does not have so sincere a votary as Algarotti has in her; and so on. But when she is about to begin her journey, the religious imagery loses its ironic edge: her journey is a pilgrimage, at the end of which he may grant her prayers; and she departs from England "with the resolution of a man well persuaded of his religion and happy in his conscience, filled with faith and hope."

When her faith and hope in Algarotti (as her Savior) collapsed, how would she "compose" the denouement of the drama that had begun five years earlier? Instead of assuming the role of a classical heroine (or hero) she calmly tells him (in French): "I have studied you, and studied so well that Sir Isaac Newton did not dissect the rays of the sun with more exactness than I have deciphered the sentiments of your soul. Your eyes served me as a prism to discern the ideas of your mind." She continues the elaborate analogy, ending with: "I see so clearly the nature of your soul that I am as much in despair of touching it as Mr. Newton was of enlarging his discoveries by means of telescopes, which by their own powers dissipate and change the light rays." The letter is a tour de force; its central imagery is especially apt when we remember that Algarotti's most famous book, published three years before, was a set of graceful dialogues on the *Optics*, entitled *Newtonianism for the Ladies*. Lady Mary had assured him, "I have read, I have re-read, and I shall re-read your book. I shall always find new beauties; none of its charms escapes me." She could not have foreseen its usefulness in dramatizing her disillusion.

When Byron read a few of these love-letters in manuscript he called them "very pretty and passionate . . . the *French* not good, but the sentiments beautiful." Taken as a group they extend our knowledge of Lady Mary's emotional and literary versatility far beyond the limits previously charted. They uncover a new dimension in her personality and her art.

Lady Mary's letters to her sister Lady Mar in the 1720's are famous for their brilliant, occasionally malicious picture of upper-class English life. Because of her sisterly affection, the letters are intimate and unrestrained. Lady Mar, who lived in Paris with her exiled Jacobite husband, suffered from melancholia which later deepened into insanity; hence Lady Mary tries to raise her from the doldrums by pointing to what was most ridiculous in the *beau monde* they both knew.

The scandal she deals with at greatest length is, in fact, her own. It is the dismal history of her involvement with a blackmailing Frenchman named Rémond—an affair which *his* letters prove to have been purely financial and not amatory. But when she turns to the scandal of other people she elevates gossip to art. With her narrative skill she can compress a whole chapter into a few sentences. Or in even briefer scope, she anatomizes a personality—as when she tells how Lord Carleton "has left this transitory world. . . . He was taken ill in my company at a concert at the Duchess of Marlborough's, and died two days after, holding the fair Duchess [of Queensberry] by the hand, and being fed at the same time with a fine fat chicken, thus dying, as he lived, indulging his pleasures." In an age of Palladian architecture Lady Mary balanced her ideas and phrases with a comparable symmetry. The Countess of

Bristol, she writes, has given up gambling for gallants, "and resolved to make up for time mis-spent, she has two lovers at a time, and is equally wickedly talked of for the gentle Colonel Cotton and the superfine Mr. Braddocks. Now I think this the greatest compliment in nature to her own lord; since 'tis plain that when she will be false to him, she is forced to take two men in his stead, and that no one mortal has merit enough to make up for him." In a similar vein Mrs. West is a great prude who has only two lovers at a time, one for use and the other for show.

Of all the social questions she deals with in these letters, marriage is foremost. The daughter of a friend was "in the paradisal state of receiving visits every day from a passionate lover, who is her first love. . . . Her Mama and I often laugh and sigh reflecting on her felicity. . . ." But the engagement of an elderly crippled couple seemed to her an *amour* "as curious as that between two oysters, and as well worthy the serious enquiry of the naturalists." If courtships had these contrasting possibilities, what she usually observed of marriages deserved her cynicism.

"To speak plainly," she writes, "I am very sorry for the forlorn state of matrimony, which is as much ridiculed by our young ladies as it used to be by young fellows: in short, both sexes have found the inconveniencies of it, and the appellation of rake is as genteel in a woman as a man of quality." She documents her generalization with "curious" examples from the world around her. In one letter she tells her sister that an acquaintance of hers "has had a small accident befallen him. Mr. Annesley found him in bed with his wife, prosecuted, and brought a bill of divorce into Parliament. Those things grow more fashionable every day, and in a little while won't be at all scandalous. The best expedient for the public, and to prevent the expense of private families, would be a general act of divorcing all the people of England. You know, those that pleased might marry over again; and it would save the reputations of several ladies that are now in peril of being exposed every day."

Her great interest in marriage probably grew out of her own, so unsuccessful when measured by her ideals. She admits as much in another of her comments, about how "one of the agreeablest girls upon earth" was "so vilely misplaced. But where are people matched!" she exclaims—and then moralizes: "I suppose we shall all come right in Heaven; as in a country dance, though hands are strangely given and taken while they are in motion, at last all meet their partners when the jig is done." Many of her poems and miscellaneous prose pieces also deal with marriage—and prove that her cynicism masked an irrepressible idealism. She once wrote a long essay in French to refute the maxim of La Rochefoucauld that marriages are convenient but not delightful. Most of those she describes seem to be neither.

If her concern with marriage grew out of her own misfortune, so did her philosophizing. On its simplest level, her cure for lowness of spirits was not "drinking nasty water but galloping all day, and a moderate glass of champagne at night in good company." In another letter she explains more fully what she calls "the true philosophy"—and it adds up to a reasonable, balanced way of life. But in spite of her recipes for contentment she was obsessed by "the damned, damned quality of growing older and older every day, and my present joys are made imperfect by fears of the future." (She was all of thirty-six at the time.)

Describing the world around her in less personal terms, she concedes that with youth and money one might be well diverted; but since it is her "established opinion that this globe of ours is no better than a Holland cheese, and the walkers about in it mites, I possess my mind in patience, let what will happen; and should feel tolerably easy, though a great rat came and ate half of it up." (What a striking metaphor, the cheese and rat! What would a psychoanalytical critic make of it?)

She expressed her most extended and "philosophic" rumination in a letter written when she was in the deepest despair because of the disappearance of her runaway son: "I have five thousand pins and needles running into my heart." She was sufficiently shaken to explore the depths of her discouragement. "This is a vile world, dear sister," she begins; and after lamenting mankind's ills, both inherited and acquired, she continues, "All these things, and five hundred more, convince me (as I have the most profound adoration for the Author of Nature) that we are here in an actual state of punishment. I am satisfied I have been damned ever since I was born, and in submission to divine justice, don't at all doubt but I deserved it in some pre-existent state. I am very willing to soften the word damned and hope I am only in purgatory, and that after whining and grunting here a certain number of years, I shall be translated to some more happy sphere, where virtue will be natural, and custom reasonable; that is, in short, where common sense will reign. I grow very devout, as you see, and place all my hopes in the next life, being totally persuaded of the nothingness of this." But then, in the same letter, she advises her sister—and herself, we can be sure—"One should pluck up a spirit, and live upon cordials when one can have no other nourishment." She was not an unregenerate pessimist.

She even enjoyed moments of happiness. From her country retreat at Twickenham she wrote: "My time is melted away here in almost perpetual concerts." In the same setting she gloated over how well she felt "in this dear minute, in this golden now." Besides, pungent common sense kept her from losing her perilous equilibrium. When told that she looked better than ever in her life, she reflected that it was "one of those lies one is always glad to hear." In the same mood of comfortable disenchantment, after witnessing the absurd airs of elderly ladies at the Coronation of George the Second, she, who dreaded "growing wise more than any thing in the world, was overjoyed to observe one can never outlive one's vanity."

"Egotism is the god that inspires the letter-writer," George Moore once remarked, "and good letters are all about the letter-writer." Lady Mary frequently writes about herself, but with a refreshing detachment free of cloying vanity. No matter how often she philosophizes she is never boring; for she avoids those *longueurs* that so easily infect introspective writers.

Her mind and style have a consonant keenness. Among the critics who have analyzed her style, Walter Bagehot awarded her "the highest merit of letter-writing—she is concise without being affected. . . . She said what she had to say in words that were always graphic and always sufficiently good, but she avoided curious felicity. Her expressions seemed choice, but not chosen." Lytton Strachey praised her for being "absolutely frank and absolutely sensible. . . . Her wit has that quality which is the best of all preservatives against dullness—it goes straight to the point."

The most varied and interesting of her informal correspondences is that with her daughter Lady Bute, carried on most abundantly during the decade near the end of her life when she lived in comfortable retirement in northern Italy. Lady Bute served as the focus of a benign affection (unlike the hysterical passion of Madame de Sévigné for her daughter); and Lady Mary took full advantage of what she called her "maternal privilege of being tiresome." She practices what George Saintsbury defines as the art of letter-writing—a mosaic or macédoine of nearly all departments of general literature: description, narrative, argument; pathos, perhaps; wit, if well managed; and the greatest negative virtue of not being *obviously* "written for publication."

As a descriptive artist Lady Mary felt the full beauty of the landscape around her; she was a pioneer explorer of the Italian lake country before that region was invaded by tourists armed with album and water colors. The village of Lovere on Lago d' Iseo resembled Tunbridge Wells, she writes, and its gardens, those on Richmond Hill: she frequently makes such comparisons, not out of invidious insularity but to bring the scene to her correspondent's eye. At other times she is forced to be poetical, and evoke all the "delightful ideas of romance" or fairy tale. But her description is more effective in concrete terms: near her farm was a little wood "carpeted, in their succeeding seasons, with violets and strawberries, inhabited by a nation of nightingales, and filled with game of all kinds, excepting deer and wild boar."

As a social historian she tells of the local gentry, peasants, and artisans, of their diversions on the lake, at the carnival, their opera and theatre productions. Here is a brief vignette with the concise charm of a drawing by Watteau: "Some ladies in the neighborhood favored me last week with a visit in masquerade. They were all dressed in white like vestal virgins, with garlands on their heads. They came at night with violins and flambeaux, but did not stay more than one dance, pursuing their way to another castle some miles from hence."

Along with her finesse in description—more effective through its casualness—she practices the art of narrative. Here her worldly detachment and wisdom keep her tales from being tedious. In one of her best, that about Signora Laura Bono, she relates how the lady's husband returned home unexpectedly and "proceeded to his chamber, without meeting anybody, where he found his beloved spouse asleep on the bed with her gallant. The opening of [the] door waked them: the young fellow immediately leaped out of the window, which looked into the garden, and was open, it being summer, and escaped over the fields, leaving his breeches on a chair by the bedside—a very striking circumstance. In short, the case was such, I do not think the queen of fairies herself could have found an excuse, though Chaucer tells us she has made a solemn promise to leave none of her sex unfurnished with one, to all eternity." Lady Mary, the heroine of this "small history," prevented the cuckold husband from killing his wife; and she adds that because the episode has remained secret, "the lady retains the satisfaction of insulting all her acquaintance on the foundation of a spotless character." Her longest story is "an adventure exactly resembling, and I believe copied from, Pamela"; she sketches it in five (printed) pages, though, she says, it would in Richardson's hands "furnish out seven or eight volumes."

It is a masterly narrative; in it the true-life Pamela is depicted as virtuous, modest, and deserving; yet at the end Lady Mary accuses her of "artifice" and a "designing head." This ambivalent attitude—her sympathy and cynicism toward the sentimental—characterizes her opinion of all of Richardson's novels. Her daughter in England supplied her with books, mostly fiction; and Lady Mary repaid her with (besides drafts on her London bank) long critiques of those books which particularly struck her. As she read *Clarissa Harlowe* and *Sir Charles Grandison* she wept; but then she called them mean, miserable stuff and violently criticized their picture of upper-class life. "This Richardson is a strange fellow," she confessed; "I heartily despise him, and eagerly read him, nay, sob over his works in a most scandalous manner." Many years before, she had assisted her cousin Henry Fielding in his career as a playwright; now she commented on his novels and on his sad death, and on Smollett's novels and Johnson's *Rambler*. She read voraciously, and her letters mention more of the ephemeral novels of the 1750's than are listed in modern bibliographies. Here, then, is her literary criticism—fragmentary and disorganized perhaps, but valuable for its acuteness.

Lady Mary also indulged in what she calls "reflections"; these are in effect brief essays on almost any subject. She drew her observations from her surroundings, from her past life so rich in activity, and from the constant reading with which she "sweetened her solitude." Her advice on the education of her granddaughter and namesake, if put together, would complement Lord Chesterfield's on the education of his son. Lady Mary recommends learning, particularly the study of languages; but the girl must "conceal whatever learning she attains, with as much solicitude as she would hide crookedness or lameness."

The theme of retirement naturally engrossed much of what she calls "thinking upon paper." "It was formerly a terrifying view to me, that I should one day be an old woman. I now find that Nature has provided pleasures for every state. Those are only unhappy who will not be contented with what she gives, but strive to break through her laws, by affecting a perpetuity of youth. . . ." She resigned herself to old age, and even to death, with a stoicism worthy of Epictetus, whom she had once translated.

She looked beyond her own philosophical threshold to generalize on society and mankind. "I have never in all my various travels seen but two sorts of people, and those very like one another; I mean men and women, who always have been, and ever will be, the same. The same vices and the same follies have been the fruit of all ages, though sometimes under different names." In her utilitarian view, religion is "a comfort to the distressed, a cordial to the sick, and sometimes a restraint on the wicked." As she surveys the history of man she finds great progress since its infancy, but remembers "the many palpable follies which are still (almost) universally persisted in"—especially war.

She does not set forth any strikingly original philosophical position, but rather what oft was thought but ne'er so well expressed-in-prose, particularly on the topic that engaged so many other minds at this time—the nature of happiness. No real happiness is to be found or expected in this world, and to think it can be secured is as childish as running after sparrows to lay salt on their tails. "Mankind," she continues, "is placed in a state of dependency, not only on one another (which all are in some degree), but so many inevitable accidents thwart our designs, and limit our best laid projects, the poor efforts of our utmost prudence and political schemes appear, I fancy, in the eyes of some superior beings, like the pecking of a young linnet to break a wire cage, or the climbing of a squirrel in a hoop. The moral needs no explanation: let us sing as cheerfully as we can in our impenetrable confinement, and crack our nuts with pleasure from the little store that is allowed us." (She wrote this four years before the publication of Voltaire's *Candide*, whose conclusion is not unlike hers.)

One doubts that Lady Mary will ever be enrolled among the philosophers of the Enlightenment (particularly since some of her precepts are so *un*enlightened); but her clear and vivid exposition of the basic assumptions of her time and of her social class gives these informal letters an interest much broader than their modest intent.

All the letters discussed so far are clearly personal and informal; the Turkish Embassy ones are relatively impersonal and formal. These, fifty-two in number, were Lady Mary's first published collection and the basis of her initial fame. They tell of her experiences and observations while accompanying her husband on his two-year Embassy to Turkey. The important question is: can these letters be considered as informal letters, when they were compiled, and transcribed in an album, by Lady Mary herself? Are they, in other words, a narrative in the form of letters, a very popular form of travel literature since the Renaissance?

That assumption cannot be entirely dismissed. The letters are evidently extracts from her journals (now lost) *and* revisions of actual letters. In one of her letters addressed to her sister she says: "I am resolved to keep the copies, as testimonies of my inclination to give you, to the utmost of my power, all the diverting part of my travels, while you are exempt from all the fatigues and inconveniencies." And she headed her transcript "Copies." She altered them, however, removing purely personal references and transposing sections from various letters. As in real letters, the contents are usually appropriate to the correspondent: for example, to Sarah Chiswell, a girlhood friend, Lady Mary addresses a homely description of a Dutch town that resembles Nottingham; to the Princess of Wales, a pathetic account of oppressed peasantry; to Pope, a gracefully modest and clever discourse on Turkish poetry; to the savant Abbé Conti, a witty analysis of the religious sects of Islam; to her "dear sister," as she repeatedly addresses Lady Mar, her observations of the fabulous luxury surrounding Turkish ladies; and so on. These letters, then, are neither actual nor artificial, but something of both. They differ, essentially, from any of her other correspondences: they are virtuoso letters in which she exploited her rich opportunities as she glittered in the courts of Western Europe, rode across the frozen, war-ravaged plains of Hungary, basked in the exotic splendor of Islam, and sailed along the classical shores of the Mediterranean.

Taken as a whole the collection does have structural elements. It starts with her departure from England, and ends with her return to Dover. The most pervasive pattern, growing out of the nature of her subject matter, is a series of contrasts between Western Europe and Turkey; and of contrasts within Europe and within Turkey. The scope of her observations, with their attendant commentaries, is immense; besides such obvious material of tourism as landscapes and buildings (from mosques and palaces to cottages and tree-houses), it includes social life, history, women's dress, religion, marriage and divorce, feminism, and poetry and fable. She had two particular advantages (beyond her sharp eye, mind, and pen) over other travel-writers: as a woman she had entrée into the harems of Islamic Turkey, and as an ambassadress into the courts of Western Europe.

In Vienna she observes the mode of gallantry where married ladies are "served" by men not their husbands (sub-marriage is what she calls it); and at the end of her journey, the same custom in Genoa, under the name of *cicisbeismo;* and in between, she discourses on Turkish marriage, concubines, divorce, and gallantry. In Adrianople she visits an old, devout lady—boring, of course, except for the splendor of her establishment—and then a young, amusing beauty; in Constantinople she again contrasts two such visits. In Sofia she visits a ladies' bagnio and then in Constantinople another. (Her depiction of beautiful Turkish ladies at their bath-ritual inspired the French painter Ingres about a hundred years later to compose *"Le Bain Turc."*)

Far from suffering from narrow insularity, like so many travel writers, Lady Mary is unabashedly open-minded. After describing Viennese sub-marriages, she concludes: "Thus you see, my dear, gallantry and good breeding are as different, in different climates, as morality and religion. Who have the rightest notions of both, we shall never know till the day of judgment. . . ." The most enlightened Moslems, she also discovers, are no different from sensible English Deists; and after describing a religious sect who go to mosques on Friday and church on Sunday because "not being skilled in controversy, [they] declare that they are utterly unable to judge which religion is best," she approves of the modest opinion they have of their own capacity. She continued to apply this comparative attitude to everything she observed on her journey; that she was not committed to any standard except reason and common sense allowed her to exploit in full her gift for witty paradox.

One of her striking paradoxes was that the Sultan of the great Ottoman Empire was himself the slave of the military Janissaries. (Voltaire borrowed this observation directly from some of her verse.) Slaves in Turkey were better treated and happier than free servants in England, she noted; and women's confinement in the harem allowed them greater opportunity for infidelity when they emerged effectively disguised by heavy veils and shapeless garments in what she calls "perpetual masquerade."

To such unifying themes as religion and feminism in the Embassy Letters, Lady Mary added her literary interests, particularly in those letters addressed to Pope. In Vienna she attends the theatre and opera; in Adrianople she observes the manners and customs of Theocritus and Homer still flourishing; and after translating a Turkish love poem literally, she transposes it freely into equivalent English. Her most elaborate literary letter is a long one (addressed to the Abbé Conti) about her voyage through the Mediterranean; and it is so densely allusive that it contains over sixty references that need to be footnoted. It is in that letter that she exclaims: "'Tis impossible to imagine any thing more agreeable than this journey would have been between two and three thousand years since, when, after drinking a dish of tea with Sappho, I might have gone the same evening to visit the temple of Homer in Chios, and have passed this voyage in taking plans of magnificent temples, delineating the miracles of statuaries, and conversing with the most polite and most gay of human kind." This passage may conjure up an amusing tea-party, but it also shows how vitally and intimately she felt the force of classical civilization.

In general, she did not use automatic devices to begin and end her letters. She did not rely on formulas, but adapted the form to the occasion and the recipient. Her salutations and conclusions are so casual and spontaneous that they escape attention. She is fond, however, of ending on a humorous note. One of her frequent conclusions is a variant of: "This letter is of a horrible length, but you may burn it when you have read enough." This warning always comes, not at the beginning or middle, but at the very end of the letter.

Compared to her unequivocally actual letters, these Embassy ones may seem exhibitionistic and self-conscious; but how well she succeeded in her purpose: to amuse and instruct her correspondents—and ultimate readers! For we, more than two centuries later, are spared moral qualms—if we have any— about whether it is proper to read other people's private letters. Lady Mary wished these to be published—and thus to be read by a wider circle than friends and family; indeed to be enjoyed by readers not confined to only one continent and one generation.

The Turkish Embassy Letters, then, are a hybrid form in which Lady Mary "crossed" actual, personal letters with a "cultivated" travel-book. In her miscellaneous prose writings she sometimes used the letter-form without any pretense of its being actual. Were these writings, we may wonder, influenced by her major literary orientation as a letter-writer?

We can begin with a literary work which precedes in date any of her surviving letters. Among her juvenilia is a brief epistolary romance, written—if we may believe her own dating —when she was fifteen. This precocious if undistinguished tale at least shows her interest in the letter as a technical device in fiction. In her maturity she made a few forays into practical journalism, and again used the letter form. (All of these literary adventures are recent discoveries.) The *Spectator* No. 516 (in 1714) contained a satiric letter about a club of nine widows; and a month later Lady Mary—as Mrs. President—answered with a letter defending widows in general and outlining in particular the marriages of the club's president. She composed another essay-letter twenty-five years later in her periodical *The Nonsense of Common-Sense*. In its third issue, again in the satirical mode, she writes a letter signed by a sculptor, who promises to construct artificial opera singers, and thus save for England the money squandered on these foreign imports. In a very different mood, she was so much aroused by the controversy about smallpox inoculation in 1722 that she contributed to the newspaper the *Flying Post* a "letter to the editor" from a Turkey merchant, explaining and defending the operation. Here, dramatically aware of her role, she propagandizes with blunt vigor.

Another variant of the literary letter she used was the "letter from another world"—three of them, characteristically light and debonair. All of these essays in the form of letters display her versatility in general, and, in particular, her skill in adapting that form to literary purposes.

These minor pieces, though not our primary concern, do show her awareness of the letter as a distinct literary type. But nowhere in her writings does she define the letter, or give its characteristics. How can there be rules for such a formless genre? Samuel Johnson, who devoted *Rambler* No. 152 to letter-writing, gave a simple enough recipe: "strict conformity to nature." (It is interesting that, according to Mrs. Piozzi, the only book he ever read through purely for pleasure was Lady Mary's Letters.) But the main burden of his *Rambler* essay was that there could be no rules for letter-writing because "Precept has generally been posterior to performance," and England had not produced any "examples of the familiar style, or models of private correspondence." The irony of his complaint is that at that very moment, although he was not aware of it, the Golden Age of English letter-writing was in progress: letters were being written by Lady Mary, Horace Walpole, Thomas Gray, Lord Chesterfield, and William Cowper, and by Johnson himself.[1]

Columbia University

RICHARDSON'S CORRESPONDENCE:
THE PERSONAL LETTER
AS PRIVATE EXPERIENCE

Malvin R. Zirker, Jr.

PROBABLY NO WRITER'S LIFE reflects such an intense and sustained commitment to the letter form as does Richardson's. It is not merely that he wrote three epistolary novels (of which only one, *Pamela,* is shorter than *War and Peace*), though the nineteen volumes of letters in the Shakespeare Head Edition of his novels are impressive enough. Richardson's attachment to the letter form begins neither with his career as novelist nor with his acceptance of the commission to write "a little Volume of Letters, in a common Style, on such Subjects as might be of Use to those Country Readers who were unable to indite for themselves." Rather, if we are to seek out the beginnings of Richardson's letter-writing career we must imagine, in so far as that is possible, a young Samuel who from his "earliest youth . . . had a Love of Letter-writing"—a Samuel not "fond of Play, as other Boys," who marked his difference from them by assigning to him the nicknames *"Serious* and *Gravity."* When but eleven years old he took up his pen "spontaneously" and made cause against a hypocritical "widow of near Fifty, who, pretending to a Zeal for Religion, & who was a constant Frequenter of Church Ordinances, was continually fomenting Quarrels & Disturbances, by Backbiting & Scandal, among all her Acquaintance." He turned, he tells us, to the Scriptures for argument and, to give force to his rebuke, assumed "the Stile and Address of a Person in Years," from which coign of vantage and safety he "exhorted her . . . [and] expostulated with her." Unfortunately, "my handwriting was known: I was challenged with it & owned ye Boldness; for she complained of it to my Mother with Tears."[1]

The anecdote is amusing—doubtless the sixty-four-year-old Richardson who recounted it found it amusing too—but it is also, in retrospect, significant: significant of Richardson's abiding moral and didactic concern, of his apparently almost instinctive impersonation in letters of imaginary personalities, and, simply but importantly, of his fascination with letter-writing—we may say, nearly, that he lisped in letters.

Richardson's youthful experience with letters was not confined to his missionary epistle to the widow. In the same letter in which he tells us of that experience (a letter to the Reverend Johannes Stinstra, Richardson's Dutch translator) we read the well-known story of his secretarial involvement with three young women of his neighborhood who turned to him for assistance in carrying on a correspondence with their lovers. As Mrs. Barbauld, the editor of his letters, says, "He was fond of two things, which boys have generally an aversion to—letter-writing and the company of the other sex."[2] Richardson, at thirteen, not only composed and corrected their love letters, but, we may infer from his description of his duties, served as apprentice as well as amanuensis to the God of Love: "I have been directed to chide, & even repulse, when an Offence was either taken or given, at the very time that the Heart of the Chider or Repulser was open before me, overflowing with Esteem & Affection; & the fair Repulser dreading to be taken at her Word; directing *this* Word, or *that* Expression, to be softened or changed. One, highly gratified with her Lover's Fervor, & Vows of everlasting Love, has said, when I have asked her Direction: 'I cannot tell you what to write; But (her Heart on her Lips) you cannot write too kindly.'"[3] One imagines that the adolescent Richardson's experiencing such titillating intimacy through letters taught the novelist the letter's power to capture a sense of emotional immediacy and confirmed his personal fondness for the letter form.

We also know that while an apprentice Richardson carried on a now lost correspondence with an unnamed "Gentleman greatly [his] superior in Degree and of ample Fortunes" who intended "high things" for him. According to Richardson this gentleman was " a Master of ye Epistolary style," and he notes regretfully that had he foreseen his future career as letter-writer he could have profited far more than he did from studying his correspondent's skill.[4] As it is, we are at least left with the knowledge that both as young man and as boy Richardson had memorable experience with letters and that that experience was intimate and emotional.

Letters remained a dominating fact of Richardson's life. They could even replace, in the instance of his business, conventional means of communication, for, we learn from Mrs. Barbauld, "in the latter part of his life, he was rarely seen among his workmen, sometimes not twice in a year, and, even when he was in town, gave his directions by little notes."[5] More importantly, with the fame that came with *Pamela*'s success, Richardson's own letters and those adulatory letters that began to flood in upon him became increasingly important to him. He began to keep copies of his own letters (as well he might when told, as he was by one anonymous correspondent that "tho' I am not Superstitious, I should regard a bit of Paper from your Hands, in the same manner as Bigots do Amulets and Relics of Saints"[6]) as well as to save those he received and, like his fictional characters, undertook what amounted to an editor's task in selecting and ordering his correspondence. Mrs. Barbauld tells us that "it was the custom of Mr. Richardson, not only to preserve the letters of his numerous correspondents, but to take copies of his own, generally by the hands of his daughters. . . . It was the favourite employment of his declining years to select and arrange them, and he always looked forward to their publication. . . ."[7]

Richardson's fascination with his own correspondence did not end with the contemplation of it. Letters were something to pass about, to comment on, to solicit comments on. "Pray be so good, when you favour me, to leave a margin at sides, top, and bottom," he writes to Miss Mulso, later the famous Mrs. Chapone, apparently in anticipation of the marginalia her unusually rich letters would inspire. He was in the habit both of asking to see the personal letters of his friends and of sending to them letters he had received from others. We find, for instance, Lady Bradshaigh writing to Richardson to thank him for sending for her perusal private letters Richardson had received: "I return you my sincere thanks for the letters you have been so kind to send, upon my earnest request. Have I not done wrong in asking those letters from you? I did it inconsiderately. But if you suspect any of your correspondents will take it amiss, or would not chuse to have their letters seen, I beg to know, and I will immediately return them."[8] Richardson assures her that all is well and that, as long as she does not take copies of them, she may show the letters to whom she will.

He is anxious to read the personal correspondence of others, as the following passage, in a letter to Mrs. Dewes, shows:

Suffer your warm, your worthy heart, to expand on paper, on a subject that must equally delight us both—on Mr. Dewes' goodness; on your family's welfare; on your own health, and matronly employments and divertisements. In short, Madam, adopt me into your worthy family as one deeply interested in its welfare: and if you will oblige me with such extracts as I may be favoured with from the letters of your excellent sister [Mrs. Delany], and with an account, as she writes it to you, of her health and the good Dean's, and of their employments, amusements, benevolencies, charities, &c. what charming subjects will here be for a correspondence—extracts without inscription, or subscription, or the form of a letter, will rejoice me, as they will give you less pain, and less attention; and I will endeavour to return extracts from some of my correspondencies: so, tho' far off, shall we be near, and mingle minds and concerns as true friends.[9]

The passage also reflects Richardson's insatiable thirst for domestic trivia—or more accurately, for unpremeditated personal comment on intimate affairs that might provide him material for his work in progress. Mrs. Dewes responded by sending Richardson those letters of her sister's which she thought most interesting, and fulfilled his request for information about her own domestic circumstances by relating her son's recovery from a fall from his horse, her sister's sufferings from a fever, and the progress of whooping cough with her two youngest children. Surely it is one of the marvels of Richardson's art that it is from such stuff as this that his novels are made.

Thus for Richardson, letters were not merely things one wrote or read. As documents demanding extraordinary time and attention they were one of life's central activities. Letters were analyzed, copied, commented on, sent about, borrowed, quarreled over, and studied.

As if in imitation of his own experience, Richardson's fictional characters expend unusual amounts of time and thought in activities relating to their correspondence. Leslie Stephen has calculated that over one three-day period Harriet Byron must have written eight hours a day to complete the physical labors her letter-writing entailed.[10] It is not merely a matter of time and labor, however. In his excellent "Epistolary Techniques in Richardson's Novels,"[11] Alan D. McKillop has shown how letters and letter-writing activities enter significantly and pervasively into the plots of Richardson's novels. In *Pamela* especially incidents involving letter-writing abound. Letters precipitate crucial action. Pamela must conceal writing materials, hide her journal, smuggle out her letters. Mr. B—'s threat to seize Pamela's journal when it is concealed under her shift suggests ludicrously an identity between her journal and her virginity. It is the reading of her journal that finally breaks down Mr. B—'s conventional prejudices, and it is Pamela's reading of his letter to her that prepares for her return to her abductor. Throughout Richardson's fictional world one finds that existence is intimately involved with letters.

In *Clarissa* the heroine's falling, however innocently, into a clandestine correspondence with Lovelace has serious consequences, especially for her family's view of her behavior. Later she suffers a cruel deception when faked letters lead her to think Mrs. Sinclair's lodgings are respectable. A fact of Lovelace's character is his fondness for writing letters, and among his many skills is the knowledge of shorthand, which allows him to indulge this fondness more easily and has the effect of adding still another weapon to his amatory arsenal. The first letter in *Grandison,* from Miss Selby to Harriet Byron, encloses a copy of a letter written by Mr. Greville about Harriet. Mr. Greville had crossed out passages in his copy of his letter, but, because he used Miss Selby's ink, which was lighter than his, they are still legible—and Miss Selby and Harriet read them with interest. Conventionally considered, the primary merit of the letter form in the novel lies in its power to convince us of the immediacy and authenticity of the subjective inner state of the writer. Although Richardson achieves this sense of immediacy, he does not do so by making us forget the form by which it is expressed. Technique becomes subject, and at times we read in Richardson's novels about their composition.

Richardson's own comments about the letter form, though interesting, do not explain satisfactorily his compulsive fascination with it. His most pertinent observations relate to what he calls *"instantaneous* descriptions" in letters. In the 1748 Preface to *Clarissa* he asserts that all the letters "are written while the Hearts of the Writers must be supposed to be wholly engaged in their Subjects: The Events at the Time generally dubious:—So that they abound, not only with critical Situations; but with what may be called *instantaneous* Descriptions and Reflections . . ." and, curiously enough, adduces in support of this technique Belford's observation (in a letter of 4 August) that *"much more* lively and affecting . . . must be the style of those who write in the height of a *present* distress; the mind tortured by the pangs of uncertainty (the events then hidden in the womb of fate); *than* the dry, narrative, unanimated style of a person relating difficulties and dangers surmounted, can be; the relater perfectly at ease; and if himself unmoved by his own story, not likely greatly to affect the reader." In the Preface to *Grandison* he makes much the same plea, this time in extenuation of the extraordinary length of that novel: "The nature of familiar letters, written, as it were, to the *moment,* while the heart is agitated by hopes and fears, on events undecided, must plead an excuse for the bulk of a collection of this kind."

Richardson's sophisticated characters share his delight in vivid representation of the present. Lovelace, for instance, to pass the time while waiting for the opportunities his "fire plot" will provide, writes to Belford, for he loves to "write to the moment." Pamela, though not verbalizing this fondness for writing to the moment nevertheless practices it constantly, and we find her on her wedding night, while waiting for Mr. B—'s appearance, writing notes to her parents at eight, ten, and eleven o'clock. Her last note, written just fifteen minutes before he arrives, takes us to the moment of love-making more provocatively perhaps than do modern instantaneous descriptions.

In the relatively infrequent comments on the nature of letters that Richardson makes in his personal letters we find again the assumption that letters are artless, that they reflect the unpremeditated outpourings of an agitated soul, that they are rich in sincerity and allow the reader to confront directly his correspondent's personality. Writing in 1750 to one of his young female admirers, Richardson assures her that she need not hesitate to write to him, artless correspondent as he is: ". . . I am one of the plainest and least accurate persons that ever took up a pen, and who have nothing but *heart* to recommend me; and, when I follow not my correspondent's lead, write whatever, at the moment, comes uppermost, trusting to that heart, and regarding not head."[12] Writing about 1748 to another admiring young lady, Richardson praises the beauties of a friendship confirmed in correspondence: "[letter-writing] is friendship avowed under hand and seal: friendship upon bond, as I may say: more pure, yet more ardent, and less broken in upon, than personal conversation can be even amongst the most pure, because of the deliberation it allows, from the very preparation to, and action of writing. A proof of this appears in [your] letter before me!—Every line of it flowing with that artless freedom, that noble consciousness of honourable meaning, which shine in every feature, in every sentiment, in every expression of the fair writer!"[13]

It is amusing to note that Richardson's praise of letters here is quite close to Lovelace's eulogy of letter-writing to Clarissa in which he too affirms the purity of personal correspondence, full of soul and not subject to the impurities that physical presence admits: "familiar letter writing . . . [is] writing from the heart (without the fetters prescribed by method or study), as the very word *correspondence* [implies]. Not the heart only; the *soul* [is] in it. Nothing of body, when friend writes to friend; the mind impelling sovereignly the vassal fingers. It [is], in short, friendship recorded; friendship given under hand and seal; demonstrating that the parties [are] under no apprehension of changing from time or accident, when they so liberally [give] testimonies, which would always be ready, on failure or infidelity, to be turned against them."[14]

Richardson agrees with Lovelace's theory here and he is as misleading as his villain when he tells his young correspondents that openness characterizes letter-writing. In his novels the reader is intended to accept the letters of Clarissa, Pamela, and Harriet, especially, as unpremeditated. Common sense, and Dr. Johnson, however, tell us that one cannot, if he has the least bit of self-awareness, write a personal letter without calculating to some degree the figure he wishes to make. If we are to read Richardson's novels as he intends us to, we must accept his convention for the letter; if we insist on retaining our real-life expectations for letters, we inevitably decide that even Richardson's good characters are calculators. The notorious difficulties with *Pamela* surely arise in large part because most readers find it impossible to believe that Pamela could present herself as she does in her letters ingenuously, though it is our acceptance of this possibility that Richardson's effects depend on.

If one grants Richardson his unrealistic theory about letters for the purposes of his novelistic art, one may nevertheless be reluctant to accept the same convention in Richardson's own letters. In fact, it is quite obvious that in much of his personal correspondence, especially that with women, Richardson is doing field work. As Joyce was to write to friends in Dublin for material for his novels, Richardson wrote to young ladies equally for the purpose of collecting data. His urging them to be frank, to write from the heart, is no more ingenuous than his asking Lady Bradshaigh to show him her diary or Miss Mulso to describe her rooms (she refused). "How," he exclaims to Lady Bradshaigh, "should I know ladies' minds, ladies' foibles, ladies' secret thoughts?"[15]—in part, we may answer, by corresponding with them.

Considering Richardson's elaborate and idiosyncratic attachment to letters both as a special kind of personal experience and as a literary form about which he was willing to theorize, one might expect that his own letters would provide a rich treasure for study of the familiar letter. Such is not the case.[16] His subject matter is by and large disappointing. There are, of course, the famous attacks on Fielding and the considerable correspondence with Young. Richardson numbered many literary figures among his correspondents—Johnson, Cave, Edwards, the sonneteer, a few bluestockings, Aaron Hill, Bishop Warburton, Cibber, Garrick—but literature or, for that matter, ideas are not significant topics in his letters. Frequently he laments (not very sincerely, one suspects) his failure to read. Speaking of Spenser, he says, "And yet, for want of time, or opportunity, I have not read his Fairy Queen through in series, or at a heat, as I may call it."[17] He tells Cave that his life has been "a trifling busy one" and that he hasn't had time to read all the *Spectator* papers. Though he prefers Johnson's *Ramblers,* he has not read through them either, saying, "I am vexed that I have not taken larger draughts of them before."[18] To Miss Highmore he confesses, "What stores of knowledge do I lose by my incapacity of reading, and by my having used myself to write, till I can do nothing else, nor hardly that. Business too, so pressing and so troublesome."[19] Though his letters are spotted with references to writers, the allusions are general and rarely reflect a real familiarity with the texts.

Politics, religion, the great public issues of his day are scarcely mentioned. After a momentary digression on a university quarrel his correspondent has introduced he exclaims, "But what am I about? Running into politics! I have long laid aside so contemptible a subject."[20] His health and the health of others, personal gossip, his own writings and everything connected with them, from contemporary criticism to his quarrel with the Irish pirates of *Grandison,* and topics that might be related to his work in progress, such as the question of learning in women, filial obedience, or popular diversions, he can warm up to. But he is cold and lifeless on the intellectual topics of the public world.

Richardson's letters to men are almost uniformly dull. They are kind, polite letters obviously intended to express Richardson's friendship and regard for his correspondent, and they continually express his willingness to be of service to his friends. He almost always is in agreement with their views on the topics they may raise, and he is always quick with praise for their triumphs and regret for their reversals. Rarely does he initiate a topic himself. His stance is that of the generous friend, but it is a stance that doesn't always catch his imagination—surely he was not thinking very clearly when, consoling Aaron Hill on a variety of misfortunes which that unhappy man had experienced, including the death of his gardener—no minor mishap, since Hill had turned from poetry to viniculture for his livelihood—he suggested that the gardener would have died a happy man had he known how great was his master's regard for him.

The style of his letters is equally disappointing. His letters generally are informal, rambling, directed closely to answering or commenting on whatever his correspondent has said. We find in them stylistic traits characteristic of his novels, such as his coy use of italics, his fondness for coining words —he is of Harriet Byron's mind when she insists, "I *will* make words whenever I please," and we find "bewailable," "accessibilities," and "unsmiling" (used transitively)—and occasionally we come upon one of those curious similes that tease some modern critics out of thought: "But shall I not affront you," Richardson writes to Miss Highmore, "if I compare you girls to spiders? Here Arachne (we will call the weaver) draws its web, spreads its snares; hangs up an entangled fly here; another there; a third, and a fourth, if she can get the buzzing insect into her purlieus; and then goes and turns one round, pats another, and enjoys her depredations as she pleases. But how miserably runs the recreant into her hole, when a powerful finger of some giant man brushes down or demolishes her cobweb!"[21] But, with some important exceptions, his style is perfunctory and disappointing.

If Richardson's personal letters are relatively uninteresting as examples of the letter form or as revelations of his own intellectual life or of that of his time, they nonetheless have a fascination of their own. They provide us, of course, with invaluable biographical data and, especially for *Grandison,* show us the writer at work, collecting his materials, trying out his ideas on his female coterie. But perhaps most interesting are the suggestions that his letters and his attachment to letters hold for our comprehension of his personality and his emotional life.

81

What catches Richardson's imagination is a correspondence with a young, nubile girl—and a Lady Bradshaigh. Writing to young ladies, Richardson comes, after his fashion, to life. He is their "dear Papa" and they his "beloved daughters." He is a playful, teasing papa, who insists on knowing just what they mean by this word and that expression, who wants to know exactly how they feel about the young men they mention and exactly what their opinion is on a multitude of essentially feminine topics.

Frequently his style becomes breathless, incomplete sentences pile up, and nearly all are found deserving of exclamation points. He produces what, in speaking of the characteristic epistolary style of *Clarissa*, McKillop has called paragraphs *de longue haleine*. Here for instance is Richardson writing to Miss Highmore to convince her that she must visit him, not he her:

> What say you to me *here*, Miss Highmore?—"Sure, if you go to Tunbridge (says a lady you dearly love, but not better than every one who has the pleasure of knowing her, loves) you will not value travelling a few miles in order to visit us." Tunbridge Wells are about thirty-eight miles distant from London: Hatch (I have enquired) is about forty; and no extraordinary roads. I, a bad traveller, cannot sit a horse—come hither to drink the waters for health-sake—can ill spare the time—propose but *three* weeks—have been here *one*, last Friday—this *my* situation.
>
> The geniuses of Hatch, how different their's! Nothing to do but study their diversion and amusement. Tunbridge, in high season, a place devoted to amusement.—Time entirely at command, though not hanging heavy; impossible indeed it should.—Vehicles, whether four-wheeled or four-legged, at will; riding, a choice.—And the worthy Dr. Knatchbull here. What says my fair correspondent?—What her worthy and kind friends to *this*?[22]

His heavy playfulness, the rather gauche archness of his tone, the insinuating informality of his argument, his citing a passage from another letter for evidence, all are characteristic of his correspondence with young women.

In his letters to them Richardson was not merely assuming a stance for professional reasons, and this part of his correspondence represents more than the novelist's experimental laboratory. As a novelist he certainly wanted to know how young ladies thought and felt about a variety of topics. But in his letters to women there is unmistakable evidence of an emotional involvement in its own right. Richardson forces a kind of intimacy with ladies by means of his style and the personality it presents. He takes whatever they may say seriously, questions their meaning whenever he finds it doubtful, returns their sentences to them with objections. Here is the opening of a letter to Miss Highmore:

"I am very much pleased, my dear Miss Highmore, with the declaration of your easy and happy state of mind. I do not take delight in finding fault with my girl; but it was because I wished you happy, and thought you ought to think yourself so, that made me take notice of an expression or two that looked another way.

"But what mean you by the word *even?* 'I behave, I hope, in a manner that even you would approve.' What mean you by this word *even*, I once more ask you?"[23]

Having presented himself as a paternal figure, and one who is artless and ingenuous, he can demand explanations, elaborations on their views of love, marriage, filial obedience. An exchange of ideas is not what results. Rather, we have a kind of dialogue between parent and child, sage adviser and young friend, lover and mistress. Richardson manages to present himself in all three roles and gives his position a further emotional coloration by the way he insinuates intimacy, by the way he attempts to creep into the emotional life of his correspondent.

Richardson wants more than information. Like Lovelace, he is an "encroacher"—Clarissa's favorite term for Lovelace because of his continual assumption of greater and greater liberties. His request for private letters, descriptions of sitting rooms, and for personal journals is one illustration of his encroaching. His playful teasing of his correspondents for more elaborate and exact explanations of their meaning is another. Richardson's compulsion to know more of his correspondent's private life and in a sense to control it by participation in it, leads him at times to a neurotic insistence on personal revelation or demand for explanation of ludicrously trivial matters. Richardson chides one young lady for her failure to take leave of him personally before setting off for Yorkshire, and her reply suggests the impatience many of his correspondents must have felt at his insistence on attention: "I am extremely sorry I can't have the pleasure of seeing you, and giving you an account of my schemes by word of mouth; but since I am so unlucky, and you seem to be curious about them, I must take this way of informing you. . . ."[24] And she goes on to outline very briefly her plans.

More striking are the letters he wrote to Miss Westcomb upbraiding her for her failure to write to him. Miss Westcomb had visited the Richardsons and then gone on a holiday trip before returning to her home, omitting for some time to write her thank-you note. In reply to this tardy note Richardson wrote an eight-page letter devoted entirely to exposing the inadequacy of her apologies. When Miss Westcomb replied with a partial apology and defense, he was not satisfied and sent another eight-page chiding letter, the tone of which is suggested by the following:

You are not in fault at all!—Not you!—Let me put a few questions to you?

Don't you think I love you dearly? With a love truly Paternal?

You know I do, you answer. Yes, my dear, all that know me know I do.

And don't you know how solicitous I was to make an opportunity to attend you to Ankerwyke?

And had you not opportunity to write when Mrs. Jodrell retired to write? when Miss Johnson retired to write to her papa?— Will you say no? Did not the former good lady remind you that you should? My concern at your slight has made me inquisitive, I can tell you that. And what then could you want but inclination?

And yet my pride (I am very proud I can tell you—and that very particularly of your favours) will hardly permit me to suppose it. Let me say, Madam, that though I may not deserve to be favoured, I cannot bear to be slighted.

What was Mrs. Jodrell's writing, to your promise of a letter, my dear girl? Answer me that,—Your voluntarily-promised letter? I thought you knew, that when we men obtain a promise of favour from a lady, we hold her to it—But I was but a papa!—Very well, Miss Westcomb![25]

The attempt at banter does not conceal Richardson's real annoyance and frustration. Throughout the rest of the letter he cites passages from her explanation and in the manner of a new critic questions their logic, their implications, their adequacy. These two letters are close to the kind of letter an uncertain lover might write to his mistress, a lover who is jealous of any private life in which he does not share.

It is tempting to explain this aspect of Richardson's personal correspondence in terms of his own life. We do not know much about Richardson's private life, but what we do know suggests that it was not particularly satisfying in its personal relationships. Richardson himself was a shy, diffident man who found it difficult to meet people socially. As McKillop and others point out, he was unable to meet such men as Garrick, Johnson, or Fielding on equal terms, and he retreated to the more congenial circle of feminine admirers and mild-mannered men who were willing to pay court to him. Even here, perhaps, he only rarely found the kind of emotional satisfaction he craved. Richardson apparently was not easy to get along with, nervous, sensitive, demanding of attention as he was, and one suspects that many of his admirers were readier to correspond than to visit with him, especially as he got older. At least we find him complaining, in 1756, of some neglect among his ladies: "I believe Miss M[ulso?], Miss P[rescott?], and that more than agreeable set of friends, and we, love one another as well as ever; I can answer, I am sure, for our side; but we meet not near so often as we used to do. The pen and ink seems to have furnished the cement of our more intimate friendship and that being over with me, as to writing any more for the public, the occasion of the endearment ceases. If this be not the cause of the distance, I know not to what to impute it, for I, and all mine, love them dearly. . . ."[26]

Both his marriages, sedate and prudent, appear to have been, if unexciting, satisfactory, though the first Mrs. Richardson's fondness for lying in bed a-mornings proved trying to a man accustomed to rising at five. The second Mrs. Richardson, who appears in his letters as "my worthy-hearted wife," remains a shadowy figure, praised for her domestic virtues but never individualized. Neither she nor Richardson's daughters entered significantly into his literary life. There is evidence to suggest that his relationship with his daughters was especially unsatisfying emotionally. As Mrs. Barbauld points out, "There appears to have been a certain formality and stiffness of manner, but ill calculated to invite his children to . . . familiarity and confidence. . . ," and she cites the letter from Lady Bradshaigh in which she criticizes the style of the letters written by one of Richardson's daughters "as too stiff, with the *Honoured Sir,* and the *ever dutiful,* constantly occurring, which, she tells him, was not likely to produce the familiarity he wished to invite; and objects, that in his writings, filial awe is too much inculcated."[27] In his answer Richardson admits that there exists too great a distance between him and his children, though he claims that he has done his best to lessen it.

Richardson's famous self-description in a letter to Lady Bradshaigh emphasizes his retiring nature and suggests a rather unpleasant sensitivity which manifests itself in sly, peeping, stealthy observation of others. Another self-portrait, less well-known, maintains this suggestion. Inviting a young lady to visit him, he promises to show her a "grotesque figure": "A sly sinner, creeping along the very edges of the walks, getting behind benches: one hand in his bosom, the other held up to his chin, as if to keep it in its place: afraid of being seen, as a thief of detection. The people of fashion, if he happen to cross a walk (which he always does with precipitation) *unsmil-*

ing their faces, as if they thought him in their way; and he as sensible of so being, stealing in and out of the bookseller's shop, as if he had one of their glass-cases under his coat. Come and see this odd figure! You never *will* see him, unless *I* shew him to you: and who knows when an opportunity for that may happen again at Tunbridge?"[28] Does not the picture Richardson gives of himself here support the conjecture that he was a man likely to seek release for his emotional life in other than the conventional forms of human intercourse?

What I would suggest is that Richardson found in letters a way to *create* for himself an emotional life otherwise unavailable to him. In his fiction letters became an artistic medium for representing real life. In his own life, letters became the equally artificial means whereby he came to live in fact an extremely important part of his life. We have seen how important, even as a boy, letters were for him and have noted the very special way both in fiction and in life letters became agents in action, became more than a medium by which experience might be conveyed and became at times that experience itself. And more. In his letters Richardson develops otherwise dormant aspects of his own personality, taps emotional resources probably largely unavailable to him in direct confrontation with other personalities. He makes come into being through letters relationships which are, especially with women, otherwise unattainable.

This special function of Richardson's personal letters is apparent if we note the resemblance of his correspondence to the fictional correspondences in his novels—a resemblance most sharply seen in his letters to Lady Bradshaigh. Lady Bradshaigh was a rather charming, eccentric, middle-aged lady from Lancashire who burst into Richardson's life in 1748 by writing to him to plead for Clarissa's life and Lovelace's as well. Her letters, especially at first, are highly dramatic and illustrate, doubtless to Richardson's delight, his theory of letters as artless and spontaneous emotional expression. In her first letter, for instance, she includes a curse for Richardson should he be so relentlessly cruel as to sacrifice Clarissa: "If you disappoint me, attend to my curse:—May the hatred of all the young, beautiful, and virtuous, for ever be your portion! and may your eyes never behold any thing but age and deformity! may you meet with applause only from envious old maids, surly bachelors, and tyrannical parents! may you be doomed to the company of such! and, after death, may their ugly souls haunt you!"[29] Her second letter—Richardson could scarcely fail to answer such a challenging correspondent—shows no flagging in her emotional state. It begins: "Let me intreat! only suppose all the good-natured, compassionate, and distressed on their knees at your feet, can you let them beg in vain? I have sometimes a faint glimmering of hope, at other times am in despair, which almost makes me mad. . . ."[30] She concludes with a promise to read *Clarissa* once every two years if he will spare the heroine. Later, when Richardson has sent her the volume relating the seduction of Clarissa, Lady Bradshaigh exclaims, "O, Sir! I have been prevailed upon to read a part of your story, that I thought would have torn my heart in a thousand pieces," and confesses that "I can scarce hold my pen. I am as mad as the poor injured Clarissa; and am afraid I cannot help hating you, if you alter not your scheme."[31]

Richardson took her letters quite seriously—his answers to her objections to his tragic ending constitute an important defense of his novel and explanation of his purposes. These letters about *Clarissa* opened a correspondence that was to continue until Richardson's death and whose importance McKillop suggests when he says, "Perhaps it is not too much to say that after 1749 Lady Bradshaigh dominated Richardson's life and work."[32]

For our purposes what is most interesting about this correspondence is its fictional character. It was, in a sense, a lovers' correspondence—McKillop calls it a "highly respectable Anglo-Saxon version of the liaisons that stud the literary history of France."[33] Lady Bradshaigh wrote to Richardson under the assumed name of Belfour. Though she lived at Haigh in Lancashire, Richardson was directed to send his letters with the inscription "To be left at the Post-office in Exeter till called for." Lady Bradshaigh's letters were dated Exeter. Only gradually did she let Richardson know details of her own life—her age, her ten-year courtship, her marriage. He had a real woman of mystery to whom he could write letters and who admired him prodigiously. It is no wonder, I think, that this correspondence fascinated him. His own letters become expansive, ranging freely over the topics that ever delighted him. He is obviously in his element. According to Mrs. Barbauld, the correspondence with Lady Bradshaigh alone is as voluminous as the six volumes of letters she chose to print in 1804.[34]

The question of a meeting between his incognita and her "sage mentor," as she came to call Richardson, inevitably arose. Lady Bradshaigh resisted Richardson's importunities for an assignation, pleading her bashfulness and timidity. His self-description, referred to earlier, was intended in part to allay her fears of his person. They finally agree that Richardson is to walk in the park on fine days between one and two and she will, unobserved herself, observe him to decide if a direct meeting would be too much for her. Rather elaborate negotiations go on, Richardson becoming more and more insistent. It becomes a lovers' meeting, the lady resisting, uncertain, afraid, the man insisting, cajoling, pleading. A rendezvous is arranged, but Lady Bradshaigh fails to appear and Richardson is left to walk, rather foolishly, alone—wondering as each carriage passes if that one contains the good lady, while he is "dining," as he says, on a sea biscuit he had brought in his pocket. This happens a second and a third time. Richardson nearly loses his patience and his fascination grows. He compares himself to Lovelace and her to Clarissa when she tells him that she has been to his very threshold but lost her nerve at the last moment:

And have you been in Salisbury-Court? upon the very steps leading to my door—the knocker in your hand? Unaccountable causeless diffidence! "But a brick-wall perhaps," says Clarissa, "between Mr. Lovelace and me!"—So near me, my incognita! I was ready to go to the steps, and to look round me there, when I read this passage, tho' at so many weeks distance, as if I had thought, that so welcome a foot had left some impressions on the stone, that might correspond with those you have in my mind. Good old soul! you will be apt to say, what ideas hadst thou in thy youth, that can have left so much force upon thee in thy decline![35]

He finally discovers her identity when she visits Richardson's friend the painter Highmore. Lady Bradshaigh gives herself away by inquiring too closely about Richardson, and one of Highmore's servants gets her name from her servant. A personal meeting still does not take place for several months, but Richardson does go to the park once more, where Lady Bradshaigh drives past him, unobserved, four times in her carriage. Richardson exasperatedly complains that he spent hours showing himself in the park, walking a total of nine miles and being worn out by the bustle of the crowd and the incessant peering that he was put to.

Lady Bradshaigh recognizes now that the game is up and in her reply invites Richardson to pay her a visit. But she cannot quite renounce the pleasures of coquetry, and her postscript to this letter is a final bantering fillip feeding the nearly spent emotions of their intrigue: "I hope, Sir, you are not very bad after your fatigue; you looked very well yesterday morning. But I dare not tell you how near I was to you."[36]

The episode is ludicrous in many ways. Richardson fifty-nine years old and Lady Bradshaigh over forty carrying on their elaborate epistolary love play and indulging themselves, largely through letters, in a series of schemes and plots after the manner of Richardson's fictional characters, make a grotesque couple. The assumed name, the feigned address, the prolonged mysteries, the foiled meetings, the artificial prolongation of artificially created suspense, the ascription to the present of emotion experienced in the past, are the materials of fiction transferred rather uncomfortably to life. The two settled down to a more prosaic relationship after their personal meeting, though Richardson tried to keep some interest up by playing on the jealousy between Lady Bradshaigh and her sister Mrs. Echlin, who began a correspondence with Richardson against her sister's wishes. But all he could provoke were some catty remarks—of her sister Mrs. Echlin says, "I cannot help but pity a creature loaded with fat."[37] Lady Bradshaigh merely threatens to write shorter letters. (Mrs. Echlin, by the way, was later to visit Richardson, insisting, without explanation, on appearing under an assumed name.)

Surely the episode demonstrates the emotional richness personal letters held for Richardson. His best letters are those to Lady Bradshaigh. By removing their relationship, through letters, from the prosaic actualities of his printer's shop and from the restraints that his personal diffidence and his restrictive sense of propriety put on direct encounters and by placing it in the semi-fictional world that he could create in letters and with letters, he lived the emotionally exciting life which he craved and which, as his novels amply demonstrate, he imaginatively comprehended. In 1750 Lady Bradshaigh commissioned a portrait of Richardson from Highmore, a portrait that was to hang incognito, of course—she told her friends that it was of a Mr. Dickenson. It is with absolute appropriateness that she requested that Richardson be pictured, not in his printing shop, not surrounded by his wife and daughters, not, even, encircled by the many volumes of his novels. Rather: "If you think proper, Sir, I would chuse to have you drawn in your study, a table or desk by you, with pen, ink, and paper; one letter just sealed, which I shall fancy is to me."[38]

Indiana University

91

"THE ART OF PLEASING":
THE LETTERS OF CHESTERFIELD

CECIL PRICE

THE LETTER FORM is infinitely accommodating. It can encompass an order of the day or a brilliant narrative. It may even contain the poignant expression of heartfelt emotion that is almost a soliloquy to an unseen audience.

For Chesterfield it was none of these, but a useful instrument in the arts of pleasing and instructing. He was always conscious of its powerful influence in civilized society and emphasized the point to his son: "It is of the greatest importance to write letters well; as this is a talent which unavoidably occurs every day of one's life."[1] Time was no more to be skimped in dealing with them than it was to be withheld from the life of the salon or the court, for letters took the place of conversation and shared its capacity to gladden men's hearts and mould their prejudices.

His axiom might well have been, "Write to others as you would have them write to you." It is certainly no accident that he is best remembered for letters that taught his son how (with the best of motives) to make friends and influence people.

In intimate correspondence it was vital "to be easy and natural, not strained and florid." To write a love letter, "you must only think of what you would say to her if you were both together."[2] He warned his son against the common error of people who "think they must write abundantly better than they talk, which is not at all necessary."[3] Clearly to be natural is to talk in the highly effective and persuasive way of well-bred men. There is even room for a little inventiveness and fancy: "tropes, figures, antitheses, epigrams etc. would be as misplaced and as impertinent in letters of business, as they are sometimes (if judiciously used) proper and pleasing in familiar letters."[4] The emphasis here lies on the word "judicious." The choice of the exact word or figure was as essential as the appropriate tone of voice. Both would delight men of discrimination, and win their favor.

If young Philip were in search of example, he need only study Cicero's letters to his friends and to Atticus: "the most perfect models of good writing."[5] If he required something lighter, he would look elsewhere. "For gay and amusing letters, for *enjouement* and *badinage,* there are none that equal Comte Bussy's and Madame Sévigné's. They are so natural, that they seem to be the extempore conversations of two people of wit, rather than letters, which are commonly studied, though they ought not to be so."[6] Chesterfield made the point again when he wrote, "I love *le style léger et fleuri.*"[7]

Now Philip became an abrupt and somewhat pedantic youth and his father soon discovered that though his letters were natural enough they fell far short of the models. They were, Chesterfield thought, "exceedingly laconic, and neither answer my desires, nor the purpose of letters; which should be familiar conversation between absent friends." He went on to advise him how to make his letters more intimate: "Tell me of any new persons and characters that you meet with in company, and add your own observations upon them: in short, let me see more of you in your letters."[8]

A question that may well have remained in the young recipient's mind was how he could show more of himself in the letters without exhibiting what his father would have called an ill-bred egotism. The answer lay in the whole system of behavior that Chesterfield inculcated. Only the man bred in courts could show himself to advantage at all times: "Nothing will do this effectually but the frequenting of good Company, and the People *du bon ton* wherever He goes."[9] The laconic is offensive because it makes one's readers strain after meaning. This is a fault to be found even in Tacitus: "He has a peculiar conciseness of style that often renders him obscure."[10] An easy clarity must be the writer's first aim.

Chesterfield's advice to Philip on these matters reflected in every way his own ambitions. It is followed most closely when Chesterfield writes letters to his friends, less closely when he writes as a teacher, and less still when he is commenting on political affairs.

He was the acknowledged leader of taste in his day, but he is careful to avoid condescension when he writes to his friends. In fact, it is not at all difficult when we read these letters to understand why Chesterfield achieved such standing among his contemporaries. Everyone who has scratched his own head and wondered how to begin a letter of apology for long silence will admire the easy opening of a note to Dayrolles: "I suspended the course of my letters for some time, from mere compassion to you."[11] It may have been true, but it reads like a most delightful—and placatory—excuse. We all of us have occasion to write letters of thanks, and they only too often lapse into commonplaces. Chesterfield's are fresh and sincere. He thanks Edward Jerningham for a poetical letter of praise and adds, "I ought to show some commonplace modesty at least, and protest to you that I am ashamed, confounded, and in a manner annihilated, by the praises you most undeservedly bestow upon me; but I will not, because if I did, I should lie confoundedly. For every human creature has vanity, and perhaps I have full as much as another."[12] This is only one passage from a most witty performance.

Another duty at which Chesterfield excelled was the writing of letters of condolence. His note to Arthur Stanhope on the death of Stanhope's wife is not lapidary in tone, but is grave, sensible, and entirely practical in approach. Of course it lacks any effort to console: "Your concern is so just, that I offer you no arguments of consolation. Time and business are the only cure for real sorrow."[13] No great comfort, but certainly true.

The rational approach, so obvious here, has its advantages when he comes to talk of his own personal difficulties. He writes to Dayrolles about the incapacitating deafness that had come upon him: "I am full as deaf, consequently full as *absurd,* as ever. I give up all hopes of cure; I know my place, and form my plan accordingly, for I strike society out of it. I must supply its place as well as I can with reading, writing, walking, riding, gardening, etc., though all these together still leave a great void, into which weariness and regret will slip, in spite of all one's endeavours to banish them. But enough of this disagreeable subject."[14] So, coolly and inexorably, he dismisses himself from an active part in that society he had led for so long. The stock opening now becomes, "As the letters of a deaf man are less troublesome than his company. . . ." Turning the greenhouse into a grape-house or trying to acquire melon seeds takes up space formerly reserved for politics or fashionable life. His existence, he thought, grew daily more like that of the cabbages at Blackheath.

His letters to his women friends differ in tone from those to men. The gift of some pineapples is described in a letter to the Marquise de Monconseil: "Cette lettre, qui va par un courier, les dévancera, j'espère, assez pour vous préparer à toutes les cérémonies requises. Au moins ne croyez pas que ces ananas soient de *Babiole,* vous feriez trop de tort à mon jardinage. Les miens sont bien autre chose. . . ."[15] He rallies Gertrude Hotham on her fussiness: "You will be extremely disappointed when you come to town by finding that I have no cough at all. I am sure you was preparing to attack me upon my ill-breeding in coughing at people unnecessarily."[16]

He enjoys exchanging chit-chat about the attractions of Bath. In 1734, he sends such a letter to Lady Suffolk giving her "the very minutes" of life there since she had left the spa.[17]

In 1771, he sends another to Gertrude Hotham: "The new rooms are really Magnificent finely finished and furnished, the dancing room, which the late Lady Thanet used to call the Posture room, particularly spacious and adorned. A large and fine play room, and a convenient Tea room well contrived, either to drink or part with that liquor. . . . In my review of the fair sex last night I did not see one tolerably handsome so that I am in no danger of falling in love this season. . . . My way is to end my letters abruptly and without a well turned period. So God bless you."[18]

Not all his letters to women are at this jocular level. He firmly supports his new daughter-in-law on the manner in which her husband is to be buried, adding the characteristic sentiment, "All I desire, for my own burial, is not be be buried alive; but how or where, I think, must be entirely indifferent to every rational creature."[19] A serious note, too, is struck in his response to Lady Huntingdon's pleas for a contribution to the Methodist chapel at Bristol: ". . . it would ill become me to censure your enthusiastic admiration for Mr. Whitefield. His eloquence is unrivalled—his zeal inexhaustible, and not to admire both would argue a total absence of taste, and an insensibility not to be coveted by anybody. Your Ladyship is a powerful auxiliary to the Methodist Cabinet; and I confess, notwithstanding my own private griefs and sentiments, I am infinitely pleased at your zeal in so good a cause. You must have twenty pounds for this new Tabernacle whenever you think proper to demand it—but I must beg *my name* not to appear *in any way.* . . . With best wishes for the success of all your disinterested acts of benevolence to the human race."[20]

The nineteenth-century editor of the work from which this is drawn saw in the letter nothing but Chesterfield's characteristic politeness and insincerity. This is hardly a fair comment. Of course Chesterfield replies politely, makes a donation, acknowledges the benevolence of Lady Huntingdon's good works and the force of Whitefield's oratory, but he nowhere pretends that he accepts the Methodist outlook. The point might be made plainer by reference to his letter to Lord Huntingdon concerning La Trappe: "I should pity those poor enthusiasts you have lately seen at La Trappe, if I did not know that enthusiasm carries along with it, not only its comforts but its joys."[21] In the same way he felt that he was in no position to censure Lady Huntingdon's enthusiasm or Whitefield's proselytizing. They were convinced of the truth of their beliefs; Chesterfield thought them fanatics. The only hope for the civilized world lay in the reconciliation of these opposites. Life was more interesting when a sympathetic understanding (not necessarily a correspondence of views) prevailed.

The tone of these letters to both men and women friends is that of good-humored conversation among equals. He claimed that he had written them without correction: "[I] am so idle and negligent in my familiar letters, that I never wrote one over twice in my life, and am consequently often guilty both of false spelling and false English."[22] This would be difficult to believe were not Chesterfield so honest, so careful, and so practised a hand.

They have little ostensible form apart from the logical connection of opinions and facts, but their diversified content is in many ways more interesting than that of the *Letters to his Son,* and those to his godson and Huntingdon. This is partly because, in teaching these young men his basic philosophy, Chesterfield repeated himself over and over again (as any good teacher will do) and partly because of the strong note of exhortation that crept into them.

Instead of the relaxed attitude we find in the letters to his friends, we are aware of a certain relentless pressure being exercised on his young readers. This comes from Chesterfield's belief that everything may be achieved by diligent attention: "I know nothing in the world but poetry that is not to be acquired by application and care."[23] He constantly practises and preaches the doctrine. All this sounds rather humorless but Chesterfield was adroit enough to find ways of making the lesson more striking by putting it in a comic light:

I knew a gentleman, who was so good a manager of his time, that he would not even lose that small portion of it which the calls of nature obliged him to pass in the necessary-house, but gradually went through all the Latin poets in those moments. He bought, for example, a common edition of Horace, of which he tore off gradually a couple of pages, carried them with him to that necessary place, read them first, and then sent them down as a sacrifice to Cloacina; this was so much time fairly gained; and I recommend to you to follow his example. It is better than only doing what you cannot help doing at those moments; and it will make any book which you shall read in that manner, very present to your mind.[24]

Under the amused tone there is still a serious purpose, and we must never forget that Chesterfield was the man who wrote, "I look upon indolence as a sort of *suicide*."[25]

The form of these letters is also loose but sometimes a more obvious pattern may be perceived. Chesterfield begins by complimenting his son or godson on his last letter, repeats some praise of the boy he has heard, or merely picks up some reference of interest to them both. All this is done to warm or quicken his young reader's attention. Chesterfield moves quickly from praise to qualification and to exhortation, illustrating his argument with examples and clarifying the theme at all points. He brings the letter to a close in a neat, unstudied fashion.

For an example of this form we need only look at his letter to his son from Bath on 28 June 1742.[26] He has been pleased with the promises in Philip's letter, but would be more gratified if they were performed. To break a promise is folly; it must always be kept—for reasons of "interest and ambition." How can Philip arrive at this desired perfection? He must respond to challenge, pay close attention when learning. If he does not do so, he will be laughed at as a dunce; but if he does so, he will learn quickly and have more time for play. So Philip must do his duty to God and man, acquire great knowledge, and be very well bred, for these qualities "comprehend whatever is necessary and useful for this world or the next."

This form is also employed in some of his letters to his god-son (notably Nos. 2541, 2546, 2563), and in letters to Hunting-don. Some change of tone, however, will be found in the latter. Although Huntingdon was only a young man, Chester-field defers to him almost as if he were a nobleman of the same age. Where deference enters (as it sometimes does), Chester-field usually creates an effect of humorous irony; but in the letters to Huntingdon, there is evident a deep desire to win his goodwill so that he will advance his contemporary, Philip, in society. Consequently the compliments that open the let-ters to Huntingdon are a little exaggerated: "I owe you what I can never pay you in value, though I can in number, two let-ters."[27] The development of the themes is as neat as ever, but Chesterfield's habitual self-depreciation becomes flattery of Huntingdon's superiority, and exhortation is more muted, even concealed, under small talk.

Where a very strong sense of form is discernible in the let-ters to his son, godson, or Huntingdon, they read almost as essays. The most obvious example is the celebrated letter on the man of pleasure. It begins strikingly with a sustained figure: "Pleasure is the rock which most young people split upon; they launch out with crowded sails in quest of it, but without a compass to direct their course, or reason sufficient to steer the vessel." The man of pleasure's normal vices—drink-ing, gaming, swearing—are then described. "Thus seduced by fashion, and blindly adopting nominal pleasures, I lost real ones." This personal statement is the link between the general theme and Chesterfield's conclusion: if he were to begin life again, he would read more, frequent good company, give him-self up to the pleasures of the mind.[28]

It is unexpected to find that this was published twenty-three years before the rest of the letters. It appeared twice in the *London Daily Advertiser, and Literary Gazette* (4 Septem-ber and 14 October 1751), and twice in the *Bath Journal* (23 September 1751 and 17 April 1752). Although it is called "A

Letter from a Nobleman to his Son," it appears in space usually occupied by essays and reviews.[29]

There are other letters to his son showing something of this form. One might be entitled "On Virtue" and another, "On Novels and Romances."[30] The opening letters which describe classical mythology or history are certainly essays, when they are not merely lessons. Many of the letters also contain passages of generalized comment on the human condition of a sort that essayists have long found agreeable. Chesterfield delighted in the development of a rational argument from a fetching opening, through the sinuosities of the subject, to the just conclusion, and if he preferred to call these exercises letters rather than essays that was because his genius lay in condensation. Not for him the genial expansiveness of the eighteenth-century essayists: he was too fond of aphorism, distilled from wise observation.

In this respect it is worth speculating how much Chesterfield owed to his maternal grandfather, the Marquis of Halifax. *The Lady's New-Years-Gift: or, Advice to a Daughter*[31] shows in its title a resemblance to Chesterfield's subject matter, and is a set of essays on a young woman's proper approach to religion, marriage, conversation, friendship, vanity and pride. Halifax is aware that young people may resent constant instruction: "There may be some bitterness in meer obedience."[32] With a sober good sense and an idiomatic turn of phrase, he seeks to persuade his daughter to accept the fruits of his experience. Some of his sentiments have a family stamp: "It is not true Devotion, to put on an angry Zeal against those of a differing persuasion."[33] When Halifax writes, "The Triumph of Wit is to make your good Nature subdue your Censure," or decides that "An Aversion to what is Criminal, a Contempt of what is ridiculous, are the inseparable Companions of Understanding and Vertue,"[34] the sound of the lines as much as their sense reminds us of Chesterfield. Yet Halifax is the essayist, graver, more discursive, in some ways more convincing in his balanced assessments. Chesterfield's letters are much briefer, more sprightly and darting, even (as he said of the letters to his godson) more jocose.

There remain to be considered the letters of business, those written on affairs of state. Once again Chesterfield stresses the importance of clarity: "Every paragraph should be so clear and unambiguous, that the dullest fellow in the world may not be able to mistake it, nor obliged to read it twice in order to understand it."[35] Diplomacy, the art of negotiation, was a futile exercise if the language used was not precise in its choice and ordering. Correspondence between political allies at home called equally for strict concentration on, and attention to, the matter in hand. "In business an elegant simplicity, the result of care, not of labour, is required."[36] This implies that a writer will establish his case if only he is careful enough in the presentation, and there is some evidence that the letters of business cost Chesterfield more pains than his familiar letters. In fact, it seems likely (though I depend on inference and do not show proof) that Chesterfield was in the habit of drafting some of the more important of his business letters, and that he could have said about them what he said about his essays, "I often scribble, but at the same time protest to you that I almost as often burn."[37] They are models of lucidity and careful ease.

His letters to the Duke of Newcastle between December 1744 and October 1746 are recognized as historical documents of considerable value, and their editor, Sir Richard Lodge, described them as "an invaluable commentary upon our foreign policy."[38] For the student of literature they have quite as much value as direct statements from a mind that delighted in observing and forecasting the ways of men either as individuals or in groups. At this time Chesterfield occupied with distinction the posts of special ambassador to the Hague and of Lord Lieutenant of Ireland, and could write freely to the Secretary of State for the Southern Department, the busy but pusillanimous Newcastle. As a man of common sense, Chesterfield saw that his own mastery of political negotiation would be completely wasted if he were not supported by a firm minister at home. Courteously but inflexibly, he gave Newcastle directions: "I would ask by what means such a decision is to be brought on next month, that will not bring it on full as well next week? I beg your Grace's pardon, but I cannot help being a little warm upon this subject, as it is of the utmost consequence to yourselves, to the nation, and to all Europe. Every hour's delay has an ill effect somewhere or other. The game is now in your hands, and if you lose it—*your enemies will tell you the rest with pleasure.*"[39]

The formal deference is there, but the real respect is missing. The tone of these letters is persuasive in argument, but the conclusions are forthright: "Your Grace says, and very truly, that the King's servants must be his ministers exclusive of all others, or they cannot remain his servants: but give me leave to say that if you do not bring that matter to a decision before the Parliament rises, you will certainly be neither, after it is up. Your strength is in Parliament, and you must use it while you have it."[40] If there is a slightly imperious tone here, that is hardly surprising. Chesterfield's invariable coolness is often mentioned by critics, but he felt strongly sometimes about the right course to adopt in certain political circumstances. Here emotion found some play.

It must be emphasized, however, that these were the comments of a man actively engaged in government service, for the use of his nominal superior. When, sixteen years later, Chesterfield was out of office and of society, the tone of his letters to Newcastle is markedly different. He knows that he is not at the center of things as Newcastle is, and he dismisses his own claims to any authority in a well-turned introductory sentence: "Your Grace's faithful servant, deafer and weaker both in body and mind than ever, will be at your orders whenever you please to signify them."[41]

Another of the rare occasions when a quiet note of emotion touches the letters occurs when he pleads for office for his son. Look at the note he sent Bute pleading that Philip's illegitimacy should be no bar to his advancement: ". . . now my Lord if Mr. Stanhope could have the happyness and the honour to succeed him [Sir Charles Hotham] in that employment [Groom of the Bedchamber], it would make him happy, for the many (probably) remaining years of his life, and me so for the few remaining months, or perhaps, only weeks or days of mine. . . . I am sensible of one great objection which may be urged against him, I mean his birth, but in Justice and Equity both the shame and the guilt are mine, not his."[42] The plea, as always, is to a dispassionate examination of the facts of the case, but a note of emotion undoubtedly enters into the pleading.

It is important to remember that these letters to his son, godson, Huntingdon, friends, and political colleagues, were not written for publication, even though a few of them were— by accident, probably—printed in his lifetime. The very idea disturbed him: "I confess, the printing of a letter carelessly and inaccurately written, in the freedom and confidence of friendly correspondence, is not very agreeable. . . ."[43] His detractors will be ready to doubt his sincerity, but it seems certain that he would have regarded publication as an invasion of privacy. He might well have seized an opportunity for revision had he known that over two thousand of his letters would eventually appear in print.

When his daughter-in-law sold the *Letters to his Son* to Dodsley, a huge sale was foreseen. In the last quarter of the eighteenth century, copies sold in thousands and the abridgments and adaptations sold in tens of thousands.[44] No work of this kind has ever achieved comparable success, though parental advice to children has been the subject of many works since medieval times. Why did it attract this attention? There was no great novelty in the ideas it contained.[45] Many of them were current in the seventeenth and early eighteenth centuries, and Chesterfield, as it were, codified them. Yet this synthesis was so deftly performed and the illustrations from his own experience were so aptly chosen, that they struck every reader with pleasure or dismay. It was impossible to ignore them.

Another reason why they provoked immediate interest lies in the fact that Chesterfield had been for many years what Samuel Johnson termed him in the famous letter on patrons: *"le vainqueur de la terre."* He was respected as a disinterested statesman in an age of venal politicians. His wit and address as well as his oratorical and conversational powers were proverbial. Colley Cibber gives us a good idea of the source of his influence: "His Expression is easy, short, and clear; a stiff or studied word never comes from him; it is in a simplicity of Style that he gives the highest Surprize, and his Ideas are always adapted to the Capacity and Taste of the Person he speaks to."[46] This passage describes Chesterfield's conversation, but it could be used with equal force to bring out the stylistic qualities of the letters, and it explains why people looked forward to reading anything that came from the hand of a man of such exquisite taste. Time often deals severely with those whose fame depends on the spoken word or the enchantment of personality, but Chesterfield's letters embalmed his best qualities and he spoke from the grave. In the two hundred years (almost) since his death, he has been ridiculed by critics as powerful as Cowper, Dickens, Virginia Woolf, and Lytton Strachey, but his work survives. Chesterfield still is, what he was in his own day, the epitome of style.

The phrase requires some elucidation. "Style," he wrote, "is the dress of thoughts."[47] It follows that a good style does not draw attention to itself but sets off the thoughts of the writer. This is very true of Chesterfield's expression.

We are aware of a series of carefully articulated sentences that follow logically one after the other, and are phrased in a lively and catching manner. If we look more closely at one particular letter,[48] we see a considerable variation in sentence length to avoid the monotony that might arise from a succession of loose sentences. Two quite long sentences are followed by "No!" After another fairly long sentence comes "Let us exemplify." Then three shorter sentences are followed by "Nothing less." This is a more striking example than most and may exaggerate a little the effect that Chesterfield tried to achieve, but there is no disputing the notion that he sought to vary and give harmony to his periods.

His diction is chosen with the same care and desire for appropriateness. He told his son that for forty years he had never spoken a word without giving himself a moment to consider whether or not he could find a better one.[49] He is sparing of adjectives, and those used are customary rather than striking: "deep learning and superior parts." His use of language is not in any sense colorful, but is plain and to the point. Pithy expression of thought suited him better than the highly original juxtaposition of epithets. He has an ear for a phrase, and his description of the House of Lords as "that hospital of incurables" is still remembered.

Sometimes he finds that a French word is the only appropriate one: "No man is *distrait* with the man he fears, or the woman he loves."[50] Usage of this kind drew an attack on him for his gallicisms, and the critic went to the absurd length of saying that Chesterfield was "only a Frenchman studying English."[51] It may be conceded that he wished to introduce into English prose the cool reasonableness, logical force, and precision of the French. In fact he recommended Philip to note that "the French . . . attend very minutely to the purity, the correctness, and the elegancy of their style, in conversation, and in their letters. . . . Form your French style upon theirs; for elegancy in one language will re-produce itself in all."[52] He himself wrote French with ease and numbered among his friends and admirers Montesquieu and Voltaire.

Perhaps the influence of the French is best seen in his concern with the elegant. Paragraphs have a finish that is never showy. Sentences have epigrammatic point. He advises his son to "talk often, but never long,"[53] and to "pocket all your knowledge with your watch, and never pull it out in company unless desired."[54] The language is thoroughly idiomatic but is ordered with skill: "Whoever is in a hurry, shows that the thing he is about is too big for him."[55] His brief statements prompt thought: "Courts are the best keys to characters."[56] True or false? While we decide the issue, we forget the admirably terse but elegant way in which the assertion has been planted in our minds. He is fond of antithesis and likes the kind of generalization that enables him to open up an argument. At other times, a generalized statement sums up his outlook: "In my mind it is only the strength of our passions, and the weakness of our reason, that makes us so fond of life."[57]

He is so candid and so penetrating that we accept what he has to say only too readily. "I have the failing of all little minds, I am to suspect and dislike whatever I do not understand."[58] We enjoy the well-phrased jest against himself, but with the uneasy suspicion that it may well be turned against us.

At lesser moments, like all wits, he played with a well-known line and gave it greater fame in its new form. The best-known example is Dryden's forgotten "Men are but children of a larger growth." Chesterfield gave it new relish by substituting "Women" for "Men."[59]

When grace and economy of effort go together, they are matchless, and so it is hardly surprising that Landor was of the opinion that in point of style Chesterfield was one of the best of our writers. Like Goldsmith, he did not depend on tricks or artifices; he repeated ideas rather than effects. He avoided the devices of declamation in his written work, for he had ample opportunity of practising the arts of the orator in the House of Lords. Yet the virtues of his speeches in Parliament are those which distinguish the letters. Lord Orrery reported one occasion when he heard Chesterfield "in all the weight of Eloquence, the superiority of Argument, the dignity of Genius, and the sweetness of Persuasion. No Syren had ever half his Powers. . . ."[60]

His secrets are open ones—good sense and good taste. What he says so well is that if we sit back and look at the ways of the world in general or in some particular set of circumstances, we are forced when we add up our perceptions to certain inescapable truths. The method is highly persuasive. Guided by the "lively but not giddy" Chesterfield, we form a judgment. We are aware at once of the orderly deployment of ideas, and an overriding concern (as in the letter to Bute) with justice and equity. We realize that tolerance, balance, and honesty are a normal part of his outlook, and that the scruples that made him resign from office were always evident when he sat down to examine his own motives. Honesty is an expensive policy, and Chesterfield has been paying for it ever since the *Letters to his Son* came out.

He once wrote that ordinary people looked upon a good speaker and a comet as "preternatural phenomena," but added that when the speaker's art was examined carefully he was found to be "a man of good common sense, who reasons justly, and expresses himself elegantly on that subject upon which he speaks. There is, surely, no witchcraft in this."[61] In many ways the description suits Chesterfield's art as a letter-writer, but there is a magic in it; otherwise any hack could entrance us. When the justness of the diction, the elegance of the phrasing, the sparkle of wit, agility in argument, and robustness of thinking have all been noted, one finds that these letters contain something beyond analysis. Writing deliberately "in minuet time," Chesterfield was in every sense of the words "expressing himself." This is what only genius does effectively.

University College, Swansea

DR. JOHNSON IN HIS LETTERS:
THE PUBLIC GUISE OF PRIVATE MATTER

PHILIP B. DAGHLIAN

THE READER CURIOUS to see Dr. Johnson without any intervening elements has three sources to examine. As long ago as 1908 Sir Walter Raleigh suggested that in the notes on Shakespeare we hear Johnson "talking without the intervention of Boswell . . ." and that "the reader who desires to have Johnson to himself for an hour, with no interpreter, cannot do better than turn to the notes on Shakespeare."[1] A second source is the *Diaries, Prayers, and Annals,* edited by Professor E. L. McAdam and the Hydes in 1958 and containing matter previously incorporated in Hill's edition of the *Prayers and Meditations,* together with much fresh material. Finally, and most important, are *The Letters of Samuel Johnson,* memorably edited in three volumes in 1952 by R. W. Chapman.[2]

Although Raleigh's claim cannot be dismissed lightly, the fact remains that the notes on Shakespeare are so restricted by their very nature that they can communicate only a single aspect of the complexity that was Johnson. The *Diaries, Prayers, and Annals,* the most intimate surviving accounts of Johnson's thoughts in times of stress, are a much more fruitful source. The record is somber and moving, but we must realize that this is an aspect of Johnson which is, strictly speaking, none of our business to know. This class of material, fascinating and valuable as it is, does not actually show us Johnson as he was, because it is too intimate to be used as evidence for what has to be a public kind of portrait. He would rather have died than to have someone reading these papers.

Johnson's letters are an ideal source for a direct view of the man. He uses correspondence as a necessary form of communication with the world at large, but there is nothing compulsive about his desire to put pen to paper. Essentially he writes only when he has something to say. Despite their utilitarian nature, Johnson's letters are highly readable, and their cumulative effect is to present a vivid and detailed impression of their author. Although he appears as essentially the same person always, the letters demonstrate how he adapts his manner to different correspondents under varying conditions.

We shall examine the range and variety as we proceed. Occasionally, and especially in the later years, the letters reveal matters as intimate as any to be found in the *Diaries, Prayers, and Annals.* But the very fact that these things were discussed in letters puts them into the public realm, since any letter would be assumed to be read by the recipient, and might of course be read by others. Thus the letters give evidence for a public picture in a way that the diaries cannot. Furthermore, if one could imagine a reader encountering Johnson for the first time only through his letters, I venture to suggest that such a reader would have a pretty accurate sense of his subject after reading them all. The picture would become infinitely fuller and more fascinating with the reading of Boswell's *Life* and of Johnson's principal works, but the essential elements would all be familiar from the letters alone.

R. W. Chapman's edition contains about 1,500 of these letters, addressed to about two hundred correspondents. Thirty-six correspondents received more than five letters each, to a total of about a thousand, or more than two-thirds of the entire edition. We find that a relatively small group of people received most of these thousand-odd letters. Well over four hundred went to various members of the Thrale family, with Mrs.

Thrale receiving about 380. Around a hundred each went to Boswell and to Dr. John Taylor, almost sixty to Lucy Porter, and thirty or more each to recipients as various as Bennet Langton, John Nichols, Frances Reynolds, and William Strahan.

One might expect Johnson to be merely conventional and formal in writing to people he knew slightly or to whom he felt he should show a particular kind of respect. It is true that he was a formal person, even for an age given to many formal observances, and that some of the diction in his miscellaneous letters is merely a more skillfully concatenated version of what the age considered appropriate to the circumstances. Nonetheless Johnson has the knack of leaving the stamp of his own personality on such conventional subjects as requests for favors, apology, or condolence. Writing on 3 November 1762 to the Earl of Bute to request that steps be taken to assure regular payment of his pension, Johnson is in rather a delicate position. After making his request, he presents his apology for disturbing a man as busy as a chief minister in terms that are politely appropriate to the situation: "To interrupt your Lordship at a time like this with such petty difficulties is improper and unseasonable, but your knowledge of the world has long since taught you, that every man's affairs, however little, are important to himself" (145).

He wrote to John Macleod, the Laird of Raasay, on 6 May 1775, apologizing for a passage in the *Journey to the Western Islands* to which Macleod had taken exception. Johnson's apology is most handsome and polite and includes an offer to have Boswell publish a correction in the Edinburgh newspapers. In his central passage he said: "Though what I said had been true, if it had been disagreeable to you, I should have wished it unsaid. . . . As it is mistaken, I find myself disposed to correct it, both by my respect for you, and my reverence for truth" (389).

Johnson's letter of November, 1775, to Mrs. Edmund Burke on the death of her father Dr. Christopher Nugent is a fine example of a letter of condolence: "Among those who really share your pleasures and your troubles, give me leave to condole with you upon the death of a Friend whom I loved much, and whom you undoubtedly loved much more. His death has taken from us the benefit of his counsel, and the delight of his conversation, but it cannot without our own fault, deprive us of the influence of his virtues, or efface the pleasing remembrance of his Worth his Integrity, and his Piety" (437.1). The precision and economy of the letter, on an occasion when precision and economy are usually not to be found, combine to create a genuinely moving effect.

The tone is courtly without being artificial as he writes on 21 December 1775 to settle a dinner engagement with Mrs. Montagu. After setting a day as she had suggested, he concludes: "Till I am favoured with your answer, or despair of so much condescention I shall suffer no engagement to fasten itself upon me" (445).

Johnson apparently made one interesting exception to his general rule of not writing a letter unless he had something to say. He felt that a letter to a friend who was far away, usually abroad, should not be short or perfunctory. As he observed on 10 June 1761 to Baretti in Milan: "A short letter to a distant friend is, in my opinion, an insult like that of a slight bow or cursory salutation;—a proof of unwillingness to do much, even where there is a necessity of doing something" (138). He reveals the same sentiment, many years later, on 19 April 1783, in writing to Sir Robert Chambers in Calcutta: "Removed as We are with so much land and sea between us, We ought to compensate the difficulty of correspondence by the length of our letters, yet searching my memory, I do not [find] much to communicate" (835.1). Johnson lived up to his prescription nonetheless, for Chapman reports that this letter is one of the longest extant.

At this point it may be instructive to investigate in some detail Johnson's letters to four of his major correspondents, who received among them considerably more than a third of all his letters. We see Johnson as he was in each of these series, though he skillfully adapts the tone and content of each letter to suit the particular recipient. I have chosen Dr. John Taylor, Lucy Porter, Mrs. Thrale, and James Boswell for consideration here. Each represents a clear and particular strand in Johnson's life. The responses these four evoked in Johnson's letters to them combine to give a remarkably strong sense of the way he must have been. Furthermore, there will be no danger of confusing the recipients. A letter to Taylor is as different from a letter to Boswell as a letter to Lucy Porter is from one to Mrs. Thrale.

One wonders seriously if Johnson would have become friendly with the Reverend Dr. John Taylor if they had first met in maturity. He seems to have been a dull and generally unattractive person who had done well for himself both in agriculture and in the church. Boswell described him as "a hearty English 'Squire, with the parson super-induced."[3] Taylor and Johnson had been schoolmates at Lichfield Grammar School, and Johnson, who had preceded him to Oxford, arranged for him to enter Christ Church, since he could not honestly recommend the tutors in Pembroke College. Taylor represents to Johnson a clear link with the past of his youth. Undoubtedly the two young men had found each other congenial, but there never developed sufficient basis for the relationship to mature as they matured, except for the link with the past. Johnson reveals an awareness of this fact in his remark to Boswell about Taylor in 1777: "Sir, I love him; but I do not love him more; my regard for him does not increase. As it is said in the Apocrypha, 'his talk is of bullocks.' "[4]

Most of the surviving letters to Taylor fall in the last twenty years of Johnson's life, and are chiefly concerned with the topic that most actively engaged the two men, the state of their health. Writing on 31 August 1772 Johnson regrets that Taylor's health is not better. Since he attributes much of the distress to Taylor's "unsettled and discontented" mind, he devotes a large part of the letter to suggesting ways in which he can "encrease the general cheerfulness of Life." The suggested "little apparatus for chimistry or experimental philosophy" probably would not have helped much, although there might have been more promise of diversion in "some little purchase at a small distance, or . . . some petty farm." Johnson's conclusion is highly characteristic: "Thus it is that the progress of life brings often with it diseases not of the body only, but of the mind. We must endeavour to cure both the one and the other. In our bodies we must ourselves do a great part, and for the mind it is very seldom that any help can be had, but what prayer and reason shall supply" (277) .

The series continues, steadily if not profusely, with Johnson varying the basic discussion of health with reports on his comings and goings. He offers abundant advice, chiefly legal and therapeutic. On 6 June 1780, after giving direction for taking mercury, Johnson concludes in terms more practical than condescending, however they may strike a modern reader: "Be sure, whatever else You do, to keep your mind easy, and do not let little things disturb it. Bustle about your hay and your cattle, and keep yourself busy with such things as give you little solicitude" (676). The advice is even more fundamental in a letter of 12 August 1782: "Be particularly careful now to drink enough, and to avoid costiveness; you will find that vexation has much more power over you, ridiculous as it may seem, if you neglect to evacuate your body" (798).

Although Dr. Taylor seems to have been a very dull man, it is perfectly easy to see why Johnson remained on friendly terms with him. With each passing year Taylor, despite his hay and his cattle and his keen alertness to possible ecclesiastical preferment, loomed larger as a link with the youthful past that was so rapidly receding.

Johnson's ties with Lucy Porter were stronger than those with John Taylor. In one sense she too was a link with the world of Lichfield and therefore of the past. But she was of course more than this. As the oldest daughter of Mrs. Porter, Lucy Porter was his stepdaughter and therefore after his mother's death in 1759 the only family he had. She had been the only one of the Porter children not to object to their mother's marriage to the strange young Samuel Johnson. Furthermore, she lived in Lichfield for many years, helping old Mrs. Johnson with the bookselling business. Lucy Porter was truly a relative to Johnson, and if the fact that she was only six years younger than he made the roles of stepdaughter and stepfather seem mildly anomalous, that was only a minor matter. The connection was there, and it was used, especially in the years after Sarah Johnson's death.

In the first letter after her death, on 23 January 1759, he writes: "I return you and all those that have been good to her my sincerest thanks, and pray God to repay you all with infinite advantage. Write to me, and comfort me, dear child" (125). On 6 February 1759 he gives a clear indication of his future relationship with her: "I had no reason to forbear writing but that it makes my heart heavy, and I had nothing particular to say which might not be delayed to the next post, but had no thoughts of ceasing to correspond with my dear Lucy, the only person now left in the world with whom I think myself connected. . . . every heart must lean to somebody, and I have nobody but you . . ." (127).

The letter of 24 July 1762 is an excellent indication of Lucy's standing in Johnson's eyes: "If I write but seldom to you, it is because it seldom happens that I have any thing to tell you that can give you pleasure, but last Monday I was sent for by the chief Minister the Earl of Bute, who told me that the King had empowered him to do something for me, and let me know that a pension was granted me of three hundred a year" (144). So far as we know, she was the only person to whom Johnson wrote to confide this important and exciting news.

On 12 April 1763 Johnson sent condolences on the death of her brother and then continued: "I wish to be informed in what condition your Brother's death has left your fortune; if he has bequeathed you competence or plenty, I shall sincerely rejoice, if you are in any distress or difficulty, I will endeavour to make what I have, or what I can get, sufficient for us both" (150). The legacy was for £10,000, and it soon became apparent that Lucy had definite ideas of what she wanted to do with it. We see from Johnson's letter of 12 July 1763 that she had decided on building a house, a course of action of which he disapproved. The lady had her own way, however, and Johnson remarked on 10 January 1764: "I was in hopes that you would have written to me before this time, to tell me that your house was finished, and that you were happy in it. I am sure I wish you happy" (164). From this point on, although Johnson is still the sovereign, Lucy has achieved a lesser sovereignty of her own. Johnson remarked to Mrs. Thrale on 20 July 1767, during the first of a long series of visits in the new house in Lichfield: "Miss Lucy is more kind and civil than I expected, and has raised my esteem by many excellencies very noble and resplendent, though a little discoloured by hoary virginity" (190).

The letter of 24 August 1779 reveals Johnson in an unusual role. General fear of French invasion had become so widespread that he apparently felt it necessary to reassure Lucy Porter and the Lichfield circle. He held to the opinion that there was not yet any danger, and he was able to reinforce this view by citing rather highly placed authority: "I had a note from Mr Chamier (the under Secretary of State) yesterday, that tells me. *The combined fleets* (of French and Spaniards) *are not in sight of land. They are supposed to be driven out of the channel by the Easterly wind. . . .* Do not pay any regard to the newspapers; you will only disturb yourself. When there is any thing worth telling you, I design to let you know it" (627.1). Here is the head of family reassuring the womenfolk in time of public danger, which is what heads of family are supposed to do.

The usual topics appear in the letters: gifts of oysters or books, plans to visit Lichfield, and, increasingly, the state of Johnson's health. Thrale's death in 1781 and Johnson's appointment as one of his executors (723,730.2) are exceptions to the normal pattern. On 10 November 1783 he comments on the deaths of Lucy's brother and of Mrs. Williams: "As we daily see our friends die round us, we that are left must cling closer, and, if we can do nothing more, at least pray for one another; and remember, that as others die we must die too, and prepare ourselves diligently for the last great trial" (898).

On 2 December 1784 Johnson writes to Lucy Porter on a matter which was a major concern of his last days and a somber reminder of the original tie between them. He had already written on that day (1040) to Richard Greene at Lichfield making arrangements for a stone and epitaph for his parents and brother in St. Michael's Church, and directing him to call on Mrs. Porter for such additional payments as might be necessary. He reported this arrangement in his letter to Lucy and then went on to tell her about the stone and inscription he had had placed "over Tetty in the chapel of Bromley in Kent." After giving an English translation of the Latin inscription he concludes the letter: "That this is done, I thought it fit that You should know . . ." (1041). As he watched the hour of death draw near, his concern was with family matters. It was completely appropriate that such business should be communicated to the surviving member of the family.

Although the relationship with Boswell bulks largest in the eyes of posterity, there is little doubt that in Johnson's own lifetime his connection with Mrs. Thrale and her family was of paramount importance in many ways. In the famous last letter to Mrs. Thrale after her marriage to Piozzi, Johnson gratefully alludes to "that kindness which soothed twenty years of a life radically wretched" (972). His letters to her make up the largest single group to any correspondent. Virtually all the letters reflect his special status as an honored and respected and beloved member of the Thrale family.

One very important aspect of Johnson's relationship with Mrs. Thrale is reflected only fleetingly in the correspondence. Only two letters by Johnson treat his break with her over

Piozzi, even though the event was cataclysmic for Johnson. Why it was cataclysmic is best explained by Miss Balderston's suggestion of a masochistic relationship between Johnson and Mrs. Thrale.[5] Coming to Johnson's letters aware of Miss Balderston's essay, with its account of whips and padlocks and the like, a reader may find himself wondering about passages such as the following: On 23 November 1772 Johnson complains about her flattery of him and continues, "Pray keep strictly to your character of governess" (287). A few days later he reports from Lichfield his plans to return "to lye in my old habitation, under your government" (289.2). And on 29 May 1773 he writes, "I wish you could fetch me on Wednesday. I long to be in my own room. Have you got your key?" (311.1).

But this kind of thing, important though it is in any total view of Johnson, falls outside our present concern with a public view of the man in his letters. By examining his letters to Mrs. Thrale in their external significance, we emphasize his status as a member of a family circle, which is what he was first and foremost. The first surviving letter to Mrs. Thrale, on 13 August 1765, sets a gallant tone which Johnson never gave up. By the time of the next letter, almost two years later, he observes that in his journey to Lichfield he has found nothing "which makes me less desirous of reposing in that place which your kindness and Mr Thrale's allows me to call my *home*" (190). On 23 May 1768 he writes, "Every Man is desirous to keep those Friends whom he is proud to have gained, and I count the friendship of your house among the felicities of life" (205).

The letters written during visits to Taylor at Ashbourne often reveal both the paucity of intellectual matters to occupy Johnson while he was there, and the intimate manner in which he takes this deficiency for granted as he writes to Mrs. Thrale. He reports on 23 July 1770, "I have seen the great Bull, and very great he is. I have seen likewise his heir apparent, who promises to inherit all the bulk and all the virtues of his Sire. I have seen the Man who offered an hundred guineas for the young Bull while he was yet little better than a Calf" (237). The following year he observes, "The great Bull has no disease but age. I hope in time to be like the great Bull . . ." (254). Some fifteen months later the report is that "our Bulls and Cows are all well, but we hate the man that has seen a bigger Bull" (282). These three passages tell us much about Johnson's attitudes toward Dr. Taylor and toward Mrs. Thrale.

The letters during the tour to the Hebrides with Boswell in 1773 are much longer than is customary for Johnson, but they served as his travel journals as well as his correspondence with Mrs. Thrale. In addition to vast amounts of topographical and biographical detail, these letters contain various touches which are authentically Johnsonian. The philosopher reflects on travel in the letter of 15-21 September 1773: "The use of travelling is to regulate imagination by reality, and instead of thinking how things may be, to see them as they are" (326). On 6 September 1773 he had already had occasion to modify this principle by describing things as they were going to be: "Near this Bridge is the fall of Fiers, a famous Cataract, of which by clambering over the rocks we obtained the view. The water was low, and therefore we had only the pleasure of knowing that rain would make it at once pleasing and formidable. There will then be a mighty flood foaming along a rocky channel frequently obstructed by protuberances, and exasperated by reverberation, at last precipitated with a sudden descent, and lost in the depth of a gloomy chasm" (323). The final sentence could not be more Johnsonian in its ring.

The long letter of 30 September 1773 contains a good example of the ironic observation of humanity which Johnson often shared with Mrs. Thrale: "At Kingsburgh we were very liberally feasted, and I slept in the bed, on which the Prince reposed in his distress. The sheets which he used were never put to any meaner offices, but they were wrapped up by the Lady of the house, and at last, according to her desire, were laid round her in her grave. These are not Whigs" (329).

What might be regarded as the happy ending of the Hebridean tour is reported in the conspiratorial intimacy of the letter describing the reception of the *Journey to the Western Islands:* "You must not tell any body but Mr Thrale that the King fell to reading the book as soon as he got it, when any thing struck him, he read aloud to the Queen, and the Queen would not stay to get the King's book, but borrowed Dr Hunter's. See now. Of the two Queens who has the better tast?

"Of all this you must absolutely say nothing to any body" (369.2).

Many of the topics treated in this particular correspondence pertain to the ordinary interests, problems, and activities of any family group. Johnson is always sincerely solicitous about illness of any kind, including Mrs. Thrale's regularly recurring pregnancies, her mother Mrs. Salusbury's losing struggle with cancer, the many illnesses of the Thrale children, and the stroke of Thrale himself, culminating in his death. Another topic is politics, especially as viewed in the light of Thrale's own public career. A good many letters, especially after Thrale's death, relate to business matters.

The letters to Mrs. Thrale reflect Johnson's capacity for the light touch, an attribute which has tended to be obscured because of Boswell's deliberately monumental portraiture. Johnson is capable not only of the polite courtliness we have already seen, but also of affectionate teasing. Letters from Lichfield written in June, 1775, twit her for being excited about a regatta. "I have just had your sweet letter, and am glad that you are to be at the regatta. . . . You that have seen the regatta will have images which we who miss it must want, and no intellectual images are without uses. But when you are in this scene of splendour and gayety, do not let one of your fits of negligence steal upon you. . . . Of the whole entertainment let me not hear so copious nor so true an account from any body as from you" (409). He continues in the next letter, "So now you have been at the regatta, . . . and were dressed fine and

fanciful, and made a fine part of the fine show, and heard musick, and said good things, and staid on the water four hours
after midnight, and came well home, and slept, and dreamed
of the regatta. . . . We make a hard shift here to live on without
a regatta" (410). Mrs. Thrale found the regatta disappointing,
a fact which evoked the following highly characteristic response: "All pleasure preconceived and preconcerted ends in
disappointment; but disappointment, when it involves neither
shame nor loss, is as good as success; for it supplies as many
images to the mind, and as many topicks to the tongue" (411).
His final word on the subject was: "Talk not of the Punick
war; nor of the depravity of human nature; nor of the slender
motives of human actions; nor of the difficulty of finding employment or pleasure; but talk, and talk, and talk of the
regatta . . ." (414).

Despite his general belief that letter-writing, like all other
forms of composition, should be engaged in only as necessary,
he devoted a goodly portion of his letters to Mrs. Thrale to
discussing subjects for letters and the rationale of epistolary
correspondence in general. Writing from Lichfield on 2 August 1775, he asked her, "Do you keep my letters? . . . they will,
I hope always be in some degree the records of a pure and
blameless friendship, and in some hours of languor and sadness may revive the memory of more cheerful times" (428).
The letter of 27 October 1777 is an extended and playful
meditation on letter-writing which skillfully conceals the fact
that Johnson had no particular message to communicate on
that particular day. Smilingly solemn, he observes, "In a
Man's Letters you know, Madam, his soul lies naked. . . . Is not
my soul laid open in these veracious pages? do not you see me
reduced to my first principles? . . . I know, dearest Lady, that
in the perusal of this such is the consanguinity of our intellects,
you will be touched as I am touched" (559). He strikes something of the same tone on 11 April 1780 when he says, "Now
you think yourself the first Writer in the world for a letter
about nothing. Can you write such a letter as this? So miscel-

laneous, with such noble disdain of regularity, like Shakespeare's works, such graceful negligence of transition like the ancient enthusiasts. The pure voice of nature and of friendship." The flight continues beyond the passage quoted, but the letter comes back to earth with the following mundane postscript: "You do not date your letters" (657). Writing from Lichfield on 20 October 1781 his quip has a rueful quality: "Now We are both valetudinary, we shall have something to write about. We can tell each other our complaints, and give reciprocal comfort and advice. . . . And so we may write and write, till we can find another subject" (742).

Unfortunately the letters of the final years do treat matters of health quite extensively, particularly his stroke in June, 1783, and the threat of surgical treatment for his sarcocele some months later. At the same time the shadow of the impending marriage to Piozzi looms larger. Consequently the light touch is considerably less frequent in these later letters.

In many respects the letters to Mrs. Thrale show Johnson at his easiest and happiest, or as close to happiness as he was capable of getting. Even when the situation contained elements of sadness, he had the great advantage of knowing that he had a fully sympathetic auditor in Mrs. Thrale. The relationship was so good for Johnson in so many ways and for so long a time that even now, after almost two hundred years, one reads his last two letters on her marriage to Piozzi with shock and sadness. On 2 July 1784 he says in his concluding paragraph, "If the last act is yet to do [marrying Piozzi], I, who have loved you, esteemed you, reverenced you, and served you, I who long thought you the first of human kind, entreat that before your fate is irrevocable, I may once more see you" (970). It was already too late, and he began the well-known last letter on 8 July 1784: "What you have done, however I may lament it, I have no pretence to resent, as it has not been injurious to me. I therefore breathe out one sigh more of tenderness perhaps useless but at least sincere" (972). The postscript assuring her that letters for him would be forwarded to

Lichfield is clear indication that the rational acceptance of adversity with which he began the letter was only a goal and not an achievement. The hurt he suffered was great and permanent.

Johnson's letters to Boswell are generally the best-known of his letters, because almost all of them appeared, in varying degrees of completeness, in the *Life of Johnson*. Though their matter may be familiar, their manner is worth particular examination at this time. Perhaps the most striking feature of the letters to Boswell is constant indication of steady affection on Johnson's part. He truly liked Boswell from the beginning. This is not to say that he was always willing to endure all of Boswell's foibles and eccentricities, because at times he was not, and he said so.

The bulk of the correspondence falls after the tour to the Hebrides in 1773. Only ten letters survive for the first decade of their acquaintance. The letter of 24 February 1773 may be said to set the pattern for the remaining correspondence. Johnson makes courteous response to Boswell's last letter, gently reproves him for having "been one of the *first* masquers in a country where no masquerade had ever been before," describes what he has done for a new edition of the Dictionary, reports on the quarrel between Baretti and Davies, tells of Goldsmith's new comedy, comments favorably on one of Boswell's legal cases, urges him to follow his father's precepts, and describes his own health. He concludes, "Write to me now and then; and whenever any good befalls you, make haste to let me know it. . . . You continue to stand very high in the favour of Mrs. Thrale" (295). All the elements of the fully developed relationship are here: personal affection, literary intelligence, concern with Boswell's professional career, and sympathetic understanding of his personal insecurities.

From the time of Johnson's return from Scotland to London late in November, 1773, until the end of 1777, he corresponded regularly with Boswell, writing him an average of about a letter a month. Johnson immediately started thinking about the book which was to become the *Journey to the Western Islands,* and he has many questions pertaining to the book. There are directions about shipping a box from Scotland, the ponderously gallant series of messages to Mrs. Boswell, and greetings and gifts to be sent to his new Scottish friends. As he observed at the end of one of these letters, "I would not wish to be thought forgetful of civilities" (348).

A long, thoughtful letter written in March, 1774, considers the question whether Boswell should go to London that spring, and examines his "fancy" that celebrating Easter at St. Paul's was "like going to Jerusalem at the feast of the Passover." Johnson reasonably advises him to forego the trip that year. "She [Mrs. Boswell] permitted you to ramble last year, you must permit her now to keep you at home." He comments on Boswell's thought concerning Easter and Passover, "if the annual resort to Jerusalem was a duty to the Jews, it was a duty because it was commanded; and you have no such command, therefore no such duty." After a thorough discussion of the "degree fancy is to be admitted into religious offices," he concludes, "Thus I have answered your letter, and have not answered it negligently. I love you too well to be careless when you are serious" (352).

Early in July, 1776, Johnson replied in rather harsh terms to one of Boswell's letters complaining about his melancholy (493). Apparently Johnson regretted what he had done, for he wrote again on 6 July: "I make haste to write again, lest my last letter should give you too much pain. If you are really oppressed with overpowering and involuntary melancholy, you are to be pitied rather than reproached. . . . Now my dear Bozzy, let us have done with quarrels and with censure" (494). The letter of 18 February 1777 is a conspicuous indication of Johnson's high regard for Boswell. "It is so long since I heard any thing from you, that I am not easy about it; write something to me next post." After discussing miscellaneous items in the body of the letter he concludes, "My dear Boswell, do not neglect to write to me, for your kindness is one of the pleasures of my life, which I should be very sorry to lose" (507). Johnson's mood could change, however, as in the letter of 3 July 1778 in which he reproves Boswell for complaining of neglect in correspondence. "When it may happen that I can give you either counsel or comfort, I hope it will never happen to me that I should neglect you; but you must not think me criminal or cold if I say nothing, when I have nothing to say." Most of the letter is devoted to arguing that true happiness is more likely to be solidly based on "the reasonable hope of a happy futurity" than on residence in London. Although Boswell may have been disheartened by this attitude, he must have been pleased to read, "I can tell you that I have heard you mentioned as *a man whom every body likes*. I think life has little more to give" (578).

The letter of 14 March 1781 finds him trying to allay Boswell's distresses, this time about Liberty and Necessity. "Do not doubt but I shall be most heartily glad to see you here again, for I love every part about you but your affectation of distress." His suggested remedy shows how well he knew his friend when he reports that he has finished the *Lives of the Poets* and has "laid up for you a load of copy, all out of order, so that it will amuse you a long time to set it right. Come to me, my dear Bozzy, and let us be as happy as we can. We will go again to the Mitre, and talk old times over" (715). On 24 December 1783 Johnson observes, "Of the exultations and repressions of your mind you delight to talk, and I hate to hear. Drive all such fancies from you." He then proceeds to thoughtful consideration of Boswell's query as to what "should be done with old horses unable to labour" (920). In the last letter that he wrote to him, on 3 November 1784, Johnson is concerned that he has not heard from Boswell. "Are you sick, or are you sullen? Whatever be the reason, if it be less than necessity, drive it away, and of the short life that we have, make the best use for yourself and for your friends" (1033).

On looking back over Johnson's letters to Boswell, one has a prevailing impression of warm and sustained affection. But there is also the constant proffering of the helping hand in times of need. Whenever Boswell is melancholy or otherwise distressed, Johnson is particularly solicitous to consider his plight seriously and thoughtfully. It has become a truism to say that Boswell found in Johnson a substitute for the father he could not get along with. But the sympathetic attention Johnson gave to Boswell's problems was much more than one might expect any father, no matter how kind, to give a son. The relation of Boswell and Johnson was not merely that of youth and age. More importantly, it was one of kinship of spirit. Both had been marked by melancholy for her own.

The story of Johnson's final years is increasingly a story of illness and loneliness. Through most of a long life dogged by ill health he had managed to survive by means of his constant fighting spirit. As late as March, 1782, he was able to tell Mrs. Thrale, "I am glad that I do not sink without resistance" (767). What with the increasing severity of his ailments and the diminution through death of his circle of intimates, the struggle became more difficult, although the resistance never ceased. The unusually large number of letters for 1783 and 1784 makes it possible to observe this process in great detail. It is almost with embarrassment, so intimate are the glimpses, that we observe Johnson in his final years, both in his own person, and as an examplar of Everyman grown old. Most human beings are subject to illness and old age. Fortunate are those who can bear these burdens with the fortitude and dignity of Johnson.

Although the paralytic stroke he suffered on 17 June 1783 was a relatively mild one, the experience must have been harrowing nonetheless. His letter to Mrs. Thrale on 19 June 1783 gives an excellent summary of the attack. The self-possession and control displayed in his account is truly awe-inspiring, and the procedures he describes clearly reflect his own scale of values. The first duty is prayer to God, asking to spare his mind, whatever may happen to the body. The next step is to test the mind by composing the prayer in Latin verse; by knowing that the lines were not very good he decided that his mind was unimpaired. Only then did he turn to his unsuccessful attempts to restore his voice, after which he slept. He did not attempt to seek external aid until light dawned. Then he wrote the notes to Francis Barber, to his neighbor and landlord Allen, and to Dr. Taylor. Against this background one is even more impressed by the powers of mind and character which triumphed over what must have been sheer terror as he wrote the note to Allen: "It hath pleased almighty God this morning to deprive me of the powers of speech; and, as I do not know but that it may be his further good pleasure to deprive me soon of my senses, I request you will, on the receipt of this note, come to me, and act for me, as the exigencies of my case may require" (847). Since the attack was not severe, recovery was fairly rapid, and by the beginning of July he was sufficiently improved to dine with the Club.

Another crisis of health loomed when on 20 September 1783 he wrote to Bennet Langton and to Taylor, reporting to each the probability of surgery. Living before the age of anesthetics, Johnson shared the common dread of surgery. But he also recognized that there were times when terrible things had to be faced. He wrote Mrs. Thrale on 22 September, "The complaint about which you enquire is a sarcocele: I thought it a hydrocele, and heeded it but little. . . . If excision should be delayed there is danger of gangrene. You would not have me for fear of pain perish in putrescence. I shall I hope, with trust in eternal mercy, lay hold of the possibility of life which yet remains" (883).

In the letters of the next few weeks Johnson consults with his physicians while the disorder fluctuates, as do the opinions of the medical men. In writing to his friends Johnson indulges in one of the few pleasures left to the more than trivially sick: he proudly reports the extreme gravity of his disease. To Taylor he wrote, "My case is what you think it, of the worst kind, a Sarcocele. There is I suppose nothing to be done but by the Knife" (885). In the course of much explicit clinical detail the possibility begins to appear by 7 October that the ailment may be improving spontaneously, so that talk of surgery is postponed (891.1). As his surgeon Mr. Pott remarked, one should not carry "fire and sword further than is necessary" (892). The letters continue to contain additional specific details, but by 1 November Johnson can report to Mrs. Thrale that "Mr. Pott bad me this day take no more care about the tumour" (897).

Once again the experience has been a harrowing one, and once again Johnson's response has been completely admirable. Unlike the stroke, this ailment carried no threat of mental incapacity. On the other hand, the possibilities of extreme physical suffering were enormous if surgery had to be performed. Johnson was fully aware of this, and yet he was willing to endure "excision" if no other viable choice existed. Happily this was not necessary, even though the reasons why were never clear. As he observed to Mrs. Thrale, "The great malady is neither heard, seen, felt, nor—understood" (895).

Johnson continued in ill-health for the rest of his life, but his ailments were less conspicuous. He was confined in the house from 14 December 1783 to 21 April 1784 (938, 955) with asthma and dropsy. He describes his condition to Mrs. Thrale on 12 January 1784: "I am confined to the house . . . my Physicians direct me to combat the hard weather with opium; I cannot well support its turbulence, and yet cannot forbear it, for its immediate effect is ease. . . . My legs and my thighs grow very tumid. In the mean time my appetite is good and if my Physicians do not flatter me, death is [not] rushing upon me. But this is in the hand of God" (925). Toward the end of February, however, his condition began to improve somewhat, and by 30 March 1784 he could write to Dr. Adams at Oxford, ". . . I was very hard beset with an Ashma and a Dropsy, from both which the Goodness of God has very much relieved me" (946.1).

Despite his improvement it was not until 21 April 1784 that he ventured out "After a confinement of one hundred twenty nine days, more than the third part of a year . . ." to return "thanks to God in St. Clements Church" for his recovery, "a recovery in my seventy fifth year from a distemper which few in the vigour of youth are known to surmount; a recovery of which neither myself, my friends, nor my physicians had any hope, for though they flattered me with some continuance of life, they never supposed that I could cease to be dropsical. . . . I hope the Mercy that lengthens my days, will assist me to use them well" (955). Even as we rejoice with Johnson in the excitement of his recovery—and perhaps smile affectionately as he describes the severity of his ailments—we are struck once again by the constancy of his religious faith. Here is a man who had within him the capacity to be as ready for his final hour as any mortal can be.

Now that we have completed our examination of Johnson's letters we have ample evidence for the claim underlying this paper, that the letters present a view of him as he was, with the difference from letter to letter governed by the nature of his activities at the time he wrote. Many of the familiar qualities may be seen: steady common sense, a wide variety of friendship, a lively and active interest in the world around him, personal and family loyalty, the capacity to triumph over many kinds of suffering, and the constant sense of sympathy with fellow sufferers. Implicit throughout his life and letters are his compassionately ironic view of his world, his realistic awareness of the vanity of human wishes, and his ever-present if sometimes tortured religious faith.

It is not difficult to find in the letters examples of the "Johnsonian" manner, both in style and in content, and we have occasionally noted some. But the letters are not essentially "literary" creations, and we do not read them as such. We read them with interest and with increasing absorption because Johnson was an interesting man, of outstanding moral and intellectual stature. If the view seems a little unusual when we first approach him solely through the letters, it is only because we have not become accustomed to the new light.

Very soon we come to see that this is the same powerful mind and rare human spirit we have always known.

Indiana University

STERNE'S LETTERS:
CONSCIOUSNESS AND SYMPATHY

HOWARD ANDERSON

THAT DISTRUST OF THE ARTFUL which increasingly characterized the eighteenth century is nowhere more evident than
in the remarks of the age upon letter-writing. Whatever tribute they felt bound to pay to decorum in other literary forms,
eighteenth-century writers insisted that "nature" must dis-
place "art" in personal letters. Conversations, not books,
should provide the models; letters should above all not be
literary. So Sterne is no exception to the rule when he de-
nounces those who "in lieu of sending me what I sat expecting
—a Letter—surprize me with an Essay cut & clip'd at all corners. to me inconsiderate Soul that I am, who never yet knew
what it was to speak or write one premeditated word, such an
intercourse would be an abomination; & I would as soon go
and commit fornication with the Moabites, as have a hand in
any thing of this kind unless written in that careless irregular-
ity of a good and an easy heart."[1] Such comments are most frequent in his letters to young ladies—whom, like Swift, he delighted to instruct. He begs his daughter Lydia to write to him
"as to a friend—in short whatever comes into your little head,
and then it will be natural" (p. 212). Later he says, "Write
soon, and never let your letters be studied ones—write naturally, and then you will write well" (p. 302). He advises an-

other young girl, Eliza Draper (who for a time replaced both Lydia and her mother in his affections), to make her letters "speak the easy carelessness of a heart that opens itself, any how, and every how, to a man you ought to esteem and trust" (p. 306).

Yet despite their apparent spontaneity, Sterne's protestations of his carelessness, and his urging of others to follow his example, it is difficult to accept his letters as merely "natural." *Tristram Shandy*, that apparently most artless of novels, bearing the author's assurance that he begins "with writing the first sentence—and trusting to Almighty God for the second,"[2] has been shown by critics in recent years to be a splendidly complex example of the art that hides art. Similarly the 222 letters, collected in the Curtis edition with the *Journal to Eliza*, provide frequent cause to question the ingenuousness of his claim that "my pen governs me—not me my pen" (Curtis, p. 394). It is not that, like Pope, he gathered and edited his own letters, recomposing some of them into a form as impersonal as the personal essay. The duty and honor of first editor fell to Lydia Sterne, and a dubious honor it has been, so poorly did she perform the duty. But Sterne's claim to absolute freshness is shadowed by a number of other devices that become apparent when the letters (and the *Journal*) are compared. His repetition of supposedly spontaneous passages,[3] his occasional liberties with fact, and his habit of sometimes drafting letters in a notebook, all make it clear that his accomplishment in letter-writing is not a triumph of artlessness.[4] If his letters appear completely spontaneous, it is not because he abandoned artistic techniques, but because he made them serve an unconventional vision of the human mind. His communication with others would be impossible without sympathy; but, equally important, his generous and subtle imagination enabled him to express his feeling for others in a style most likely to ensure their sympathetic response.

In a revealing letter to Eliza, Sterne shows an awareness of the value of a high degree of art in letter-writing, while he is yet unwilling to credit it to any source but nature:

131

The observation was very applicable, very good, and very elegantly expressed. I wish my memory did justice to the wording of it.—Who taught you the art of writing so sweetly, Eliza?—You have absolutely exalted it to a science! When I am in want of ready cash, and ill health will permit my genius to exert itself, I shall print your letters, as finished essays, "by an unfortunate Indian lady." The style is new; and would almost be a sufficient recommendation for their selling well, without merit—but their sense, natural ease, and spirit, is not to be equalled, I believe, in this section of the globe. . . . I only wonder where thou could'st acquire thy graces, thy goodness, thy accomplishments—so connected! so educated! Nature has, surely, studied to make thee her peculiar care—for thou art (and not in my eyes alone) the best and fairest of all her works. (pp. 320-321)

The passage maintains Sterne's usual loyalty to nature first, but clearly nature is here methodized. If Eliza is the Goddess's favorite, the sign of it is the "wording" of her letter; she is accomplished in the "art of writing," possessed indeed of a style. There is no mention of incompatibility between premeditation and spontaneity, elegance and sincerity, for Eliza's "style" is the vehicle of "sense, natural ease, and spirit." Even such natural virtues, then, require a style. She has had to learn to write so sweetly, her graces are acquired. It would be pointless to expect that Sterne would try in this passage to reconcile nature and art, carelessness and "trim'd edges," the letter and the essay. His first intention, after all, is somewhat indiscriminate praise of a girl with whom he is infatuated. The passage serves, rather, as an implicit recognition that writing natural letters requires considerable art.

This is not to accuse Sterne of mere lip service to the natural. Clearly he means something when again and again he discounts art in correspondence; if he in fact uses rhetorical techniques to spurn rhetoric, his real interest may be not to ignore art, but to replace old art with new.[5] Like Pope, Sterne insists upon artless letters. But in an unexpected way, the letters of both men (very different from one another) are very much like their other literary work. If Sterne's usually seem closer to "the easy carelessness of a heart that opens itself, any how, and every how" it is not because he ignored art but rather because his whole effort was spent in making his art do something which Pope's did not do. Specifically, he achieved means of communicating an impression of intimate sympathy and greater imaginative understanding—the impression of conversation with someone totally present. This aim was not confined to his correspondence.

Nor did Sterne accomplish this impression by merely resorting to formless outbursts of feeling. The letters do not contain a discussion of the role that art plays in letter-writing, but in view of the similarity between the aims of Sterne's novels and his letters, and of the contemporary commonplace that letters are another form of conversation, a well-known passage in *Tristram Shandy* on the nature of polite talk and its relationship to writing is relevant:

Writing, when properly managed, (as you may be sure I think mine is) is but a different name for conversation: As no one, who knows what he is about in good company would venture to talk all; —so no author, who understands the just boundaries of decorum and good breeding, would presume to think all: The truest respect which you can pay to the reader's understanding, is to halve this matter amicably, and leave him something to imagine, in his turn, as well as yourself.

For my own part, I am eternally paying him compliments of this kind, and do all that lies in my power to keep his imagination as busy as my own. (pp. 108-109)

This passage is one of the most significant of Sterne's many comments on his method in *Tristram Shandy* and it also shows something of his conception of himself as a correspondent. It was once taken for granted that Sterne was the most self-revelatory of writers; his name has been nearly a synonym for a lack of inhibition. Yet Henri Fluchère, at the end of the biography in his recent study of Sterne, suggests that a certain "sentiment de la solitude" is perhaps the most important characteristic of Sterne's consciousness.[6] This preoccupation with himself is even at best dangerously close to solipsism; at times in the *Journal to Eliza* it collapses into that condition. But the passage from *Tristram Shandy* reveals that Sterne's self-consciousness was equaled by an awareness of the necessity for conversation with others and of the profoundly social nature of talk and writing. Tristram's self-consciousness is balanced by his consciousness of the person to whom he speaks. Complete self-revelation is no compliment to the other person; the polite man does not bare his soul—what a bore he would be if he did. Rather, "Leave something to imagine" (or *give* something to imagine?) and thereby recognize the reader as a human being possessed of a mind of his own.

It is this remarkable tact that distinguishes Sterne from his Augustan predecessors. However elegant they were in conversation, Pope and Swift often find it difficult to avoid preaching when they write; their letters, charming as they often are, are characteristically rational structures, designed to convince. Sterne was certainly no less eager to make a point, but he did so by a different method. Though he and Pope would agree about the proper study of mankind, one used his mind to scorn the irrational, the other to exploit irrational links between human beings. His novels, his sermons, and his letters leave little doubt that Sterne shared the Augustan determination to improve society, but his faith in human improvability exceeded theirs, and he sought this improvement through mutual understanding and sympathy. His extraordinary self-consciousness, despite its dangerous inclination, was the cause of his equally remarkable perception of other people.

"The world has imagined," Sterne commented to a titled correspondent some months before he died, "because I wrote Tristram Shandy, that I was myself more Shandean than I really ever was—'tis a good-natured world we live in, and we are often painted in divers colours according to the ideas each one frames in his head" (pp. 402-403). Such was indeed the case, but if Sterne was habitually identified with Tristram and Yorick, he was himself responsible. Probably for commercial reasons he had published his sermons as "Yorick's" and his social as well as his financial success came to depend on this identity. Whatever the cause, the confusion of his public role and his private being was unquestionably greater than is usually the case with writers. Not only for his distant readers, but for people who came to be his intimate friends (and received his letters), Sterne *was* Tristram or Yorick. Like Byron and Hemingway, he was the product of his own imagination.

Thus Sterne could not help giving thought to his identity. His consciousness of himself as an individual person, of his inner feelings and private thoughts, could only be heightened by the image of himself that was constantly presented to him by other people. What those private thoughts were, and the extent to which his public identity constrained him, it is impossible to tell. The remark that I have quoted is scarcely anguished, and it is the only one extant in which Sterne deliberately separates himself from his creation. He had been shrewd enough to face the world in a character of almost unlimited freedom, one whose dominant qualities are improvisation and frankness, and he seems to have lived with that character quite comfortably. It is difficult to imagine one more versatile.

His awareness of his own identity, as he sketches it in the letter to his titled friend, depends upon his awareness of the workings of the minds of others: this world being what it is, every man sees things "according to the ideas each one frames in his head." Contemplating his own identity leads him to that of other people. Sterne aroused distinct responses in other people; the nature of those responses revealed to him (if he did not already know it) the individuality, the eccentricity, of human beings that resulted in the creation of his eccentric Shandeans and also in his ability to recognize other people as individuals. But his ability to make people respond to him depended upon his awareness of similarities between himself and others, of habits of mind shared by all. From his letter-writing methods we can learn a great deal about his view of himself and about his view of human nature and the mind.

His style is the vehicle he devised for those views, and it is our best access to them.

Before analyzing the elements of that style, I shall comment briefly on the difficulties and limitations of the text of the letters as we have them. The degree of identity between Sterne's letters and his other works may be heightened by the fact that many of his most personal letters have not survived. Mrs. Sterne's brother-in-law, John Botham, took it upon himself[7] to go through Shandy Hall after Sterne's death and burn what he found offensive. Presumably the burned letters included some of those which would provide a most intimate view of Sterne.[8] So much very personal material survives, however (notably the *Journal to Eliza,* which was not at Shandy Hall when Botham set to work), that the nature of the burned letters would probably not surprise us. Another textual difficulty, though one that does not bear directly upon this analysis, results from Lydia's tampering with many of the letters when she edited them in 1775; most of the damage she did, however, is confined to eliminating personal names, or, in the case of the letters to Eliza, changing her father's occasionally unflattering references to Mrs. Sterne. Finally, the question of forged letters is, for reasons already mentioned,[9] a serious one in the case of Sterne.

Sterne's characteristic method in his letters is to face his reader with a mind actively at work. The desired effect is immediacy. So while some of his letters begin with a conventional reference to the receipt of one, his typical opening is sudden: "of the two bad cassocs, fair Lady which I am worth in the world, I would this moment freely give the better of 'em to find out by what irresistable force of magic it is, that I am influenced to write a Letter to you upon so short an Acquaintance—*short,* did I say—I unsay it again: I have had the happiness to be acquainted with Mrs Vesey almost time immemorial" (p. 137). He launches in without pausing even to capitalize. Or to his Parisian banker: "After many turnings (*alias* digressions) to say nothing of downright overthrows, stops, and delays, we have arrived in three weeks at Toulouse, and are now settled in our houses with servants, &c. about us, and look as composed as if we had been here seven years" (p. 182). Just as Sterne complained about letters that look like essays, he detested those that begin "in the honest John-Trot-Style of, *yours of the 15th instant came safe to hand*" (p. 120, and cf. p. 117).[10] His swift beginnings seem to pick up the thread of a broken conversation, with or without a hurried explanation of the interruption; they do not allow the reader to become conscious of the space and time that separate him from Sterne. Their informality breathes life into the paper and ink: rules follow man in the proper Shandean order.

The impression of immediacy which seems to unite writer and reader is often gained by a number of skilfully handled dramatic techniques. Sterne is adept at rendering a scene so that the reader quickly takes part in it, rather than presenting a description from which he can stand aside. If a friend finds himself imposed upon in the financial arrangements for his prospective marriage, it is not enough for Sterne to give "the coolest & most candid Consideration . . . [to] every Movement throughout this affair." He dramatizes it, with the prospective bride's "Grand Mama standing first in the Dramatis Personae, the Lôup Garôu or raw head & Bloody bones to frighten Master Jacky into silence & make him go to bed with Missy, *supperless* and in Peace. Stanhope the Lawyer behind the Scenes ready to be call'd in to do his part either to frighten or outwit You. . . . Miss's Part was to play them Off upon y^r good nature" (p. 58). Sterne finds a way of thoroughly occupying his reader's mind by placing him in the midst of an action which is at once amusing and threatening.

Another dramatic method that Sterne uses to reduce the distance between his reader and himself is mimicry. The ability to capture idiom is everywhere apparent in his novels. It is an ability that he uses in his letters to make his reader share his own experiences; Sterne and Garrick together observe the affectation of fashionable French women in this passage:

I hear no news of you, or your *empire,* I would have said *kingdom* —but here every thing is hyperbolized—and if a woman is but simply pleased—'tis *Je suis charmée*—and if she is charmed 'tis nothing less, than that she is *ravi*-sh'd—and when ravi-sh'd, (which may happen) there is nothing left for her but to fly to the other world for a metaphor, and swear, qu'elle etoit toute *extasiée*— which mode of speaking, is, by the bye, here creeping into use, and there is scarce a woman who understands the *bon ton,* but is seven times in a day in downright extasy—that is, the devil's in her—by a small mistake of one world for the other—Now, where am I got? (pp. 161-162)

The element of reportage in such a passage should not make us forget that its effectiveness rests not only in Sterne's re- markable ear, well tuned to hear and reproduce what it hears, but also in a mind capable of selecting from endless hours of idle talk just the most revelatory bits. His selection here is anything but random, despite its apparent offhandedness. The effect is that of a shared experience *and* a comment upon it; a complex and absorbing effect.

This comic flight, ending in double entendre, also shows Sterne's characteristic verbal associationism—the quality that ruined his reputation among the Victorians, but which mod- ern critics have seen as basic to his conception of the human mind.[11] Beginning with "I hear no news of you," he does not go on with the expected series of questions about Garrick's health and work; a different train of thought is begun by the word *empire,* and he is on his Shandean way. This way delib- erately plays off his individuality against the conventional. But it is more than individual: Sterne's associations are not simply personal, for when he sets off on his associational course he is careful to select one which he knows his reader will be able to follow. More often than not, the basis of his association is sexual; it is grounded, that is, in faculties which are irrational, but which are shared by—and of interest to— everyone. Because of this assured participation, he can assume that his reader will be able to follow his sudden imaginative leaps. And the reader is flattered by shared awareness, not condescended to with elaborate and tiresome explanations.

Closely related to Sterne's illogical associationism is his habitual allusiveness. The letters abound in direct (though not always accurate) quotations, usually from the Bible and from Shakespeare; his wide familiarity with Shakespeare is far more apparent in the letters than in the novels. And at least as often as he quotes, he alludes to these favorite books indirectly, fusing his own words with those of a biblical or Shakespearean passage: "There is a blessing in store for the meek and gentle, and Eliza will not be disinherited of it" (p. 324); "God made us not for Misery and Ruin—he has orderd all our Steps—& influenced our Attachments for what is worthy of them" (p. 352); and, near the end of his life, "Yet I feel my Existence Strongly, and something like revelation along with it, which tells, I shall not dye—but live——& yet any other man w^d set his house in order" (p. 416). He adapts the Ghost's speech from *Hamlet* to tell Eliza he will always remember her (p. 346); he borrows Iago's sentiments on his "good name" (p. 357); and he fancies himself, rather like Falstaff, "sad as a cat" (p. 376). This use of biblical and Shakespearean language has two effects. As Curtis remarks in his introduction (p. xxix), the cadences of the King James version and of Shakespeare balance the extremely rapid rhythms of Sterne's usually colloquial English, contrasting with them, often ironically setting off the tone of Sterne's language. But the allusions do not only influence Sterne's tone: however ironic their effect, they add weight to Sterne's thought, as well. Like Tristram and Yorick (and Falstaff), he plays the *wise* fool, and that character is made the more impressive by his familiarity with the two greatest traditional repositories of wisdom in English. The undeniable air of learning makes Sterne's brilliance respectable; it gives the reader reason to look for a method in the apparent madness. It prevents him from laughing at Sterne, leads him rather to share the privileged amusement of the wise fool. And again, Sterne pays his reader the compliment of assuming that the allusions will be recognized, and so establishes common ground.

Associationism and allusiveness are methods dependent specifically upon Sterne's psychological insight; he has also further dramatic techniques which make the reader ignore the distance between him and the writer. Sterne's mimicry often extends to dialogue. He uses a "transcription" of an interchange between himself and his archdeacon's agent as a way of explaining how he seemed to insult the archdeacon. His aim is not merely to avoid an apology, but to avoid the very break between them which would require an apology:

[The agent] thus opens his Commission. Sir—My Friend the A. Deacon of Cleveland not caring to preach his Turn, as I conjectured, Has left me to provide a Preacher,—But before I can take any Steps in it with Regard to You—I want first to know, Sir, upon what Footing You and Dr Sterne [L. Sterne's uncle with whom he had quarreled] are?—upon what Footing!—Yes Sir, How your Quarel Stands?—Whats that to you?—How our Quarrel stands! Whats that to You, you Puppy? But Sir, Mr Blackburn would know—What's that to Him?—But Sir, dont be angry, I only want to know of You, whether Dr Sterne will not be displeased in Case You should preach—Go Look; Ive just now been preaching and You could not have fitter Opportunity to be satisfyed.—I hope, Mr Sterne, You are not Angry. Yes I am; But much more astonished at your *Impudence.* (p. 26)

Sterne could do much better than that when ten years later he began to write *Tristram Shandy,* but even this somewhat clumsy dialogue accomplishes his purpose of making the archdeacon laugh at the unflattering remark. It has the appearance of a real record, immediate and lifelike. Sterne does not hide the remark that might have been offensive to his friend; he places it in the context of his anger at the agent's impudence and makes it palatable through the vigor of the whole scene. A mere description of the quarrel might seem to leave something out or otherwise to distort the situation in Sterne's favor. The dialogue appears simply to present evidence, requiring the reader once again to make his own judgment. It presents the evidence in such a way that the reader's judgment will almost necessarily coincide with the writer's, but the reader is unlikely to question its authenticity. Reader and writer watch the quarrel together. This is, of course, only possible because Sterne knows the archdeacon well enough to be sure that they share righteous indignation at over-personal questions and bumbling inefficiency.

Nothing contributes more to the convincing spontaneity, the apparent immediacy of Sterne's letter-writing technique than his witty indecision. Far from giving the impression of having logically thought out everything he wants to say, he typically is of two minds on a subject. This double point of view convinces the reader that Sterne has not rehearsed his letter. Through this technique he coolly and objectively undercuts his own apparent enthusiasms, and at the same time broadens his perspective on the subject: "An urn of cold water in the driest stages of the driest Desert in Arabia, pour'd out by an angel's hand to a thirsty Pilgrim, could not have been more gratefully received than Miss Macartny's Letter—pray is that Simile too warm? or conceived too orientally? if it is; I could easily mend it" (p. 117). He has the best of two worlds: the gallantry of a compliment and the shrewdness to smile at such raptures, combining Don Quixote and Sancho in a single man. Sterne complicates his personality for his reader by showing her that he is consciously playing a role in offering the compliment. He will not have her think that he is incapable of a sparkling phrase—but he makes clear that he is not an empty-headed beau who is blind to the comedy of social forms. He seems to achieve sincerity by openly recognizing his own possible insincerity. His first letter to David Garrick makes use of the same device: "I know not what it was (tho 'I lye abominably,' because I know very well) which inclined me more to wish for your approbation than any Other's" (p. 86). As in his "transcription" of dialogue, he seems to hide nothing. He reveals not only the smooth exterior of the social being, but also some slightly rough edges that are usually tucked out of sight (or "clip'd at all the corners") in society. He does so through an art that laughs at art.

Thus we seem to have the whole man before us: an effect which is heightened by a final dramatic technique. As in his novels, Sterne frequently describes in his letters the setting and pose in which he finds himself. He remarks upon the way he is sitting at his desk or what he is looking at, or he mentions to Eliza that "the sky seems to smile upon me, as I look up to it" (p. 312). This inclusion of gesture and situation makes the reader *see* Sterne working and gives to the letter an element invariably present, if unnoticed, in conversation. It helps to make Sterne's correspondence a dialogue.

These techniques give the letters the appearance of "nature" despite the self-consciousness which we are justified in seeing behind Sterne's re-use of passages, his distortion of facts, and his letter book. Dominating his singular ability to create a living man in his letters is Sterne's realization, demonstrated fully in *Tristram Shandy,* that the mind does not work in a systematically reasoned way. This is what Sterne—and perhaps his contemporaries—meant when they said that letters are not essays; if a letter is to evoke a mind operating freely (rather than the organized result of that operation), then the principles of the letter's construction will not be simply logical ones. Sterne's understanding of the unreasoned forms of thought and conversation made it possible for him to give the appearance of artlessness to his letters and his novels. Their movement is lucid, but the lucidity is not usually that of logic.

His superior sense of the way people ordinarily think and talk enabled him above all to please his reader. In his letters, Sterne devised a way of making his reader feel that the whole attention of a real and vital human being is centered upon him. This aim is not, of course, entirely selfless. As Henri Fluchère comments in an essay on Sterne as a letter-writer, "avec plus ou moins de constance dans la lucidité, il pensera à la valeur littéraire de ce qu'il écrit, à la façon dont sa lettre pourra être utilisée pour, ou contre lui-même."[12] Certainly the use Sterne made of his Shandean identity in his private life reveals a writer who sustained himself (and not only financially) by his writing. And we have seen that he employed his art in writing letters as well as novels. The egoism implicit in Sterne's determination to impress his personality upon the recipients of his letters in an unforgettable way is something more, however, than a calculation of how best to influence people in his own behalf.

In a celebrated letter to David Garrick, Sterne shows what that combination of attitudes and technique which he called Shandeism meant to him: "I Shandy it more than ever, and verily do believe, that by mere Shandeism sublimated by a laughter-loving people, I fence as much against infirmities, as I do by the benefit of air and climate" (p. 163). His particular method of writing, which merged with his manner of dealing with people, was a game that made his painful life bearable and replaced his illness as the object of his attention. As in any game properly played, the delight of one player depends upon that of the other. The egoism apparent in his desire to exist brilliantly for other people is great, but it is benign when compared with the egoism of the invalid against which he used it as a shield: compare the letters and the *Journal to Eliza*. Sterne in the letters does not characteristically lose sight of the world beyond himself; his humor frequently results from his dry perception of how he looks from the outside. He is quick to perceive his own ridiculousness, to make himself the object of a joke. Thus with a grin he admits his tardiness in answering a letter: " '*God, be merciful to me a sinner*'—or sometimes, dear Sir, or dear Madame, be merciful, &c. (just as the case happens) is all I have gen^{lly} to say for what I do, and what I do not" (p. 213). Or he joins his archbishop in smiling at his own exaggerations in a letter asking leave to stay away from his parish: "I have preached too much, my Lord, already; and was my age to be computed either by the number of sermons I have preached, or the infirmities they have brought upon me, I might be truly said to have the claim of a *Miles emeritus*, and was there a Hotel des Invalides for the reception of such established upon any salutary plain betwixt here and Arabia Felix, I wᵈ beg your Grace's interest to help me into it" (p. 196). Of course such lines are intended to accomplish a purpose; they accomplish it by an amusing perception of the writer's own human weakness, which he engagingly reveals. He can admit these weaknesses because they are human ones that link him with, rather than separate him from, other people. Sterne exploits the erratic nature of the mind and the various weaknesses of the flesh as the bases of a common understanding. They are funny—even worthy of satire—but they are first of all human.

The *Journal to Eliza* is the only prolonged lapse of Sterne's imagination.[13] This account of the "castles" that he built, with Eliza as "corner stone" (p. 371) of them all, is another effort to protect himself from the dangers of the illness that was destroying him. As Tristram's Uncle Toby turned from King William's wars to his amours with the Widow Wadman, so Sterne in the last year of his life devotes his imagination to a new love. But, again like Uncle Toby, Sterne's pleasure in this affair seems to have been more in his fancy than in the woman herself. "In proportion as I am thus torn from yʳ embraces—*I cling the closer to the Idea of you*" (p. 376), he writes during the summer after their separation, and he seems indeed through most of the *Journal* to be lost in his "ideas," devoid of that perception of the world beyond himself which had given Shandeism its objectivity and humor. Nowhere is Sterne more open than in the *Journal*, nowhere more devoted to his reader, less concerned with art. Paradoxically, it is just here that, for all his obvious sincerity, he is most wrapped within himself, least in touch with the real girl whom he presumably addressed.

No better proof of the seriousness of Sterne's illness could exist than some of the pathetic fantasies which he constructs in an effort to realize his dream of a reunion with Eliza. Sentimental fictions which would have been wryly undercut in earlier days here pass for possibility; during the year before his death Sterne could stand very little reality:

Some Annotator or explainer of my works in this place will take occasion, to speak of the Friendship wch Subsisted so long & faithfully betwixt Yorick & the Lady he speaks of—Her Name he will tell the world was Draper—a Native of India—married there to a gentleman in the India Service. . . . It was ab^t three months before her Return to India, That our Author's acquaintance & hers began. Mrs Draper had a great thirst for Knowledge—was handsome —genteel—engaging—and of such gentle dispositions & so enlightend an understanding,—That Yorick . . . soon became her Admirer —they caught fire, at each other at the same time—& they w^d often say, without reserve to the world, & without any Idea of saying wrong in it, That their Affections for each other were *unbounded* —Mr Draper dying in the Year xxxxx—This Lady return'd to England, & Yorick the year after becoming a Widower—They were married—& retiring to one of his Livings in Yorkshire, where was a most romantic Situation—they lived & died happily.—and are spoke of with honour in the parish to this day. (pp. 358-359)

In preparation for this happy event he spends days furnishing and decorating a room for Eliza; he walks as often as he can to the nearby ruins of a convent to confide his loneliness to the spirits of the nuns; he dreams of what "will be the golden Age when You govern the rural feast, my Bramine" (p. 371).

Yet even when addressing Eliza, Sterne can occasionally rally some of his old clear sight, and the humor that attends it. When their separation was only beginning, he could achieve a degree of candor rare in any letter. Of two portraits of her which he has recently seen, he says he prefers the one in which she is *not* "dressed in smiles, with all the advantages of silks, pearls, and ermine" (p. 312); her natural appearance is far better. Then he continues: "When I first saw you, I beheld you as an object of compassion, and as a very plain woman." The conventional compliment that he pays her later—that he has now seen the inner beauty that makes her the rarest of women—can be counted on to redeem him with Eliza; yet even with that compliment in store such a remark is uncommon.

Most writers would have recourse to the formula whereby the lady's beauty is outdone only by her virtue. Instead, Sterne pays Eliza a true compliment—its originality and honesty apparent precisely in contrast to conventional flattery. And in the *Journal* Sterne tosses Eliza a bit of double entendre reminiscent of John Donne and certainly worthy of better days: "Yʳ little Temple I have described—& what it will hold—but if it ever holds You & I, my Eliza—the Room will not be too little for us—but We shall be *too big* for the Room" (p. 367). There are other moments of wit that may or may not be conscious. An account of a bad siege of illness in the *Journal* has the hysterical immediacy that Fielding laughed at in *Shamela*. As Fielding's heroine scribbles a letter in bed while Mr. Booby approaches, so Sterne recounts a different sort of close call:

> Ap:24
> So Ill, I could not write a word all this morning—not so much, as Eliza! farewel to thee;—I'm going— (Ap 25) am a little better—
> —So Shall not depart, as I apprehended— (p. 329)

The business-like bathos of the last line would have delighted Fielding, or Sterne in better health; but in this context it is difficult to judge whether Sterne had achieved that distance from himself which he formerly shared so easily with his readers.

The *Letters* and the *Journal to Eliza* show how little distance lies between the healthy imagination and the sick, between structures that allow the artist to converse with the world and those that turn him toward solipsism. The letters themselves dispel once and for all the notion that true communication is gained by speaking "any how and every how." Sterne's counsel that letters should be easily careless recognizes the fact that artfulness can be carried too far, ending in mere self-amusement. He advises "carelessness" in an effort to do away with superficiality. Mere artfulness, like the fancies of the pedants in *Tristram Shandy,* builds a wall between one man and another. But the letters themselves illustrate how proper art achieves precisely the objectivity, the distance from self, which is necessary for true sympathy. Sterne in his letters crosses the space between himself and his friends, and from that new vantage point they look out together. Thus consciousness, not carelessness, accounts for Sterne's success in reaching the hearts of his readers. Sincerity is not just openness—if it were, the *Journal to Eliza* would be a great letter. Rather, sincerity, beginning in proper self-awareness, leads to sympathetic awareness of others.

Such sincerity and sympathy are not easily achieved and maintained, but to the invalid Sterne they were necessary as weapons against his infirmities. In a letter dated shortly before his death, he writes, "Tell me the reason, why Cervantes could write so fine and humourous a Satyre, in the melancholly regions of a damp prison—or why Scarron in bodily pain" (p. 416). Humor arises from melancholy in Sterne, objectivity from egoism, sympathy from selfishness. In his letters Sterne has found a style which makes him exist richly—but he is able to do so only because other people first exist for him.

Indiana University

THE POET WHO SPOKE OUT:
THE LETTERS OF THOMAS GRAY

R. W. Ketton-Cremer

I

The letters of Thomas Gray may be read, and indeed it is right that they should be read, for the sheer enjoyment of their excellence as letters—their wisdom, their humor, their critical insight, the unfailing ease and grace of their expression. But since the publication of my life of Gray in 1955, I have never been able to read his letters without recalling the years during which I lived with them, trying to understand and to portray the man who wrote them. In consequence this essay, for better or for worse, is written primarily from the biographer's point of view.

Some biographers have had to lament that few letters or none from their subjects have survived the chances of time. At the opposite extreme the next biographer of Horace Walpole, thanks to the labors of Mr. W. S. Lewis, will have more than four thousand letters to aid him in his task. The existence of a great body of correspondence does in fact put an additional responsibility upon the biographer, and raises all sorts of problems of selection, and, above all, of interpretation. Has one put the right emphasis upon the right letters? When there are contradictory statements or expressions of opinion, as there quite often are, which is one to believe? One has got to re-

148

member that, with a few outstanding exceptions, a letter-writer is seldom deliberately addressing posterity. At the time of writing he may be tired, he may be ill, drunk, in a vile temper, dazed with happiness, intoxicated with success, in any sort of mood. Only the most self-conscious of men are always mindful that posterity may take an interest in them, and compose their letters accordingly. But the letters of a great writer, however perfunctory or perverse or indiscreet, do tend to get preserved: and after his death they find their way into "cold irrevocable type": and by them he is judged.

Hence, of all the pitfalls that may entrap the biographer, one of the most dangerous is the importance that he may wrongly attach to some random, throw-away phrase. Idiom, expression, the nuances of language are always changing. We have seen it in our own generation—how much more in the two hundred years between Gray's lifetime and our own. Yet the jokes and the nonsense of the eighteenth century have to be expounded, learnedly, gravely, and sometimes with extreme misapprehension, by the editors and the thesis-writers of the twentieth. One casual sentence, mistakenly interpreted, can distort the whole image of a man or woman in the eyes of posterity.

Thus Matthew Arnold based his famous explanation of Gray upon four words into which, I am convinced, he read a good deal more meaning than they can bear. A few days after Gray's death his good and faithful friend James Brown, afterwards Master of Pembroke College, wrote: "He never spoke out, but I believe from some little expressions I now remember to have dropped from him, that for some time past he thought himself nearer his end than those about him apprehended." I do not think that anyone with an ear even faintly attuned to eighteenth-century speech could mistake Brown's meaning. He intended to say that Gray never spoke out about his awareness of his declining health: just that, and nothing more. But Arnold took the words "He never spoke out" as the text of his whole interpretation. "Let us dwell upon them," he wrote, "and press into their meaning, for in following it we shall come to understand Gray." And those four insignificant words have stuck in the popular mind ever since. Arnold was a great man, whose critical pronouncements were made with all the majestic certainty of his age. There is much in his essay on Gray that is illuminating and just. We must remember, too, that to all but his closest friends Gray was notably reticent in his speech—prim, shy, unresponsive. Walpole recorded how at a gay party beside the Thames he only once opened his lips: and that was in reply to a question: and all he said was "Yes, my lady, I believe so." But in his letters he certainly did speak out. No poet of comparable importance, perhaps, has left so small a body of verse. On the other hand, some five hundred of his letters have survived: and here, in contrast to his long-pondered and carefully polished verse, he said what he wanted to say with spontaneity, with ease, and often with surprising frankness.

Even so, one must interpret these letters with caution, and be very sparing of conjecture. Many of them are a tissue of jokes and private allusions and subtle shades of meaning, known only to his correspondents. The humor that plays incessantly over them, and that will suddenly light up their most sombre expressions of melancholy, is not a thing to be solemnly dissected. It would be delightful to know why Mason was nicknamed Skroddles: and what Mr. Senhouse's acoustic warming-pan may have been: what was the whale in pickle that had just come from Ipswich, what the curled dog, what the red nightingale. But it is not very profitable to guess. The letter of 11 September 1746, with its description of one of Gray's dreams, could provide a rich quarry for the psychoanalyst. "I thought I was in t'other world and confined in a little apartment much like a cellar, enlightened by one rush candle that burn'd blue. On each side of me sate (for my sins) Mr. Davie and my friend Mr. Ashton: they bow'd continually and smil'd in my face, and while one fill'd me out very bitter tea, the other sweetened it with a vast deal of brown sugar. In the corner sat Tuthill very melancholy, in expectation of the tea-leaves." No doubt, when Gray's biography is written from a strictly psychological approach, this passage will figure prominently. But personally I have a strong suspicion that the dream was all made up on the spur of the moment to amuse his correspondent Thomas Wharton.

II

One must always remember that letters are private and personal documents, and that their survival is very much a matter of chance. One man will take special care to arrange that his letters are preserved by their recipients, or will keep copies of them himself. Horace Walpole was the supreme instance of the deliberate letter-writer: and Mr. Lewis has shown how carefully, and how effectively, he made certain that his letters would reach posterity. Another man will do everything in his power to ensure that his letters are destroyed: for there are those who cherish their personal privacy beyond the grave. But there are also men who prefer to commit the whole matter to the discretion of a trustworthy executor: and this was the course adopted by Gray. In his will he bequeathed to his friend and executor William Mason "all my books, manuscripts, coins, musick printed or written, and papers of all kinds, to preserve or destroy at his own discretion."

All biographers are very conscious of their predecessors. They may regard them with varying degrees of admiration or exasperation, but they can seldom ignore them. If their subject was a great letter-writer, they will be similarly conscious of the editors to whose labors they are so much indebted—their varying personalities, the varying ways in which they tackled the problems of assembling and editing and annotating the letters. The editors of Gray's correspondence were a diverse and remarkable band: and it is fitting that I should say something about each of them.

And first of William Mason. No writer of the eighteenth century, once widely esteemed, now receives quite such a bad press. As H. W. Garrod once said, "Nobody likes him: and nobody trusts him." But the odd thing is that Gray himself both liked and trusted him—trusted him, as we have seen, with all his papers, including his letters, to preserve or destroy at his own discretion. In his *Memoirs of Gray,* Mason did what he could, according to his lights, to justify the confidence reposed in him. It is all very well for us to assume that the entire private papers of a great writer ought to be consigned intact to posterity: but the great writers, and those who wish them well, sometimes do not see the matter in quite the same light. Posterity is not always a kindly or a sensible or even a just tribunal. Gray himself put it in a nutshell—"As to posterity," he wrote, "I may ask (with somebody whom I have forgot) what has it ever done to oblige me?" There were occasions in his life, as there are in the lives of most of us, when he did not appear at his best. One of them was his rather undignified departure from Peterhouse to Pembroke, caused or at least accelerated by the horseplay of some rowdy undergraduates, taking advantage of his known timidity about the danger of fire. I do not suppose that Gray gave his biographer any instructions as to how this and one or two other passages were to be handled: but I think he relied on Mason's discretion and good feeling, and not in vain.

On the other hand, Mason took liberties with the letters which later generations can never forgive. He mutilated some, transposed passages in others, strung together portions of quite different letters, and in many cases destroyed the originals after printing extracts from them. By the standards of modern scholarship, he committed every possible editorial crime. But Mason was not thinking of his admired friend and mentor as a subject for Ph.D. theses, for Freudian interpretations, for articles in the learned journals of two hundred years later. It was his purpose to show Gray, both to his contemporaries and to posterity, as what he essentially was—"a virtuous, a friendly, and an amiable man." He would allow Gray to speak, within the limits which he thought advisable, through the medium of his own letters—"in a word, Mr. Gray will become his own biographer." And thus was composed one of the earliest and most influential biographies in the English language—the book which, on Boswell's own admission, served as the model for his *Life of Johnson.*

To Johnson himself, and to other contemporaries who knew Gray only by hearsay as a finical and affected Cambridge recluse, these letters came as an impressive surprise. They did portray a virtuous, a friendly, and an amiable man. They revealed also, as Johnson wrote in the *Lives of the Poets,* Gray's unlimited curiosity, his cultivated judgment, the grasp of his mind. No one would ever again dismiss him contemptuously as "delicate Mr. Gray." To that extent Mason had succeeded in what he set out to do. Nevertheless his treatment of the text of the letters obviously had to be rectified: and Gray's next editor, the Rev. John Mitford, made it his aim to print every procurable letter in its entirety. Mitford was not a very assiduous clergyman—Charles Lamb described him, in fact, as "a pleasant layman spoiled"—but one cannot be too grateful for his devoted and lifelong labors on Gray. The whole long succession of the letters to Thomas Wharton was now printed, and all the delightful letters to Gray's younger friend Norton Nicholls, of which Mason had only used six, and fragments of them at that. Mitford also printed the letters to Bonstetten, which had appeared in the appendix of a book published in Switzerland—those letters, only three in number, which reveal so much about the emotional crisis of Gray's last years.

Later in the century, Gray's letters were edited afresh by an ambitious and able young writer named Edmund Gosse. Here we have another literary figure, like Mason greatly admired in his own day, whose laurels have withered somewhat in the eyes of posterity. With all his merits, Gosse could be quite extraordinarily careless and inaccurate: and over Gray's letters he had one of the worst mishaps of his career. Mitford, an excellent editor in so many respects, was not impeccable: and it became necessary to re-transcribe the correspondence with Wharton, which had now come to rest in the British Museum.

Unfortunately Gosse handed over the task of transcribing these letters to a hack: and still more unfortunately the hack, after copying the first dozen or so from the originals, preferred the comfort of his own fireside to the austerities of the British Museum Reading Room, and calmly transcribed the remainder, errors and all, from Mitford's printed edition. Gosse was completely taken in. He did not bother to check the transcript: yet in his preface he assured his readers that "I have scrupulously printed these letters, as though they had never been published before, direct from the originals . . . in the manuscript department of the British Museum. The Wharton letters are so numerous and so important, and have hitherto been so carelessly transcribed, that I regard this portion of my labours, mechanical as it is, with great satisfaction." This remarkable piece of disingenuousness remained undetected until sixteen years later, when the admirable Duncan Tovey brought out the first volume of his edition of the letters. Tovey thoroughly enjoyed his task of exposing Gosse, which he did in a long and elaborately sarcastic appendix to his first volume. But Gosse had now become so great a pundit that he was able simply to brush the matter aside: and he did not, in his next edition, even alter the passage that has just been quoted.

Tovey's edition was excellent—very accurate, very judicious. But there was still room for improvement, and unpublished letters of Gray turned up in quite considerable numbers early in this century. Dr. Paget Toynbee, whose wife was responsible for the edition of Walpole's correspondence which is only now being superseded by that of Mr. Lewis, turned late in life from the study of Dante to the study of Walpole and presently of Gray. There is a most engaging portrait of him in Mr. Lewis's book *Collector's Progress*. He first edited in two volumes the correspondence between the four friends who at Eton formed the "Quadruple Alliance"—Gray, Walpole, West, and Ashton: and then he embarked upon a definitive edition of the correspondence of Gray. In the meantime a Fellow of Pembroke, Leonard Whibley, after a lifetime of tutoring in classical literature, had become deeply interested in Gray. He and Toynbee decided to collaborate. Toynbee died in 1932, and three years later Whibley completed and published the edition, with its superb annotation and its detailed appendices on every important aspect of Gray's life. It is with gratitude and affection that many scholars still remember Leonard Whibley today.

III

Gray's qualities as a poet revealed themselves slowly and belatedly. Before 1742, when he reached the age of twenty-five, he had written a good deal of excellent Latin verse, but no original English poetry at all. And the few poems which he did achieve in all his lifetime were the result of long and anguished struggles. Yet in his letters, from the very first, he showed himself able to handle his native language with complete confidence and ease.

Walpole remarked more than once that Gray was never a boy. Many of his earlier letters to Walpole, with all their comical prefixes and suffixes, are boyish enough in tone—bubbling over with nonsense, sometimes exploding into the wildest fantasy. But on occasion he could be astonishingly mature, and this is what Walpole perceived. The power of self-analysis is not often granted to the young: but there are passages in Gray's early letters which show the clearest insight into his own character and the characters of other people. There is one letter in which he draws with perfect good-humor the contrast between Walpole and himself: the rich young man of the world and the retiring scholar, shy in large companies, clumsy in social life. "Bear I was born, and bear, I believe, I'm like to remain: consequently a little ungainly in my fondnesses: but I'll be bold to say, you shan't in a hurry meet with a more loving poor animal, than your faithful creature, Bruin."

There are many such passages, full of the humor which irradiates all his letters. Even when melancholy and heavy-hearted, he would write with an enchanting lightness of touch. We shall never know the extent of the stresses and strains between him and Walpole during their two years' Grand Tour together. And we do not have the letters in which he must undoubtedly have explained to his parents and to West why he quarreled with Walpole and parted from him in the spring of 1741. Thanks presumably to Mason, his wonderful series of travel-letters stops dead just at that time. But there were two letters in which his graver note was sounded, and his insight into human character revealed. The first is the long letter written from Florence to West on 16 July 1741. West had fallen into a mood of despondency and lassitude, was talking of giving up the study of the law before he had really begun it, and in general was imperiling his future prospects. Letters of good advice can be a bore to write, and still more so to receive. But this particular letter of Gray's is so outstanding in its sympathy, its wisdom, and its warmheartedness, that it cannot have failed to encourage and refresh poor West. A few months later it was Gray's turn to look into his own heart, at the end of almost two years of travel, when an open quarrel with Walpole was only a month ahead. The result was another of these remarkable passages of self-analysis, almost of autobiography:

Methinks I ought to send you my picture. . . . You must add then, to your former idea, two years of age, reasonable quantity of dullness, a great deal of silence, and something that rather resembles, than is, thinking: a confused notion of many strange and fine things that have swum before my eyes for some time: a want of love for general society, indeed an inability to it. On the good side you may add a sensibility for what others feel, and indulgence for their faults or weaknesses, a love of truth, and detestation of everything else. Then you are to deduct a little impertinence, a little laughter, a great deal of pride, and some spirits. . . . Think not that I have been obliged for this reformation of manners to reason or reflection, but to a severer schoolmistress, Experience. One has little merit in learning her lessons, for one cannot well help it; but they are more useful than others, and imprint themselves in the very heart.

The travel letters, with their instant response to the beauties of nature and of art alike, are everywhere full of the poetry which had so far found no other means of expression. "There is a moon! there are stars for you! Do not you hear the fountain? do not you smell the orange flowers?" All these letters contain immensely quotable descriptions of landscape and townscape—the Alps, Genoa, Lombardy, Rome, Naples, all viewed with those fresh and searching eyes. And there is the famous and significant passage: "In our little journey up to the Grande Chartreuse, I do not remember to have gone ten paces without an exclamation, that there was no restraining: Not a precipice, not a torrent, not a cliff, but is pregnant with religion and poetry. There are certain scenes that would awe an atheist into belief, without the help of other argument."

All these letters were written when Gray was a young man, seemingly without literary ambition or the least expectation of fame, with creative powers so dormant as to be unsuspected by himself as by the rest of the world. In 1742 came the first flowering of his genius, with the "Ode on the Spring," the "Eton Ode," the "Hymn to Adversity," the sonnet in memory of West, perhaps the first tentative lines of the "Elegy." In 1750 the "Elegy" was completed: the next year its publication set him at the head of living English poets. He had written a poem which, in the words of Johnson, "abounds with images which find a mirrour in every mind, and with sentiments to which every bosom returns an echo." He had reached and touched the heart of the common man.

A poet, however modest and retiring, who has thus caught the attention of his age, must surely have some thoughts of posthumous fame, some inkling that his letters would be of interest to posterity. Gray knew Pope's letters well, and how solicitously Pope had tidied them up for publication. It is possible that he was aware of the manner in which Walpole's letters were to be preserved for the enlightenment of posterity. Yet I do not think one can perceive in his own letters the smallest trace of self-consciousness, of literary devices or deliberate "fine writing." His fame made no more alteration in the manner of his correspondence than in the conduct of his daily life. The quality of his letters remained astonishingly consistent, from his obscure youth to the European celebrity of his mature years.

Perhaps the quality that strikes one most is the sympathy, the warmth of understanding that Gray reveals time and again. This reticent and unapproachable man—as the world regarded him—was intensely concerned with the welfare of his friends, their successes and their troubles: Walpole's health, Wharton's children and his family happiness, Nicholls's prospects in life. This solicitude was extended even to people well outside his intimate group of friends. When Boswell's friend Temple, a clergyman in Devonshire, quarreled with his patron Lord Lisburne, Gray sent through Nicholls pages full of sympathetic advice on this and all his other troubles. And in times of misfortune he was able to give comfort and strength. The letter to William Mason at the time of his wife's death is a memorable example. "I break in upon you at a moment, when we least of all are permitted to disturb our Friends, only to say, that you are daily and hourly present to my thoughts. If the worst be not yet past: you will neglect and pardon me. But if the last struggle be over: if the poor subject of your long anxieties be no longer sensible to your kindness, or to her own sufferings: allow me (at least in idea, for what could I do, were I present, more than this?) to sit by you in silence, and pity from my heart, not her, who is at rest; but you, who lose her. May He, who made us, the Master of our pleasures, and of our pains, preserve and support you!" The manuscript of the letter still bears Mason's endorsement: "This little billet which I received almost at the precise moment when it would be most affecting, then breathed and still seems to breathe the voice of Friendship in its tenderest and most pathetic note."

The power of self-analysis, to which reference has already been made, remained with him through life. At the age of twenty-five he could define, in a letter to West, his usual condition of mind as "a white Melancholy, or rather Leucocholy, for the most part: which though it seldoms laughs or dances, nor ever amounts to what one calls joy or pleasure, yet is a good easy sort of a state, et *ça ne laisse que de s'amuser.*" But he went on to describe, most revealingly, his fits of the true Melancholy, "black indeed . . . for it believes, nay is sure of everything that is unlikely, so it be but frightful: and, on the other hand, excludes and shuts its eyes to the most possible hopes, and every thing that is pleasurable. From this the Lord deliver us! for none but he and sunshiny weather can do it." Sixteen years later he was still describing the horrors of Melancholy in similar terms: "Heavy, lifeless, without form and void: sometimes almost as black, as the moral of Voltaire's *Lisbon,* which angers you so." And this was the man who never spoke out!

But there were long spells of sunshiny weather in his life: and no reader of the letters as a whole could suppose them to be the work of a man whom Melancholy had marked for her own. Their earliest readers, the people who first bought Mason's *Memoirs,* were astonished by their gaiety and lightness of tone, their humor, their wit. It is the interplay of wit that makes his correspondence with Walpole a dialogue so perfectly matched. When he wrote to younger friends, to Mason and above all to Nicholls, he could become frivolous to a degree that might have disconcerted some of those who thought of him as "the sweetly plaintive Gray." Take, for instance, his explanation to Mason of his refusal to become Poet Laureate. "Though I very well know the bland emollient saponaceous qualities both of sack and silver, yet if any great man would say to me, 'I make you rat-catcher to his Majesty with a salary of £300 a year and two butts of the best Malaga: and though it has been usual to catch a mouse or two (for form's sake) in public once a year, yet to you, Sir, we shall not stand upon these things', I can not say, I should jump at it. Nay, if they would drop the very name of the office, and call me Sinecure to the King's Majesty, I should still feel a little awkward, and think everybody I saw, smelt a rat about me . . . for my part I would rather be Serjeant Trumpeter, or Pin-maker to the Palace."

This wit, and this occasional frivolity, give a particular flavor to the literary criticism which is scattered so abundantly through his letters. Unlike some critics in every age, not excluding our own, Gray was never arrogant or pontifical: yet how often his lightly aimed shafts hit the mark. Take the letter in which he discussed with Walpole the first volumes of Dodsley's *Collection*. On Matthew Green: "There is a profusion of wit every where: reading would have formed his judgement, and harmonized his verse, for even his wood-notes often break out into strains of real poetry and music." On Johnson's *London:* "I am sorry to differ from you, but *London* is to me one of those few imitations, that have all the ease and all the spirit of the original." On *Grongar Hill:* "Mr. Dyer has more of poetry in his imagination than almost any of our number." On Lady Mary Wortley Montagu's *Town Eclogues:* "The Town is an owl, if it don't like Lady Mary." His criticism was equally to the point in later letters. "There is Mr. Shenstone, who trusts to nature and simple sentiment, why does he do no better? he goes hopping along his own gravel walks, and never deviates from the beaten paths for fear of being lost." "There is much good fun in *Tristram Shandy,* and humour sometimes hit and sometimes missed. . . . Have you read his *Sermons,* with his own comic figure at the head of them? They are in the style I think most proper for the pulpit, and show a very strong imagination and a sensible heart: but you see him often tottering on the verge of laughter, and ready to throw his periwig in the face of his audience." "I think you will like Sterne's *Sentimental Travels,* which though often tiresome, are exceedingly goodnatured and picturesque."

No one, in fact, ever better exemplified the old *cliché,* "He wore his learning lightly." Temple in his character-sketch of Gray suggested that he was "perhaps the most learned man in Europe." Of course on a literal basis such a claim was nonsense. How could one possibly tell? What standards were there to go by? But reading through Gray's letters, with their extraordinary range of topics and interests, one does appreciate what Temple was trying to say. And this view of his learning is reinforced by a perusal of those amazing notebooks of his, whether he was dealing with the dialogues of Plato, or the geography of the ancient world, or the architecture of English cathedrals, or—the especial passion of his later years—the whole vast subject of natural history.

Every summer Gray would leave the sober levels of Cambridgeshire, and make a tour in search of the picturesque. He explored the Lakes, the Peak, the Wye valley, and many other parts, once even venturing far into Scotland: and he described what he saw, for the benefit of Wharton and other friends, with great feeling and power. A good deal of eighteenth-century writing about natural beauty was curiously pompous—the sort of thing satirized by Peacock in *Headlong Hall*—wranglings about the definition of what was sublime, what was beautiful, what was picturesque, and so forth. Gray, on the contrary, was seeing mountains and trees and streams, and describing them to his private friends, with a very different vision. The nearest comparison, perhaps, is with those wonderful diarists Dorothy Wordsworth and Francis Kilvert, who in years to come would depict the beauties of nature in the privacy of their diaries with the same exquisite freshness. Some of these passages are almost too well-known for quotation—that about Netley Abbey, for example: or that which describes the advance of evening in Borrowdale, the sunlight fading from the hills, the murmuring of waterfalls inaudible by day. But passages less famous have the same mysterious quality. On the morning of 3 October 1769, Gray rose at seven, and walked out into the autumnal morning.

A heavenly day. The grass was covered with a hoar-frost, which soon melted, and exhaled in a thin blewish smoke. Crossed the meadows obliquely, catching a diversity of views among the hills over the lake and islands, and changing prospect at every ten paces

. . . our path here tends to the left, and the ground gently rising, and covered with a glade of scattering trees and bushes on the very margin of the water, opens both ways the most delicious view, that my eyes ever beheld . . . to the left the jaws of Borrowdale, with that turbulent chaos of mountain beyond mountain rolled in confusion: beneath you, and stretching far to the right, the shining purity of the lake, just ruffled by the breeze enough to show it is alive. . . . Oh Doctor! I never wished more for you.

Finally there are the three letters, or portions of letters, to Charles-Victor de Bonstetten. They were all written within the space of a few weeks, just after his young friend had left England in the spring of 1770. There is in them an emotional intensity which appears nowhere else in the letters of Gray. "Never did I feel, my dear Bonstetten, to what a tedious length the few short moments of our life may be extended by impatience and expectation, till you had left me: nor ever knew before with so strong a conviction how much this frail body sympathises with the inquietude of the mind. . . . The strength and spirits that now enable me to write to you, are only owing to your last letter, a temporary gleam of sunshine. Heaven knows, when it may shine again! I did not conceive till now (I own) what it was to lose you, nor felt the solitude and insipidity of my own condition, before I possessed the happiness of your friendship." Or again, a few weeks later:

I am return'd, my dear Bonstetten, from the little journey I had made into Suffolk without answering the end proposed. The thought, that you might have been with me there, has embitter'd all my hours. Your letter has made me happy; as happy as so gloomy, so solitary a Being as I am is capable of being. I know and have too often felt the disadvantages I lay myself under, how much I hurt the little interest I have in you, by this air of sadness so contrary to your nature and present enjoyments; but sure you will forgive, tho' you can not sympathize with me. It is impossible for me to dissemble with you. Such as I am, I expose my heart to your view, nor wish to conceal a single thought from your penetrating eyes.—All that you say to me, especially on the subject of Switzerland, is infinitely acceptable. It feels too pleasing ever to be fulfill'd, and as often as I read over your truly kind letter, written long since from London, I stop at these words: *La mort qui peut glacer nos bras avant qu'ils soient entrelacés.*

These letters to Bonstetten are tantalizing documents, and they have reached us in what appears to be a truncated form. But even in their imperfect state they seem to me the final refutation of the view that Gray never spoke out.

IV

Further letters of Gray may yet be found. After all, the Boswell papers now at Yale, and the Walpole manuscripts which continue to arrive at Farmington, are instances of the treasure that may still be concealed in cupboards and lumber-rooms anywhere in the world. It is not impossible that further correspondence with Bonstetten may turn up in some remote corner of Switzerland. Only one letter has so far been printed of those which Gray wrote to his friend the Rev. "Billy" Robinson, the brother of Mrs. Montagu. Robinson did not think Mason equal to writing Gray's biography, and refused to let him use these letters, which have since vanished. Only one letter, again, survives of his correspondence with Dr. John Clerke, for whose wife he wrote a beautiful epitaph. It was described by William Gilpin as being a particularly entertaining collection, and to have included "a description of a haughty fellow of a college, soliciting a piece of university preferment." Then there was the series to a Cornish clergyman, the Rev. William Carlyon, which is said to have been in existence early in this century, and in one of which Gray described "with much vigour of language" the practical joke which led to his removal from Peterhouse to Pembroke. We may hope that some at least of these correspondences may one day come to light.

But whether they do or not, Gray's letters are among the classics of eighteenth-century literature. One of his lesser-known friends, Dr. Thomas Gisborne, wrote shortly after his death: "I believe he has not left his equal: his thoughts on all

subjects were so exceedingly good, and so purely his own."
Artlessly and unconsciously, Dr. Gisborne summed up what I
have been endeavoring to express about his quality as a letter-
writer. His thoughts were so exceedingly good, and so purely
his own.

Felbrigg Hall, Norwich

WALPOLE'S LETTERS:
THE ART OF BEING GRACEFUL

William N. Free

THE RESEMBLANCE between the form and content of Horace Walpole's letters and his journals of the reigns of George II and George III has often been noticed. Both correspondence and journals present vivid and entertaining, although not always extremely accurate, narratives of contemporary life. They reveal concern with the texture of the events they describe, an awareness of people and of the social milieu, which often seems uniquely Walpolian. Together they offer a double-edged chronicle which in the journals cuts through surfaces and reveals the inner movements of political life, and in the letters lays open the manners and morals of the age. They complement each other. The journals did not allow Walpole so much freedom to exercise wit or cultivate some of the arts which he most admired; the letters could not provide the coherent account of motives, actions, and events necessary to a true history.

Walpole's choice of correspondents, as R. W. Ketton-Cremer shows in his biography, admirably suited his self-created role as chronicler of eighteenth-century life.[1] The best correspondences are with people whom Walpole saw rarely. They contain so small an amount of purely personal ephemera that one feels that Walpole could as well have been writing to his other, greater audience, posterity, as to the individual correspondents. Whether he figures rather largely in the gossip to Horace Mann, the envoy to Florence through almost the entire period of the correspondence, or gaily coins words for George Montagu, dozing into oblivion in the country during most of the thirty-two years that Walpole sent letters to him, Walpole himself remains a character in the historical panorama of the letters. This character does not change from one correspondence to another, although different sides of it might receive emphasis at different times. Of course, some correspondents were more fit to receive certain kinds of news than others. Hence antiquarian interests were communicated to Cole, social news to Montagu, the major events of the day to Mann. But with few exceptions Walpole intended to present himself as the well-rounded man, enjoying his many capabilities and varied interests. Always he seems at ease, conversing in a manner not much different from that of the polite assembly. Even in the short exchange with Chatterton, one sees him carefully protecting his reputation as a gentleman, apparently playing a role for future generations as well as removing a present nuisance.

Walpole's epistolary manner seems to have been closely related to what hints we have of his aesthetic convictions, which, of course, are everywhere controlled by the facts that he was of the eighteenth century and a gentleman. From his letters emerges the perfect image of a gentleman: easy, witty, urbane, with enough learning to give him perspective on his own age but not enough to make him a pedant, with a moral sense but also a sense of detachment, and with a notion of his usefulness but no feeling of commitment. Always he wishes to entertain and often to communicate solid information. He delights in variety, and indeed plays the Renaissance man, albeit on a reduced scale appropriate to his time. Lacking the speculative and contemplative bent of the seventeenth century, he is of the eighteenth century in his worldliness, his social-mindedness, and his self-absorption. It is typical of his gentlemanly ideas that in preparing his *chef d'œuvre* for posterity he apparently had little concern for form in the classical sense. He did not set out to imitate models, to refine them and adjust them to the needs of the present. Nor, as I have said, did he deliberately manage his role. But everywhere he was himself, and this, given his awareness of his station, becomes a kind of structural principle.

Walpole himself had a word for the manner that went with this role. He called it "grace." For a rationale of his attitude we cannot turn to a statement of theory but must gather what we can from letters and conversations, none of which are characterized by thorough and systematic analysis. Of these gleanings the most revealing appears in a letter to John Pinkerton, a protégé. Dated June 26, 1785, this letter was a courteous reply to some of Pinkerton's most extravagant criticism in his book, *Letters of Literature*.[2] Walpole concerns himself with the issue of whether content and style alone determine the quality of a work. He disputes Pinkerton's conclusion that certain authors whose fame is established, among them Virgil, do not deserve their reputation, since they were not original thinkers or stylists. Although he refuses to esteem Virgil very highly—a sign of his breeding and of his concern for his correspondent's feelings—he finds a quality in the Roman poet that turns one's attention from his limitations. This quality is "grace."

The principle of gracefulness is announced in a gentlemanly manner. Immediately, in fact parenthetically, Walpole feels it necessary to assure his correspondent that he is not a disciple of Lord Chesterfield nor is about to commit himself in an ungentlemanly, pedantic way to the belief that grace is a "capital ingredient of writing." But, having deferred to his reputation as a gentleman by relieving himself of the odious title of critic and the accusation of being too cavalier, he proceeds to enlarge the notion of grace until it becomes somewhat more than an off-handed attempt to protect the reputation of a classic. Cowley, Pope, Swift, Racine, Madame de Sévigné, and others are drawn into the argument until it becomes a justification of a lower order of art and an adumbration of its principles. Clearly Walpole himself and his artistic career are also involved. The grace which he feels so strongly in others is part of himself.

Walpole's "grace," like most key terms in eighteenth-century criticism, is highly ambiguous. It refers to the properties of a work, to a way of thinking, and to the creative process. One is reminded of Pope's famous lines on ease in the *Essay on Criticism*.[3] When Walpole calls a few of Waller's "small pieces" "as graceful as possible," he focuses primarily on the works themselves, but when he agrees with Addison that Virgil in the *Georgics* "tossed about his dung with an air of majesty," he makes a connection between the work and the habits of mind it reveals, as he does when he goes on to say that Virgil had the ability to captivate a lord of Augustus's bedchamber and tempt him to listen to themes of rusticity, while Statius and Claudian so lacked grace that even though "talking of war, they would make a soldier despise them as bullies." What he seems to suggest is that Virgil's poetry always possesses that complex of virtues called *sprezzatura* in the Renaissance. Along with perfect ease (Hoby's *recklessness*) go the perfectly civilized attitudes, the awareness of the true quality of subject matter, the understanding of his age and its values which prevent him from descending to gross and disgusting imagery and ideas. Significantly, Walpole points out that grace must be distinguished "even from style, which regards expression," for it belongs to "manner."

Addison and Fielding seemed to Walpole to offer much the same kind of contrast as Virgil and Statius. Ease and gentleness cause Addison "to excel all men that ever lived, but Shakespeare, in humour by never dropping into an approach toward burlesque and buffoonery, even when his humour descended to characters that, in any other hands, would have been vulgarly low." But Fielding, although possessing humor in abundance, has no idea of grace and is "perpetually disgusting. His innkeepers and parsons are the grossest of their profession; and his gentlemen are awkward when they should be at their ease." No matter how "gross" or "awkward" extremes of behavior might in fact be, the author must portray only that which accords with good breeding. This gentlemanly milieu and its imaginative and aesthetic "middle way" are Walpole's version of "nature," for in his opinion the use of extremes results in the distortion of experience and a failure to assert order or establish perspective. From this point of view Fielding is not only guilty of bad taste, but his coarseness turns his characters into caricatures.

Only when the author works at ease without excessively "studying" his ideas or his expression can graceful writing flow from a graceful mentality. Excessive polishing seems to have been as abhorrent to Walpole as pedantry. In this matter, however, his practice reveals much more than his critical pronouncements. The great number of letters that have survived to our time testify to the speed and ease with which he must have written. The letter to Pinkerton itself is a good example of Walpole's unannounced principle. In form it fits well within the context of the preface to *Walpoliana*, which idealizes the enjoyment of careless and easy conversation.[4]

What Walpole means by "grace," then, is clearly not what others meant by "a grace beyond the reach of art." Far from being the *je ne sais quoi* which lies beyond the scope of critical analysis and distinguishes the masterpiece from mere craftsmanship, it is only "a perfume that will preserve from putrefaction." Furthermore, it is inappropriate to the sublime. Walpole implies that it would be wrong for Swift, rising to a tragic vision, to leave an impression of ease and carelessness or to limit himself to ideas of the middle sort. He must cast aside restraint, urbanity, detachment. And Milton's lofty mind and style must create a majestic air foreign to grace, except in poems like "L'Allegro" and "Il Penseroso" which are informed by humor and pathos of a different sort. On the contrary Addison must, if we use Walpole's own metaphor of the swan, exhibit an ungainly walk, must soar with difficulty, must become shrill when he writes outside of his true humor, *The Spectator*. Grace seems to be reserved for smaller minds and lesser inventions. It suits the polishers and refiners, not original and sublime geniuses.

Besides Fielding, Walpole selects two other figures to attack in the letter to Pinkerton—Abraham Cowley, who mistakenly affected grace, and Samuel Johnson, who mistakenly affected dignity or majesty. Cowley seemed to Walpole to be constantly attempting to display certain gentlemanly qualities, such as ready wit, without understanding that true art demands a subordination of all parts to the whole. In contrast to his "pertness" Johnson exhibited a "bearish" or "ridiculously awkward" manner. His "pedantry" produced an "erroneous dignity," which prevented grace. Like Cowley's "pertness" it was to Walpole a mannerism, a violation of the principle of easy expression, genteel mind, and proper selection and use of matter.

All of this Pinkerton had in mind when in the preface to the volumes of *Walpoliana* he explained that Walpole "was not one of those who regard conversation as an exercise of gladiatorial talents, or who study moral maxims, and arrange bon mots, to be introduced into future colloquies. Complete ease and carelessness he regarded as the chief charm of conversation."[5] Against the personal mannerisms of Johnson stands a more generalized, socially oriented notion of manner. When Pinkerton refers to *Walpoliana* as a "little *lounging* miscellany," he means that the book is suited for the genteel because it is careless and easy in method and because none of the ideas have been thought out or polished. If Boswell could not understand why Chesterfield reacted as he did to Johnson's celebrated letter, Walpole was equally unable to comprehend the Johnsonian code and the acquiescence of the Club in it. A man willing to base his permanent reputation on his letters would naturally find it hard to understand the ways of the "great Cham of literature." That Johnson's posthumous repu-

170

tation should have rested for so long on Boswell's record of his conversation would have seemed a great irony to Walpole.

Since grace is somewhat opposed to eloquence, it must discover a narrower range of emotion and the self-confidence, the detachment, the faith in reason and rational control which are the essence of the comic vision. This idea informs the comments on Madame de Sévigné's letters in the letter to Pinkerton and also suggests the nature of Walpole's own monolithic correspondence. Walpole thought that Madame de Sévigné best exemplified graceful letter-writing because she could "shine" in both grief and gaiety and through a wide range of ideas. Although she was sensitive, she never disgraced herself by pitiful lamentation or excessive joy, and though intelligent, she never committed herself too deeply to her ideas. When she expressed what could easily have become too much sorrow, she relieved the tension through new turns, new images, through wit. In other words, she had the reserve, the detachment of the comic author.

The praise of Madame de Sévigné in the letter to Pinkerton calls our attention to another of Walpole's characteristics as a letter-writer and journalist. History, he seems to say, has vitality only when it possesses the easy manner, when it is "unstudied." This is especially true when the historian is recording contemporary events. By pondering his subject, he removes himself from it. The more he depends on abstractions, generalities, and research, the further he departs from an intimate contact with reality. The gentleman thus occupies a significant position as a chronicler of contemporary life. Aware of the world and educated in the right traditions, he is best able to record for posterity events as they really occurred.

Walpole's letters describe life as a mid-eighteenth-century gentleman ought to know it. Gone are the horrors of Gin Lane, the ecstasies of Methodism, the drama of exploration and conquest. They are replaced by the comedy of Cock Lane, the transports of a trip through the Alps, and the activities of government officials and the fashionable world. When the sublime creeps in, as in the well-known letter to West from a picturesque "Hamlet among the Mountains of Savoy," it does not really seem out of place, because it has so well been absorbed by the "graceful" mind.[6] As noble as the scene may be, the description is animated not by terror or rapture (Gray in his famous letters comes closer to them) but by the well-cultivated sensibilities of the gentleman—one might even say "aesthete" were not the associations so improper.[7] If the ideas are graceful—that is, well chosen, balanced, fresh—the manner is easy. It recognizes the sublime but does not respond fully to it. Furthermore, the description is not firmly structured, moving as it does from the scene to self, to West, to Heaven, to the mundane fact of the trip from France to Switzerland. The tone is as varied, for it is dictated by whatever happens to strike the mind: from sublime, to picturesque, to half-stated inquiry about West's health, to facetious grandiloquence, to absurd but facile anticipation of the letter to follow, then to a few quick turns, and finally to a very flattering and ingenious expression of esteem for West and his friendship. The list with which the passage opens ("Precipices, mountains, torrents, wolves, rumblings, Salvator Rosa") well presents a jumble of feelings which dramatizes the effect of the sublime, but the note of reckless abandon is much more characteristic of youth and the gentleman. It might be said that the tone and form of the letter were dictated by the need to humor West, but we will see that high spirits pervade much of the correspondence, and not only the letters of Walpole's youth. They exist side by side with other gentlemanly qualities, such as a keen awareness of incongruities, of the difference between expectation and fulfillment, and of the variety of emotions which the sensitive mind undergoes. Walpole might be overwhelmed by the "sounding cataract" or a sharp and perilous turn in the road which reveals a sublime prospect, but they cannot obliterate the sense of the picturesque, nor can they keep him from seeing the Grande Chartreuse as it really is: "large and plain" with "nothing remarkable but its primitive simplicity" and inhabited by "awkward," uninteresting people. As memorable as the prospect are the "neat" manner in which Walpole was entertained and the "stupidity and brutality" of two mottoes written by fellow Englishmen in the register of visitors at the abbey.

If the moderation, the harmony, the colloquial ease, the wit of Walpole's style seems inappropriate as a vehicle for treating the sublime, they remind us of the eighteenth-century ideal of the rational man who is able to place everything in perspective. They are necessary to detachment, which is itself a pre-condition to seeing things wholly, but they do not exclude feeling, hence the occasional use of exclamation. Nevertheless, they appear to greater advantage when, to re-emphasize Walpole's own metaphor, the swan is back in the water. When Walpole is describing people and human conduct, there is nothing awkward in his manner, and there are no halting attempts to soar.

About four years after the Chartreuse letter, Walpole, now twenty-five years old, wrote to John Chute in a vein reminiscent of the character tradition.[8] Commenting on Chute's belief that temperance has made him "stupid," Walpole sets forth the character of intemperate eaters, or, as he calls them, "beefs."

I have such lamentable proofs every day before my eyes of the stupefying qualities of beef, ale, and wine, that I have contracted a most religious veneration for your spiritual nouriture. Only imagine that I here every day see men, who are mountains of roast beef, and only seem just roughly hewn out into outlines of human form, like the giant-rock at Pratolino! I shudder when I see them brandish their knives in act to carve, and look on them as savages that devour one another. I should not stare at all more than I do, if yonder Alderman at the lower end of the table was to stick his fork into his neighbour's jolly cheek, and cut a brave slice of brown and fat. Why, I'll swear I see no difference between a country gentleman and a sirloin; whenever the first laughs, or the latter is cut, there runs out just the same streams of gravy! Indeed, the sirloin does not ask quite so many questions. I have an Aunt here, a family piece of goods, an old remnant of inquisitive hospitality and economy, who, to all intents and purposes, is as beefy as her neighbours. She wore me so down yesterday with interrogatories, that I dreamt all night she was at my ear with 'who's' and 'why's,' and 'when's,' and 'where's,' till at last in my very sleep I cried out, 'for God in heaven's sake, Madam, ask me no more questions!'

Here form provides an air of detachment necessary to the urbane chronicler of manners, but it does not conceal Walpole's personality, nor does it prevent him from establishing a point of view. He is disgusted with the coarse, unimaginative hedonists who surround his father. That they should be the only ones to behold the matchless collection of paintings at Houghton seems the height of absurdity. But disgust implies a commitment requiring more eloquent expression than family loyalty or good manners allow. Therefore Walpole's character of a beef is whimsical, not slashing; the use of the grotesque is too fanciful to be shocking. In the next paragraph whimsicality becomes the dominant characteristic:

Oh! my dear Sir, don't you find that nine parts in ten of the world are of no use but to make you wish yourself with that tenth part? I am so far from growing used to mankind by living amongst them, that my natural ferocity and wildness does but every day grow worse. They tire me, they fatigue me; I don't know what to do with them; I don't know what to say to them; I fling open the windows, and fancy I want air; and when I get by myself, I undress myself, and seem to have had people in my pockets, in my plaits, and on my shoulders! I indeed find this fatigue worse in the country than in town, because one can avoid it there and has more resources; but it is there too. I fear 'tis growing old; but I literally seem to have murdered a man whose name was Ennui, for his ghost is ever before me. They say there is no English word for *ennui;* I think you may translate it most literally by what is called 'entertaining people,' and 'doing the honours': that is, you sit an hour with somebody you don't know and don't care for, talk about the wind and the weather and ask a thousand foolish questions, which all begin with, 'I think you live a good deal in the country,' or, 'I think you don't love this thing or that.' Oh! 'tis dreadful!

Pope also found the air of quizzical detachment and the theme of getting away from people a useful one for establishing the pose of the satirist, but these had to undergo a change in order to fit the role of the correspondent, the vehicle for public utterance that Walpole came to choose. The Horatian mode of satire comes closer to Walpole's method than others, but even it, though friendly and colloquial, bespeaks less intimacy than Walpole needs to show. To preserve the right atmosphere, he often describes himself with the same quizzical tone, itself a proof of self-control, that the graceful manner usually reserves for the description of others. We are allowed to discover some of the idiosyncrasies which lent charm to his personality, but we never discover the whole man or penetrate to the recesses of mind and imagination. This can be seen in the letter written to Conway on August 29, 1748, in which he separates himself from the foolishness of others but nevertheless hints at his own absurdity: "In short, these are the people I live in the midst of, though not with; and it is for want of more important histories that I have wrote to you so seldom; not, I give you my word, from the least negligence. My present and sole occupation is planting, in which I have made great progress, and talk very learnedly with the nurserymen, except that now and then a lettuce run to seed overturns all my botany, as I have more than once taken it for a curious West Indian flowering shrub. Then the deliberation with which trees grow, is extremely inconvenient to my natural impatience."

The letter to Conway is to a friend of long standing with whom Walpole was considerably more intimate than he was with more "public" correspondents like Horace Mann. The natural reserve that he feels in such cases enriches the letters as a whole by reducing facetiousness and whimsicality and deepening the significance of his detachment. In the letter of April 2, 1750, describing the psychological effects of the recent earthquake, he falls naturally into the role of cynical commentator. His satire makes use of the freedom of the epistolary medium to attack personalities, and the usual quizzical turn of wit serves well to establish a note of sanity amid the hysteria that he describes.

> You will not wonder so much at our earthquakes, as at the effects they have had. All the women in town have taken them up upon the foot of *judgments;* and the clergy, who have had no wind-falls of a long season, have driven horse and foot into this opinion. There has been a shower of sermons and exhortations: Secker, the Jesuitical Bishop of Oxford, began the mode; he heard the women were all going out of town to avoid the next shock; and so, for fear of losing his Easter offerings, he set himself to advise them to await God's good pleasure in fear and trembling. But what is more astonishing, Sherlock, who has much better sense, and much less of the popish confessor, has been running a race with him for the old ladies, and has written a pastoral letter, of which ten thousand were sold in two days; and fifty thousand have been subscribed for, since the two first editions. You never read so impudent, so absurd a piece! This earthquake, which has done no hurt, in a country where no earthquake ever did any, is sent, according to the Bishop, to punish bawdy prints, bawdy books (in one of which Mrs. Pilkington drew his Lordship's picture) gaming, drinking— (no, I think, drinking and avarice, those orthodox vices, are omitted) and all other sins, natural or not, which he makes a principal ingredient in the composition of an earthquake, because not having been able to answer a late piece, which Middleton has writ against him, he has turned the Doctor over to God for punishment, even in this world.

It would seem that anecdote, the use of which has always been considered one of the most attractive aspects of Walpole's art, occupies so important a place in the letters because it admirably suits the graceful mind and graceful manner. One of the reasons that he liked Madame de Sévigné's letters so well was that she never allowed narrative to become dull or historical. Not only did she avoid the pedantry of excessive attention to factual detail, but she also had the art of acquainting the reader with the people she described. She described great events with the warmth of a dramatist, not with the chilling impartiality of an historian. By avoiding excessive commitment to research and analysis of fact, anecdote gets at the spirit of things, the drama of a situation, which seldom can be conveyed by the cold facts and abstractions of the scholar. Aside from revealing Walpole's gentlemanly disdain for pedantry, it brings into play all of the graces which distinguish polite conversation: quickness of perception, sense of form, polished expression, all, of course, delivered with ease and spontaneity, not with the contrivance of *Jean Bull, philosophe.*

Consider, for example, the way in which history comes to life in the description of the funeral of George II included in a letter to George Montagu.[9] After describing the "solemnity and decorum" of the Abbey and the dignity of the procession, Walpole swiftly moves to the riot within the Chapel of Henry VII: ". . . people sat or stood where they could or would, the yeomen of the guard were crying out for help, oppressed by the immense weight of the coffin, the Bishop read sadly, and blundered in the prayers, the fine chapter, *Man that is born of a woman,* was chanted, not read, and the anthem, besides being unmeasurably tedious, would have served as well for a nuptial." Then in a passage which recalls the grounds for his praise of Madame de Sévigné, he contrasts the Duke of Cumberland with his favorite target of abuse, the Duke of Newcastle:

The real serious part was the figure of the Duke of Cumberland, heightened by a thousand melancholy circumstances. He had a dark brown adonis, and a cloak of black cloth with a train of five yards. Attending the funeral of a father, how little reason soever he had to love him, could not be pleasant. His leg extremely bad, yet forced to stand upon it near two hours, his face bloated and distorted with his late paralytic stroke, which has affected too one of his eyes, and placed over the mouth of the vault, into which in all probability he must himself so soon descend—think how unpleasant a situation! He bore it all with a firm and unaffected countenance. This grave scene was fully contrasted by the burlesque Duke of Newcastle—he fell into a fit of crying the moment he came into the chapel and flung himself back in a stall, the Archbishop hovering over him with a smelling bottle—but in two minutes his curiosity got the better of his hypocrisy and he ran about the chapel with his glass to spy who was or was not there, spying with one hand and mopping his eyes with t'other. Then returned the fear of catching cold, and the Duke of Cumberland, who was sinking with heat, felt himself weighed down, and turning round, found it was the Duke of Newcastle standing upon his train to avoid the chill of the marble.

There is none of the cold impartiality of the historian here. Walpole penetrates the characters, and though he takes sides he doesn't caricature. Newcastle's fear of catching cold adds a totally unexpected complexity to the portrait, as does the merging of the pathetic and ludicrous when Newcastle stands upon Cumberland's train. The concluding sentences of the paragraph touch in some other contrasts in tone: "It was very theatric to look down into the vault, where the coffin lay, attended by mourners with lights. Clavering, the Groom of the Bedchamber, refused to sit up with the body, and was dismissed by the King's order."

It is not hard to see why Walpole praised *The Rape of the Lock* so highly, why to him it was the very model of grace and elegance. Both poet and letter-writer display an acute sense of the incongruities of life which set the observer or commentator apart from the observed. But, characteristically, incongruity remains as such; it does not extend into paradox, a province of reality which lies beyond graceful writing. Within its range, however, it reveals the rational control of the observer, especially to a mind and ear educated in the rhetorical tradition. In both Pope and Walpole it leads to a complex art. The central antithesis between dignity (the procession, the Duke of Cumberland) and disorder (the interior ceremonies, the Duke of Newcastle) is shaded by many other contradictions. If the pomp fills Walpole with noble ideas and impressions, it also seems uncomfortably Catholic, as the ironic terminal clause of the following sentence reveals: "There wanted nothing but incense, and little chapels here and there, with priests saying mass for the repose of the defunct—yet one could not complain of its not being catholic enough." The courage of the Duke of

Cumberland is cut across by grotesqueness, and the hypocrisy of Newcastle by his curiosity. The magnificence of the whole is shot through with blundering, selfishness, and the petty worries of mourners like Walpole, whose primary emotion seems to have been the "dread of being coupled [in the procession] with some boy of ten years old."

In Walpole's well-known account of the execution of Lord Kilmarnock and Lord Balmerino the technique is similar.[10] Contrast between two central figures, the use of the unexpected, and sudden shifts in tone result in a complex and richly ambiguous description in which fear combines with dignity and composure with bravado and insensibility. Balmerino generates mixed feelings with his final gesture of contempt: "As he walked from his prison to execution, seeing every window and top of house filled with spectators, he cried out, 'Look, look, how they are all piled up like rotten oranges!'" But contrast and climactic events were not always available as means of revealing character and giving structure to descriptions. Often Walpole must create his own pattern. In his portrait of Simon, Lord Lovat, another defendant in the trials which followed the rebellion of 1745, he begins with some generalizations, then gives substance to them with a series of anecdotes, and concludes with an outburst of Lovat's which is as final and as disconcerting as Balmerino's:

The old creature's behaviour has been foolish, and at last, indecent. I see little of parts in him, nor attribute much to that cunning for which he is so famous; it might catch wild Highlanders; but the art of dissimulation and flattery is so refined and improved, that it is of little use now where it is not very delicate. His character seems a mixture of tyranny and pride in his villainy. I must make you a little acquainted with him. In his own domain he governed despotically, either burning or plundering the land and houses of his open enemies, or taking off his secret ones by the assistance of his cook, who was his poisoner in chief. He had two servants who married without his consent: he said, 'You shall have enough of each other' and stowed them in a dungeon, that had been a well, for three weeks. When he came to the Tower, he told

them that if he were not so old and infirm, they would find it difficult to keep him there: they told him they had kept much younger: 'Yes, said he, but they were inexperienced: they had not
broke so many jails as I have.' At his own house he used to say, that
for thirty years of his life he never saw a gallows but it made his
neck ache. His last art was to shift his treason upon his eldest son,
whom he forced into the rebellion. . . . He has a sort of ready
humour at repartee; not very well adapted to his situation. . . .
The first day, as he was brought to trial, a woman looked into the
coach, and said, 'You ugly old dog, don't you think you will have
that frightful head cut off?' He replied, 'You damned ugly old
bitch, I believe I shall.'[11]

The strength, composure, contempt, bravado, and shockingly
bad taste well shown by Lovat's retort excite a mixed response
in the reader, who becomes aware of many shadings between
the extremes of heroism and buffoonery that color the portrait.

If detachment and awareness of the imperfections in one's
self and one's fellow men are attributes of the gentlemanly
mind, a touch of cynicism seems also to be necessary. We have
already seen it in the letter describing the reactions of various
people to the earthquakes of 1750. But it appears with greater
charm when there is less animosity, when, as in a letter to Montagu written in 1760, Walpole is recording his entertainments
for the amusement of a friend. He had recently paid a visit
with a distinguished company, among them Prince Edward,
Lady Northumberland, Lady Mary Coke, Lady Hertford, and
Fanny Pelham, to the Magdalen House, an institution for re-
formed prostitutes. The situations demands a light, playful
tone:

This new convent is beyond Goodman's Fields, and I assure you,
would content any Catholic alive. We were received by—oh! first,
a vast mob, for princes are not so common at that end of town as
this. Lord Hertford at the head of the Governors with their white
staves met us at the door, and led the Prince directly into the
chapel, where before the altar was an armchair for him, with a
blue damask cushion, a prie-dieu, and a footstool of black cloth
with gold nails. We sat on forms near him. There were Lord and
Lady Dartmouth, in the odour of devotion, and many City ladies.

The chapel is small and low, but neat, hung with Gothic paper and tablets of benefactions. At the west end were enclosed the sisterhood, above an hundred and thirty, all in greyish brown stuffs, broad handkerchiefs, and flat straw hats with a blue ribband, pulled quite over their faces. As soon as we entered the chapel, the organ played, and the Magdalens sung a hymn in parts; you cannot imagine how well. The chapel was dressed with orange and myrtle, and there wanted nothing but a little incense, to drive away the devil—or to invite him. Prayers then began, psalms, and a sermon; the latter by a young clergyman, one Dodd; who contributed to the Popish idea one had imbibed, by haranguing entirely in the French style, and very eloquently and touchingly. He apostrophized the lost sheep, who sobbed and cried from their souls—so did my Lady Hertford and Fanny Pelham, till I believe the City dames took them both for Jane Shores. The confessor then turned to the audience, and addressed himself to the Royal Highness, whom he called, most illustrious Prince, beseeching his protection. In short, it was a very pleasing performance, and I got *the most illustrious* to desire it might be printed. We had another hymn, and then were conducted to the *parloir*, where the Governors kissed the Prince's hand, and then the lady abbess or matron brought us tea. From thence we went to the refectory, where all the nuns, without their hats, were ranged at long tables ready for supper. A few were handsome, many who seemed to have no title to their profession, and two or three of twelve years old: but all recovered, and looking healthy. I was struck and pleased with the modesty of two of them, who swooned away with the confusion of being stared at—one of these is a neice of Sir Clement Cotterel. We were showed their work, which is, making linen and beadwork; they earn ten pounds a week. One circumstance diverted me, but amidst all this decorum I kept it to myself. The wands of the governors are white, but twisted at top with black and white, which put me in mind of Jacob's rods that he placed before the cattle to make them breed. My Lord Hertford would never have forgiven me if I had joked on this; so I kept my countenance very demurely, nor even inquired whether among the pensioners there were any *novices* from Mrs. Naylor's.[12]

The reference to Mrs. Naylor is beautifully annotated by a saucy passage from a letter to Horace Mann written in 1750: "He [Naylor] has a wife who keeps the most indecent house of all that are called decent: every *Sunday* she has a counterband assembly: I had a card for *Monday* a fortnight before. As the day was new, I expected a great assembly, but found scarce six persons. I asked where the company was—I was answered—'Oh! they are not come yet: they will be here presently; they all supped here last night, stayed till morning, and I suppose are not up yet.' In the bedchamber I found two beds, which is too cruel to poor Naylor, to tell the whole town that he is the only man in it who does not lie with his wife!"

Walpole's characterizations are more liberally salted with Madame de Sévigné's love of scandalous particulars than with Pope's and Addison's love of general truth. Nevertheless, Walpole shows great concern for the essential traits which result in peculiarities, and he always strives to reveal the wholeness of events and people. Notice, for example, how well he conveys the chaos of elements unharmoniously confused that make up the character of Lady Mary Wortley Montagu.

Lady Mary Wortley is arrived; I have seen her; I think her avarice, her dirt, and her vivacity are all increased. Her dress, like her languages, is a galimatias of several countries; the groundwork, rags; and the embroidery, nastiness. She wears no cap, no handkerchief, no gown, no petticoat, no shoes. An old black laced hood represents the first, the fur of a horseman's coat, which replaces the third, serves for the second; a dimity petticoat is deputy and officiates for the fourth, and slippers act the part of the last. When I was at Florence, and she was expected there, we were drawing *Sortes Virgilianas*—for her, we literally drew
Insanam vatem aspicies—
it would have been a stronger prophecy now, even than it was then.[14]

Another aspect of the gentlemanly mind can be seen in the substantial amount of literary criticism in Walpole's letters. To be graceful, criticism must show ready wit, a command of particulars, and an understanding of principles. It must not be scholarly or pedantic, although it must reveal a well-read and well-bred taste. Flashing insights and urbane generalities are the matter of gentlemanly criticism, which has as its end revealing the sensibility of the critic. Indeed, to understand many pronouncements we must supply their background and often provide links between phrases. The gentlemanly manner applied even when Walpole intended to be helpful to an author who had sought his advice. Although the comments to Robertson on his *History of Scotland* do list Scotticisms and other stylistic flaws, they lack structure and deep thought and focus on the general merit of the work.[15] Interestingly enough, the *History* proves to have many of the qualities of Walpole's letters: "The style is most pure, proper, and equal; is very natural and easy, except now and then, when, as I may justly call it, you are forced to *translate* from bad writers. You will agree with me, Sir, that an historian who writes from other authorities cannot possibly always have as flowing a style as an author whose narrative is dictated from his own knowledge. Your perspicuity is beautiful, your relation always interesting, never languid. . . ." Of course, the shrewd insights and well-turned phrases which take the place of research and careful analysis throw the major emphasis on wit. Sometimes the rhetoric even recalls the couplet: "I had been told that Mr Bourk's history was of England, not of Ireland—I am glad it is the latter, for I am now in Mr Hume's England, and would fain read no more—I not only know what has been written, but what would be written. Our story is so exhausted, that to make it new they really *make* it *new*. Mr. Hume has exalted Edward II and depressed Edward III. The next historian, I suppose, will make James I a hero and geld Charles II."[16] Admittedly this is an extreme example and is found in a letter to Montagu. But throughout the letters the same tendency toward balance, contrast, and sententiousness is present.

Although wit pervades Walpole's best letters, he can, like Madame de Sévigné, excel in describing the pathetic, for this, it should be remembered, is also part of the graceful manner. When describing the pathetic or terrible, the graceful writer has to avoid the excesses of maudlin sentiment and eloquence while revealing a keen sensibility. An anecdote, for example, must conclude in such a way as to sustain tension without turning into bombast, hence the use of understatement and the grotesque in the following description of the death of Lady Besborough, which comes from the same letter that contains Walpole's anecdote about the Magdalen House:

It was the same sore throat and fever that carried off four of their children a very few years ago. My Lord now fell ill of it, very ill, and the eldest daughter slightly. My Lady caught it, attending her husband, and concealed it as long as she could. When at last the physician insisted on her keeping her bed, she said as she went into her room, 'Then, Lord, have mercy on me, I shall never come out of it again,' and died in three days. Lord Besborough grew outrageously impatient at not seeing her, and would have forced into her room when she had been dead about four days—they were obliged to tell him the truth—never was an answer that expressed so much horror! He said, 'And how many children have I left?'— not knowing how far this calamity might have reached.[17]

Walpole's skill in using the rhythms of language to heighten tension in this passage also deserves notice. The sentences build up in intensity to the last series, in which dashes take the place of the usual marks of punctuation and connectives. The passage as a whole is so natural that it seems artless. Typical of the whole is the quotation, which has the ring of truth; it seems to record faithfully what was actually said. Yet the economy and simplicity of statement so well express intense feeling that they raise the ordinary to art.

Although the rhythm of Walpole's narrative and quotations, as natural and sensitive as it may seem, is undoubtedly contrived, it reminds us of the essential character of grace, for it seems to be the idiom into which the cultivated gentleman most easily falls. Walpole's admiration of this idiom and the manner it presupposes may be attributed to the pervading rationalism of the eighteenth century. For Walpole, like the greater men of the century, Pope in particular, gives form to the myth of the rational man in an orderly universe. His buoyant wit shows the same faith in the potentialities of the cultivated mind, the same enjoyment of ideas, and the same scorn of those who fail to bring order out of chaos. To this faith may be attributed his impatience with "people that don't write just as they would talk" and his belief that the cultivated writer need never apologize by erasing, since his ideas, though they may be simple, or even nonsensical, will never be stupid or absurd.[18] In Walpole we catch the enthusiasm of the age, which has been captured in those extremely suggestive, though somewhat romantic metaphors, *Aufklärung* and *Éclaircissement*. Yet in him we feel the warmth without being exposed to the full energy of the sun. A full apprehension of the possibilities of reason demands more profound psychological or emotional commitment than mere exercise of a cultivated mind will allow. It needs eloquence, not elegance.

At his best Walpole makes the letter an eclectic form, a personal synthesis of many current modes. Of course, anyone in describing experience automatically gives concrete form to his philosophical, moral, and ethical convictions. As an author who has chosen to express himself publicly through the letter, however, Walpole raises this usual condition to an art. There are affinities with the novel in his emphasis on the problems of character and the social milieu and the interaction of the two. Certainly there are signs of the historian in the attention to factual detail. The essay contributes an interest in the general significance of the moment and the mood of quizzical detachment. But the enduring popularity of the letters rests not on their manipulation of these forms, but on their graceful manner, which, even though it reveals a high degree of self-consciousness, seems to suggest itself as the way all civilized men ought to communicate. The naturalness of the letters puts them in the middle range of literature, not completely unlike the poetical essay, and establishes them as a symbol of the truly "gentle" mentality.

Indiana University

THE LETTERS OF EDMUND BURKE: "MANLY LIBERTY OF SPEECH"

JAMES T. BOULTON

"A LETTER IS WRITTEN as a conversation is maintained, or a journey performed; not by preconcerted or premeditated means, a new contrivance, or an invention never heard of before,—but merely by maintaining a progress, and resolving as a postillion does, having once set out, never to stop till we reach the appointed end."[1] These are Cowper's, not Burke's, words, and it is significant that for a memorable description which one can apply to the statesman's youthful letters, one has to turn to remarks not his own. He has little to say about the art of letter-writing. "I always Like that the Letter Should contain the thoughts that at that time employ me; . . ."[2] "Correspondence is to me what a flow is to water, while it runs it is clear and plentiful but whenever it is stopp'd it stagnates and stinks: . . ."[3] Such incidental asides are both infrequent and undistinguished; there is none that compares for imaginative inventiveness with Cowper's or with many in Pope. Indeed Burke presents a face totally different from those letter-writers of his century who are esteemed for their rapid flow of wit, spontaneous vivacity, or attractive intimacy. Even when, as a young man, he recounted gossip—or what Garrick called "trash"—to his school-friend, Richard Shackleton, the seriousness of the later politician was always likely to emerge. He was not content lightly to discuss with Shackleton the details of a local scandal and charges of "fornication and murder" against a tailor, Peter Widdows; he must add: "Most of the misfortunes which we daily hear complaind of proceed either from our Pride, which suffers us to think nothing good enough for us, or from some imaginary Evils which our Discontedness never fails to shew us in the most glaring colours. . . . Human sufferings call for human compassion, we should rather Pity the wretched man than condemn him if we consider'd how easily we ourselves yield to vice, how strong temptation and how weak human nature!"[4] He stopped short at this point— "I find that I am moralizing, a thing I am uncapable of"—but what might have been irony was unintentional. Introspective remarks both accurate and valuable on his use of the letter-form are scarcely to be expected from such a young man.

Burke did not, then, feel "obliged under penalties and pains to be witty";[5] yet it would be false to claim that he was never so. Much depended on his correspondent. Though he could not match Garrick's extraordinary capacity for adapting himself to the temperament of the recipient of his letters, he was not insensitive to the person addressed. Garrick, indeed, provides a useful test-case. He wrote to Burke in 1768: "My dear Friend If you had a house in the Fens of Lincolnshire, or on the Swamps of Essex, where you were oblig'd to drink brandy, by way of small beer, to keep the ague out of your bones, I should long to be with you; but hearing what a Sweet place you have, with everything right about you, I am with twins, till I am well deliver'd at Gregories [Burke's house in Buckinghamshire]. But I reserve you for a bonne bouche my good Friend, and will certainly not touch your Mutton and Poultry, till I have revel'd at Mistley [the seat of Garrick's friend, Richard Rigby]."[6] Burke's reply, written immediately after he received Garrick's letter, begins: "Well, since we are to see you, I am satisfied. I think on the whole you have disposed your matters with judgment. You first sate yourself with Wit, jollity, and Luxury; and afterwards retire hither to repose your person and understanding on early hours, boild Mutton, drowsy conversation, and a little Clabber Milk."[7] Garrick was evidently presupposing a livelier personality in his friend than emerges from Burke's correspondence generally or in the specific reply to his own letter. His humorous resource, almost Elizabethan gusto, and boisterous affection are unmatched: Burke's is a more restrained good humor; he is more ponderous, and his language is more consciously chosen. The very reminder in his words of Harriet's vivid description of life in "that sad place," the country, at the end of Etherege's *Man of Mode,* emphasizes Burke's lack of the élan which is an essential element in spontaneous wit.

Garrick provides another means of assessing Burke's manner in letters to his intimate friends. Both men corresponded with Mrs. Montagu and it is useful to compare two of their letters. Garrick's (second) letter to Mrs. Montagu concerns a play she had submitted to him; it was presumably her own, though she had concealed the identity of the author. He wrote:

I will shew my regard to You, by my Zeal in promoting Its Success: Should I think Otherwise, I should pay a very ill compliment to your friendship, & my own Sense of it, if I did not speak to You, as your Shakespeare phrases it, *as to my thoughts, as I do ruminate.* Sorry, very Sorry am I to hear both for yᵉ Sake of yᵉ Author, Stage, & Manager, that a certain Lady has not had, ev'n yᵉ tip of her Finger in the Dramatic pye—if she had I would have underwritten it unseen, & unheard—

You have had such wondrous Success in Smuggling, I could wish that you would try another Venture, & take me into partnership—but what a parcel of stuff I am writing, & in the mid'st of much Company, without fear, or Wit. . . . Pray, dear Madam, accept of this galloping &, I am afraid *you'll* say, Stumbling Epistle, as yᵉ mere overflowings of a Warm heart, highly sensible of Your friendship, & favour—You see, how I can trust Your feelings, while I am afraid of Your Understanding— . . . upon reading over my hasty letter, I find I have impertinently offer'd myself as a partner in Smuggling—that is—wishing You would as secretly write a play, as you did a certain Essay [on *the Writings and Genius of Shake-speare*], & that I, as Manager, might partake of yᵉ plot & yᵉ **Profits.**[8]

Burke's fifth letter to Mrs. Montagu, written in 1763 shortly after the furore over Wilkes's *North Briton* No. 45, contains the following passage:

I think to try my hand at invective, and to sketch out a North Briton which shall equal the spirit of the celebrated and indeed *golden number, 45.* The subject of it shall be, for we scorn blanks and dashes,—Mrs. Montagu herself. After a few preceding touches upon Scotchmen and Excise, I intend to observe on the scandalous neglect of our Board of Treasury, who have suffered the most valuable staple products of the kingdom to be carried out with[out] the least opposition. I shall show that France has of late discovered that she wants our wisdom as much in her manufactories of policy in War, as she does our wool in her clothes and stuffs; and yet that I could prove our Ministry suffered to be shipped for Calais in one vessel and in one day more genius, more learning, more wit, more Eloquence, more Policy, more Mathematics, more Poetry, more Philosophy and Theology than France could produce in a century. I shall point out that Mrs. Montagu who has long been a clandestine dealer in goods of this sort, and who had several of them about her person at the very time, was the capital smuggler on this occasion and carried off all the rest.[9]

The differences in tone and manner are clear at once. Where Garrick is impetuous, hasty—"hurry Scurry as usual" he says elsewhere[10]—and instinctively witty, Burke's humor is more deliberated; he is intent on working out a premeditated idea even if the details grow under his hand. He pays Mrs. Montagu (then on a Continental tour) a pleasant compliment, but it lacks the spontaneity of Garrick's; his reference to her smuggling activities is prepared for by the preceding remarks on France and springs naturally from them, whereas Garrick's use of the same term is an unpremeditated invention of the moment. Garrick is fascinated by his invention and returns to it impulsively in his postscript; Burke, having introduced the idea with care, logically makes it the springboard for the paragraph that follows. Furthermore, there is an underlying seriousness to Burke's view of France's anxiety to import from England. He returns, in fact, to an analogous kind of imagery in the *Reflections on the Revolution in France,* to carry his gibes at the Constitutional Society's propagandist zeal: "Possibly several of [the books circulated by the Society] have been exported to France; and, like goods not in request here, may with you have found a market. I have heard much talk of the lights to be drawn from books that are sent from hence. What improvements they have had in their passage (as it is said some liquors are meliorated by crossing the sea) I cannot tell."[11] Apparently the attitude underlying Burke's good humor in his letter to Mrs. Montagu, under different circumstances could assume a more serious significance; it was not at any rate, like Garrick's, invented merely to satisfy the need for fleeting pleasantries.

In quality of mind a marked difference between the two men is revealed in their letters. Clearly Burke has greater intellectual steadiness, a firmer grip on his material, and a sense of purposive movement towards a predetermined end. For this reason, among others, he is not seen to advantage in intimate personal letters but rather in correspondence with his political associates whose important concerns exercised his capacity for profound ratiocination. The few extant letters to his wife, while deeply affectionate, comprise a succession of brief, informative sentences; ideas or argument were not called for and Burke therefore felt no need of careful rhythmic modulations in his prose or balanced sentences within a weighty paragraph. "I am in my writing, in the same Case that I am in my Conversation,"[12] he remarked to Shackleton, and one is reminded of Johnson's comment to Boswell: "When Burke does not descend to be merry, his conversation is very superiour indeed. There is no proportion between the powers which he shews in serious talk and in jocularity."[13] This substantiates the claim already made. On trivial subjects which, on the evidence of his letters, included domestic matters, Burke was not at his best; his wit was often forced into overelaboration;

whereas in "serious talk" he revealed that copiousness of mind to which his contemporaries paid tribute.

Burke knew his own strength well enough. Towards the end of a long political career he told Sir Joshua Reynolds' niece that he was accustomed to having "some substantial matter of praise or blame to express according to [his] powers, with force and clearness"; but "as to mere compliments or pretty turned phrases, [he] never had any hand at them."[14] It was an accurate assessment. Burke wrote with the greatest confidence and distinction on grave issues which had absorbed his attention at the level of general principles before he put pen to paper. His son Richard dispels any doubt about the truth of this assertion, in a letter rebuking Sir Philip Francis for his censures on the draft of the *Reflections:* "My father's opinions are never hastily adopted, and even those ideas which have often appeared to me only the effect of momentary heat, or casual impression, I have afterwards found, beyond a possibility of doubt, to be the result of systematic meditation, perhaps of years; or else, if adopted on the spur of the occasion, yet formed upon the conclusions of long and philosophical experience, and supported by no trifling depth of thought."[15] Burke's mature epistolary style itself would lead one to this view; but his son's remark also reminds one of the practice of Johnson and Gibbon. According to Arthur Murphy, Johnson "never took his pen in hand till he had weighed well his subject, and grasped in his mind the sentiments, the train of argument, and the arrangement of the whole";[16] Gibbon claimed that, when writing *The Decline and Fall,* he invariably cast a paragraph in his mind before penning a single word.[17] I do not suggest, of course, that Burke approached the composition of every letter with this degree of premeditation; I do suggest that the prose norms of his age, his predilection for basic political principles, and his training in public speaking and writing, made habitual a formal and weighty epistolary style. It was in this mode that he achieved his distinctive contribution to the eighteenth-century letter as a literary form. In it his quality of mind found its natural expression for thoughts on matters of public consequence. And when he told a correspondent in 1793, "My pen goes in the track of my thoughts,"[18] the implication was that the track was well defined through familiar country; his pen was accustomed accurately to follow its course; and the interdependence had been established by continuous exercise over more than thirty years.

The track of Burke's thinking during this period had been predominantly political and concerned with practice as well as theory. No closet philosopher, Burke was the man to whom the Duke of Richmond wrote: "Indeed Burke you have more merit than any man in keeping us togather."[19] A great deal of his energies and scores of his letters were directed to this practical end, trying to get the Rockingham Whigs to act (in Richmond's words) "like men of Sense," stimulating their thinking on important issues, and in particular exercising his influence on Rockingham himself. It also satisfied Burke's love of ceaseless activity as well as his desire "to see some effect of what [he was] doing."[20] There was little use, then, for Pope's ideal of the personal letter: ". . . so many things freely thrown out, such lengths of unreserved friendship, thoughts just warm from the brain without any polishing or dress, the very *déshabille* of the understanding."[21] Such informal spontaneity was usually irrelevant to Burke's situation. His ideas were generously "thrown out," but more formality and premeditation than Pope envisaged were essential even in Burke's letters to close political friends. There was a time for what he described to Rockingham as "political Chat"[22]—to have appeared too frequently and obviously as a mentor would have been tactless; but more often there was the need for what Burke, in 1777, described as his "cheif employment . . . that woful one, of a *flapper*" (i.e., a person who rouses the attention).[23] Despite the frustrations resulting from the noble lords' natural indolence, their seeming preference for horse-racing or hunting, their "Ill success, ill health, minds too delicate for the rough and toilsome Business of [their] time," Burke acted his part until he was "like a dried spunge."[24] Then again, political necessity frequently required him to correspond with influential men on the edge of or outside the central Rockingham group. For them the private-formal mode had to give away to the near-public voice. And yet again there were occasions when Burke addressed a large audience through the medium of the personal letter; here the public voice appeared as, for example, in the *Letter to the Sheriffs of Bristol* (1777), or the *Letter to a Noble Lord* (1796), or—at its furthest remove from a personal letter though still carrying important traces of that form—the *Reflections* (1790). Inevitably there were fine gradations between the types of letter here roughly sketched; consequently there were different degrees of formality required; but the experience of responding regularly to the social and political demands of these varied situations made a formal style habitual.

"Political chat" and personal correspondence shared some common ground. Two extracts will serve to illustrate the point. The first is taken from a personal letter to the painter James Barry, a friend and the irascible protégé of Burke; the second from one to Rockingham, a letter of the kind in which Burke acted dynamically on policy matters for the Whig group. They were written within a year of one another (1769-70). To Barry he wrote:

Believe me, my dear Barry, that the arms with which the ill dispositions of the world are to be combated and the qualitys by which it is to be reconciled to us, and we reconciled to it, are moderation, gentleness, a little indulgence to others, and a great deal of distrust of ourselves; which are not qualities of a mean Spirit, as some may possibly think them; but virtues of a great and noble kind, and such as dignifye our Nature, as much as they contribute to our repose and fortune; for nothing can be so unworthy of a well composed Soul, as to pass away Life in bickerings and Litigations: in snarling, and scuffling with every one about us. Again, and again, Dear Barry, we must be at peace with our Species; if not for their sakes, yet very much for [our] own. . . . Remember we are born to serve, or to adorn our Country and not to contend with our fellow

Citizens: and that in particular, your Business is to paint and not to dispute.[25]

The letter to Rockingham concerned the proposal by a Yorkshire committee to make a public expression of grievances consequent upon governmental action over Wilkes and the Middlesex elections.

I make no Doubt that your Plan will be judiciously settled, and spiritedly pursued. If no step at all had been taken during the Summer, I should be apprehensive, that such a stagnation would have been little less than fatal to the Cause. The people were very much and very generally touchd with the Question on Middlesex. They felt upon this, but upon no other Ground of our opposition. We never have had, and we never shall have a matter every way so calculated to engage them; and if the spirit which was excited upon this occasion were sufferd to flatten and evaporate, you would find it difficult to collect it again, when you might have the greatest occasion for it. Opposition is upon narrow and delicate Ground; especially that part of opposition which acts with your Lordship; you and your friends having exceedingly contracted the field of operation upon principles of delicacy; which will in the End be found wise, as well as honourable: However the scantiness of the Ground makes it the more necessary to cultivate it with vigour and diligence, else the rule of *exiguum colito* will neither be good farming nor good Politicks.[26]

The natural cast of Burke's mind was clearly to advise or admonish, and to stimulate moral or political thinking. In both cases he writes from what he refers to later in the second letter as "a strong conviction"; he rarely wrote on any subject without it. There is certainly a tonal difference between the extracts: Burke was Barry's patron and intimate, but he was Rockingham's social and political inferior. Yet the styles have much in common. Neither is "scribbled with all the carelessness and inattention imaginable," as Pope claimed of his letters;[27] in both letters Burke was determined to reinforce by stylistic means the gravity of the matter. The opening sentence in the first passage is somewhat unwieldy; one feels that it grew under Burke's hand rather than being completely organized before he wrote it down; yet it is weightily expressed, it closes effectively, and it is consciously set off by the brevity of the next sentence. The final sentence quoted shows a fine balance between general principle and the particular situation; there is nothing hasty or ill-considered about it. Indeed it is a private version of the public statement in *Thoughts on the . . . Present Discontents* (1770): "We are born only to be men. We shall do enough if we form ourselves to be good ones. It is therefore our business carefully . . . to bring the dispositions that are lovely in private life into the service and conduct of the commonwealth."[28] The expression of this important principle in Burke's political philosophy, suitably modified for the occasion, harmonized perfectly with his manner in a personal letter.

The extract from the letter to Rockingham shows equal care. It noticeably gathers weight and momentum as it proceeds, working from the brief, largely factual statements with which it begins, to the longer, more elevated character of those which bring it to a close. One senses in the first extract a speaking voice with an audience of one; in the second the same voice is present at the outset, but this gradually modulates into the orator's with an audience co-extensive at least with the whole Rockingham group ("you and your friends"). And as this more public voice takes control, so the imagery appears, carries the weight of the argument (as it often does in the *Present Discontents*), and makes it memorable.

There are, then, differences between the personal letter to a friend and the epistle to a political intimate, but it is easy to see how the style of one merged into that of the other. Even in a letter to Lady Rockingham, with whom Burke appears to have been more at his ease than with her husband, he obviously felt conscious of its formal structure. The two opening paragraphs of his letter to her on 3 October 1779 provide what he called "a proper quantity of Preface, to whet or to damp (as it may happen) [her] Curiosity";[29] the main body of the letter informed Rockingham (through his wife) of negotiations with the Dukes of Devonshire and Grafton; but at the end Burke reveals his awareness that he had been using the particular literary manner he described as "the Pulpit Style." No doubt he is speaking of his advantage over a captive audience, but the element of self-consciousness demonstrates that there was a minimum of casualness even in a letter which gave news rather than views. Admittedly the letter betrays Burke's sense of importance in participating in the Dukes' conversations—one realizes that the "Pulpit" he alludes to was that in an aristocrat's private chapel; yet, although he was on terms of personal friendship with Lady Rockingham and was not over-awed by her social superiority, he did not feel able to relax his formal manner. Garrick's penchant for "mixing trash with ye Affairs of a Nation"[30] in his letters to the Marquis of Hartington was not Burke's; it would have been like laughing in church.

The formal structural elements in the letter to Lady Rockingham required suitable strengthening when the issues involved were more serious; an increased urgency of tone demanded stylistic modifications. Thus in letters of the kind written to Rockingham on 27 April 1782 we come closer to the style used for addressing men on the periphery of Burke's political circle. That letter opens:

My dear Lord, Be so good as to give a few minutes attention to what I am going to submit to your Judgment. I know your Mind is occupied on many and great Objects; and in my opinion, the Salvation of the Country depends on the success of your Endeavours. But you know, that those who attend to real Business, and are anxious about it, are sometimes a little apt to neglect the intrigues that are going on, and not to be quite alert enough about the management of men. However these intrigues, sooner or later, give power; and that gets the dominion of Business, and takes it out of the honest hands, that love it for the good purposes it may answer, to put into those who care no further about it, than as it leads to new intrigues, new power, and the attaching of new connexions, and the making a faction as strong as possible. So much for preface.[31]

If "preface" was a term somewhat jocularly used in the letter to Lady Rockingham, here it is employed advisedly. Though the manner is intimate, the tone is increasingly solemn and this opening passage is designed to lay open the general principle governing Burke's argument in the paragraphs which follow. Thematically it is central. Rockingham's attention is drawn to the intrigues of Lord Shelburne; he is warned that, without immediate action, his parliamentary influence is doomed.

> If the Advocate [Dundas] should get to be firmly united with that noble Peer, I promise your Lordship, that there is wherewithal in the house of Commons to form such a Cabal as may shake the whole of that power, which, but a week ago, made you, through the medium of the Majority of that house, irresistible in every other Quarter.
>
> I am sorry, that your Lordship thinks slightly of India in the Scale of our politicks. I assure you that those who wish to wrest it out of your hands, have a very different opinion of its importance. . . . I see distinctly that Lord Shelburne, the Advocate and his party, (which is by no means small,) and the Debris of the Bedfords, coaliting as fast as possible; and it is upon this Indian Ground they will make the first essays of their opposition; What Strength they may gather from rallying together the routed Corps of the late Ministry, and from the secret Support of the Court, you may easily guess.

As in the earlier letter to Barry, so here we have a private version of the theory stated in the *Present Discontents*. In that pamphlet Burke argued that the individual with his "single, unsupported, desultory, unsystematic endeavours" is powerless "to defeat the subtle designs and united cabals of ambitious citizens"; here was a particular example. "When bad men combine," he said in 1770, "the good must associate; else they will fall, one by one, an unpitied sacrifice in a contemptible struggle."[32] In the letter the suggestion of this kind of evil power, determined to subvert the influence of Rockingham's party, is carried in a series of strong verbs; the imagery is submerged, appearing only through military allusions, but these are designed to precipitate bold action. If Dundas were attached to Rockingham, "I do not see even the possibility of any opposition, either of Cabal, or of decided contradiction in the House of Commons. *There* is the only firm Basis we have had; I see, I feel it shaking." Burke's earnest appeal—modulating in these phrases into that of the impassioned orator—is sustained to within five brief sentences from the end; only then does he relax the tension and conclude "with cordial attachment." The gravity of the situation made the tone of "political Chat" inappropriate; Rockingham had to be apprized of "the true Temper of the time and Country."[33] One can readily appreciate how letters written frequently in this calculated, thrusting manner left Burke feeling "like a dried spunge."

Vigorous and admonitory though this letter was, it was permissible within a relationship of "practised friendship and experimented fidelity."[34] Burke would expect to share with Rockingham the attitude later expressed to a correspondent who differed from him over the French Revolution: "Your freedom is far from displeasing to me,—I love it; for I always wish to know the full of what is in the mind of the friend I converse with. I give you mine as freely, and I hope I shall offend you as little as you do me."[35] He was extremely sensitive to the manner suitable for private as opposed to public or near-public correspondence. He remonstrated with Sir Philip Francis, for example, over a letter criticizing the *Reflections:* "Your remarks are, indeed, made with great skill and ability; but they hardly seem to be penned for my private and particular instruction. . . . Your paper has much more the character of a piece in an adverse controversy, carried on before the tribunal of the nation at large, than of the animadversion of a friend on his friend's performance."[36] In the light of such a statement it is interesting to watch Burke's stylistic response to a situation in which he was alert to that "tribunal" in the sense either of a public who would read his letter or of a recipient through whom he might influence a wider audience.

The series of letters written to Edmund Sexton Pery, Speaker of the Irish House of Commons, is relevant here. The matter of some letters—parliamentary debates, motions, amendments and the like—confined Burke to reportage; the sentences are brief as a result, and the only heightening of style occurs when personal feelings intrude. But in the letter of 16 June 1778, concerned with the Irish Parliament's bill for Catholic Relief, we gradually become aware that Burke was imagining a parliamentary audience behind Pery:

My dear Sir, Many, very many thanks for your goodness in turning your mind for a moment towards me in the midst of the important Business which engages your present attention. You have a Gigantick prejudice to encounter; But your Victory will be full of honour. It is no trifling matter to restore to civil Society so many hundred thousands of human Creatures, who, without any guilt, are made slaves under a constitution of Freedom; aliens in their native Country; and outlaws without charge or process. I ought to be ashamed to interrupt you for a moment in such Endeavours.

I had much rather see the act without the Clause about the Children; but if I remember right, it is somewhat less exceptionable, than the Law as it stood before. It however shows an hankering after our old unfortunate System of promoting the purity of religion by the corruption of Morality. To corrupt family relations is to poison fountains; for the scources of the commonwealth are within the Households; and errours there are irretrievable. The interest which a community has in its morals is much greater than is commonly imagined; and when the Laws endeavour to subvert that, which with all their force they are scarcely able to sustain, degeneracy will proceed with an accelerated motion, and the State will be precipitated along with its manners. . . . any thing which tends to reverse the order of Providence, to give youth a coercive power over age, to give passion and dissipation a censorial authority over prudence and foresight, and to set Children above parents, is to give new Life to the disorder and profligacy which are destroying us. We do not give Credit enough to our original and genuine affections. Nature is no bad Chancellour.[37]

The political morality of the statement is worthy of comment; it is related to the views Burke expressed on the disintegration of family ties after the French Revolution; but our primary concern here is with style. It is noticeable how quickly Burke abandons the direct address to Pery; "You have a Gigantick prejudice to encounter," Pery is told, but almost at once Burke adopts the impersonal mode and directs his attention to general principles. This was his forte. Emotive nouns ("slaves," "aliens," "outlaws") immediately assume the forceful positions in the sentence; the Aristotelian-sounding antithesis—"promoting the purity of religion by the corruption of Morality"—adds persuasive vigor; imagery appears; and sentences are rhythmically balanced internally as well as being counterbalanced. It is indeed as if Pery were made the recipient of "Hints towards a Speech on the bill for Catholic Relief."

Burke was conscious of another kind of "tribunal" when writing (c. 9 November 1771) his remarkable letter (which exists in draft form) of over 14,000 words to Dr. William Markham, Bishop of Chester. He had tried to enlist Markham's support in his efforts to deny his authorship of the Junius letters; his former friend had replied with a bitter denunciation of the private and public life of Burke, his son Richard, and his kinsman William; and Burke felt compelled to write in his own, as well as their, defense. His material was necessarily ordered with care. At the outset Burke is direct and personal: "Your Lordships unkindness has attacked me on a side, on which I was absolutely unguarded; and I bear it like a Girl";[38] "I . . . felt it on the naked nerve, and with the quickest and sorest sensibility."[39] The tone is appropriate to the sense of injury. It develops a greater astringency when, on behalf of his son, Burke comes to defend the reputation of the whole family against "the very person who answered for [Richard] at the font": "that the innocent child may know, as I trust the world, will know and acknowledge that he has not crept into it from an hole of adders to which your Lordship (I leave you to feel with what humanity and Justice) has thought proper to compare his fathers house."[40] Personal honor, public career, private emotion—all are now involved.

Inevitably Markham had become the representative of all those in public life who felt any kind of animosity against the *"Novus Homo"*[41] as Burke once described himself; and the private letter was a means of bidding them defiance. They were the "tribunal" of which Burke was aware when writing, and he naturally assumes a quasi-public voice in which to address them. He takes the indictments against him under three headings: questions relating to his "political connections," matters charged to his personal account, and finally "the various crimes . . . collected from the private conversations of [his] nearest freinds and relations."[42] One extract from this last section will illustrate the quality of the whole letter.

I will always speak what I think without caring one farthing what is the bon ton upon the subject either at Court [or] in Coffee houses, untill all honest freedom of disquisition and all manly Liberty of speech shall by legal or other power be conclusively put an End to. . . . To this freedom your Lordships friends the antients (in a Language you understand much better than I do) gave an Honourable name and classed it among the Virtues. But whether a *Virtue,* or only an *Enjoyment* I assure your Lordship that neither Courts nor town Halls with all they could give of gold Boxes or Pensions could indemnify me for the want of an Hours use of it. . . . My principles enable me to form my judgement upon Men and Actions in History, just as they do in current life; and are not formed out of events and Characters, either present or past. History is a preceptor of Prudence not of principles. The principles of true politicks are those of morality enlarged, and I neither now do or ever will admit of any other. But when your Lordship speaks of tests of publick principles, there is one which you have not mentioned but which let me say is far above them all. The actions and Conduct of Men. . . . The principles that guide us in publick and in private, which as they are not of our devising but moulded into the nature and essence of things, will endure with the Sun and Moon, long very long after Whig and Tory, Stuart and Brunswick, and all such miserable Bubbles and playthings of the Hour are vanished from existence, and from memory.[43]

It is a memorable passage on account of the vigorous manifestation of that "manly Liberty of speech" which Burke claims as a human right, as well as his assured movement between direct self-justification and defense of the principles underlying his political beliefs and conduct. He is compelled to answer specific charges; consequently he must write on issues which are involved with his deepest emotions; but, because of his conviction of the interdependence between public and private morality, the quality of his emotional response becomes evidence of political integrity. Burke maintains the fluency of a personal letter while at the same time giving powerful expression to politico-moral principles which the tribunal of "the world will know and acknowledge" to be just.

The combination of qualities to be found in the letter to Markham accounts in large measure for the distinctive character of Burke's publications which were cast in the letter-form. Whether we consider the *Reflections,* the *Letter to a Noble Lord,* or the *Letters on a Regicide Peace,* what is especially striking is the stylistic demonstration of political conviction—through imagery, irony, the balanced structure of paragraphs, the heightening of significant passages to focus salient features of the argument, and above all, the communication of passionate feeling. Even if we are not intellectually convinced we cannot escape the literary "experience." For Burke wrote most brilliantly when he was involved emotionally and intellectually in the matters at issue. "I cannot see the dignity of a great kingdom, and, with its dignity, all its virtue, imprisoned or exiled, without great pain. I cannot help making their case my own, and that of my friends who adhere to the same cause."[44] So he wrote to a French nobleman in 1793. The remark was particularly relevant to his concern with French affairs, but one can generalize from it. Whether the situation provoked self-justification as in the letter to Markham, or stimulated a deep concern for religious education as in the lengthy epistle to Viscount Kenmare in February 1782,[45] or concerned the status of the Rockingham Whigs and their centrality in political society—whenever personal feeling and political conviction fused with maximum intensity, these occasions were likely to produce Burke's finest writing both public and private.

It would be futile, of course, to claim that cause and effect invariably worked in this way. Letters written between 1789 and the end of Burke's life in 1797 were often marred by outbursts of uncontrolled feeling, debating tricks, and forced eloquence. Raw, undisciplined emotion is evident in the rebuttal of Sir Philip Francis's suggestion that Messalina could be defended on the same grounds on which Burke had apostrophized Marie Antoinette in the *Reflections*;[46] at the other extreme, as in the letter to Depont, November 1789, Burke forced his thought and emotion into a rigid oratorical mould which produced extended conditional sentences, with the main verb delayed sometimes for over two pages.[47] In sharp contrast are two earlier letters: to Samuel Span in 1778 (subsequently published with another as *Two Letters from Mr. Burke to Gentlemen in the City of Bristol*), and to Dr. John Erskine in 1779.[48] Here, as in the letters to Francis and Depont, Burke was maintaining a case against opposition; here too his emotions were strongly engaged; but their intensity was equaled by his literary control. He could, therefore, write to Span and condemn selfish, violent commercial acts against Ireland, or oppose Erskine's views on the riots in Edinburgh and Glasgow over "the Popery question," and at the same time contrive to make his style a warranty for the genuineness of the principles he advanced. His condemnation of immoderate action is matched by stylistic restraint; he advocates tolerance and his tone towards his opponents remains courteous; and his style generally demonstrates the careful discrimination of the man whose judgment his correspondents were being asked to accept.

Implicit in the foregoing argument is a claim for Burke's understanding of the appropriateness of style to circumstances. This sense of decorum appeared over political questions as well as showing itself in tactful handling of stylistic detail. For example, Rockingham, in 1779, sent for Burke's comments a resolution on the distresses of Ireland prepared by Lord Camden. A reply came by return of post. "I am quite amazed at the motion Lord Cambden has drawn. One would imagine, by the Style and manner, that he had found it in Lord Chathams Portfolio."[49] Burke's objection was certainly political but also, in an interesting way, literary and moral. We know from other letters that he distrusted Chatham, considering him unscrupulous, ambitious, and opportunist.[50] Burke himself sympathized profoundly with the Irish, but he had an equally profound reverence for Parliament; in his view the style of a parliamentary motion should mirror this respect even while being critical of governmental action. "... in Gods Name where is the Necessity that Parliament should lose all appearance of Grace and dignity in the manner of making its concessions? Fallen we certainly are; and a pompous language ill becomes our Condition; but still there is a decorum, even in the humility of decayd greatness, which ought never to be parted with." "Pompous language" was appropriate to a hypocrite; the "simplicity and gravity" Burke proceeded to recommend to Rockingham were essential if the style of the resolution was to reflect the party's honesty of purpose.

The detail of his epistolary style demonstrates the same understanding of the necessary organic relation between style and matter. One notices, for instance, how rare it was for Burke to quote vulgar statements even of men he disliked. It is true that he related to his friend, Charles O'Hara, the message sent through a servant to Lord Camden (who had just become Lord Chancellor) by "Old sarcasms," Lord Northington: "Go tell your Master that if he begins his Office by giving up his Measures, I shall see his A–se and his Mace in the Kennel within a fortnight, by God."[51] But this is almost the sole example. Nor did he make frequent use of anecdote—a letter to Fox, in November 1788, contains a rare instance[52]—or of colloquialisms.[53] Burke's letters were invariably concerned with matters of great consequence and vulgarisms would have been out of place. Similarly, though literary allusions and quotations are often used to brilliant effect in his published works, they do not appear with equal frequency or subtlety in the letters. Here they serve to provide analogies, somewhat to increase the pungency of a remark, or to furnish a synonym,[54] but for the most part they are commonplace references and lack the seeming spontaneity or witty sharpness of which he is capable in, say, the *Reflections*.[55] This too shows decorum. To have exploited literary references with the deliberate purpose he displays in works calculated for public persuasion would have been quite inappropriate in personal letters, however persuasive their aim. To have created the impression that he wished to parade his learning would have been equally unfortunate.

Literary tact also dictated a different use of imagery in the letters from that which was appropriate in published works. There were times when he relied on the imaginative "set piece," but they were rare. One such occasion was the letter in which he respectfully informed the Duke of Richmond:

You people of great families and hereditary Trusts and fortunes are not like such as I am, who whatever we may be by the Rapidity of our growth and of the fruit we bear, flatter ourselves that while we creep on the Ground we belly into melons that are exquisite for size and flavour, yet still we are but annual plants that perish with our Season and leave no sort of Traces behind us. You if you are what you ought to be are the great Oaks that shade a Country and perpetuate your benefits from Generation to Generation. In my eye—The immediate power of a D. of Richmond or a Marquis of Rm is not so much of moment but if their conduct and example hands down their principles to their successors; then their houses become the publick repositories and offices of Record for the constitution, Not like the Tower or Rolls Chappel where it is searched for and sometimes in Vain, in rotten parchments under dripping and perishing Walls; but in full vigour and acting with vital Energy and power in the Characters of the leading men and natural interests of the Country.[56]

It is an unusual passage for the extent to which Burke elaborated his imagery. One suspects that, while the image of "the great Oaks" unquestionably expressed his real veneration for an hereditary nobility, perhaps some embarrassment in comparing his position as a *"Novus Homo"* with that of Richmond and his kind had led him to adopt and then to take full advantage of an imaginative mode of statement. But for the most part the imagery in Burke's letters is much less monumental. Readers of his published works will be familiar with its principal areas of reference—in nature, building, medicine, war, or domestic processes, for example—but whereas in those works Burke exploits the philosophic and general significance of his images, in the letters he is usually content to establish particular points through them. An illustration occurs in Burke's advice to Rockingham to avoid involvement in any administration formed by Chatham in 1769: "If indeed a change is thought on, I make no Doubt but they will aim at the Choice of him as the puller down of the old, and the Architect of the New Fabrick. If so, the Building will not, I suspect, be executed in a very workmanlike manner; and can hardly be such as your Lordship will choose to be lodged in, though you should be invited to the State Apartment in it."[57] Compare this with his warning in the *Reflections:* "It is with infinite caution that any man ought to venture upon pulling down an edifice, which has answered in any tolerable degree for ages the common purposes of society, or on building it up again, without having models and patterns of approved utility before his eyes."[58] The tone of each passage is appropriate to its context. The first, more intimate as befits a personal letter, does not attempt to enforce a fundamental principle but is specific in its purpose. Perhaps Burke's enthusiasm for the image sprang from his recent purchase (in 1768) of Gregories, his Buckinghamshire estate. It is certain, however, that the personal significance of this acquisition would diminish and one notices the general theory which lies behind the second passage gradually attaching itself to the architectural image as it reappears in the letters over a number of years. A parallel development can be traced in Burke's use of natural imagery. The movement is from a passage quoted earlier (p. 194) where Rockingham is warned that "the scantiness of the Ground"—the specific situation in 1770—"makes it the more necessary to cultivate it with vigour and diligence," to the following brief extract from the letter (intended for publication) to Samuel Span in 1778: "If men are suffered freely to cultivate their natural advantages, a virtual equality of contribution will come in its own time, and will flow by an easy descent through its own proper and natural channels. An attempt to disturb that course, and to force nature, will only bring on universal discontent, distress, and confusion."[59] Here again the general theory has become central; it was appropriate for a more extensive audience than the single correspondent; and the impress of Burke's enthusiasm for farming (evident in several lengthy letters to Arthur Young and Charles O'Hara, 1768-72) has taken second place.

Burke's language is notable both for its argumentative vigor and for its allusiveness to the actual world with which he himself, his policies, and the associates whom he urged into action were involved. For the Rockingham Whigs it was a world concerned not only with politics but also with farming large estates, maintaining noble mansions, and the enjoyment of aristocratic sports; Burke brought other features to the attention of his correspondents. To the city merchant, John Bourke, he could allude to the notorious gormandizing of the upper classes in a reference to "the Shelburne faction"—"having overloaded the Stomachs of their adherents they were vomited up with Loathing and disgust";[60] by contrast he spurred the Duke of Portland into activity through an allusion (reinforced by biblical language) to a more general level of starvation: "Little more time remains for us. [Inactivity] will not be borne by the people, who are hungering and thirsting after substantial reformation, that we should balk their appetite with a long Grace, or with a formal laying on the dishes. We must let them instantly fall to."[61] Commonplace facts of human existence provided Burke with vivid imagery. The Duke of Richmond was reminded that he found it as difficult to secure privacy as Burke to obtain public notice—"It is as hard to sink a Cork as to buoy up a Lump of Lead";[62] another correspondent was assured that every party must expect some unreliable adherents—"I will say nothing about that Tail, which draggles in the dirt. . . . *That* can only flirt a little of the Mud in our faces now and then";[63] and Lord Grenville was warned that the English Jacobins remained a significant menace—"The fire is still alive under the ashes."[64] Part, too, of the commonplace was the brutality of Burke's world. He told Bishop Hussey that he felt compassion not for "pride, cruelty, and oppression" but rather for those who suffered, through whatever form of government, from "these vices": "I would not put my melilot plaister on the back of the hangman, but on the skin of the person who has been torn by his whips."[65] And, in an increasingly industrialized age, the machine frequently provided Burke with pertinent images. They range from the early reference to his lack of parliamentary influence—"I cannot move the machine, or even grease the wheels";[66] through a casual statement about the constitution in 1780—"The *Machine itself* is well enough to answer any good purpose, provided the *materials* were sound";[67] to the final usage in a letter to William Windham in 1797— "They must be singularly unfortunate who think to govern by dinners and bows, and who mistake the oil which facilitates the motion, for the machine itself."[68] This favorite source of imagery had, meanwhile, been of service in the *Reflections* in that contemptuous dismissal of the revolutionary version of monarchy, kept for the sake of pageantry: "Such a machine . . . is not worth the grease of its wheels."[69] Imagery like this was philosophically appropriate to one who insisted on the central significance of "not only the fixed but the momentary circumstances" of any event or issue;[70] it was also part of the armory of a man who, by the quality of his writing in public or in private, was determined to keep his readers in constant touch with the actual world in which his policies were designed to operate. "It has that in it which I always consider as a mark of Genius—the turning to account the images and objects that one is familiar and conversant with—and not running all into repetition, or over improvement (if that were possible) of the images which have struck others in other places and times."[71] These were Burke's words about the writings of a friend; they may justly be applied to his own.

University of Nottingham

COWPER'S LETTERS:
MIRROR TO THE MAN

William R. Cagle

THE INTENSELY PERSONAL NATURE of Cowper's letters is their most distinctive characteristic. Few men, if any, have dwelt so extensively or with such feeling on their inner and personal life in their correspondence as did this deeply troubled poet of Olney. To all of those within his circle of correspondents, though to some more than others, he wrote with a noticeable lack of restraint not only of the commonplace matters which normally make up the body of private correspondence—of likes and dislikes, the state of his health, finances or friendships—but of matters of a more personal nature: of the state of his soul, his attitude toward God and of what he perceived to be God's attitude toward him. His preoccupation with the notion that he was unacceptable to his God and consequently irrevocably damned is the background against which his whole adult life was lived and is a recurring theme in his correspondence. Sometimes it is only a passing reference: "My dear cousin, dejection of spirits, which, I suppose, may have prevented many a man from becoming an author, made me one. I find constant employment necessary, and therefore take care to be constantly employed" (II, 364).[1] Or it may be a more anxious complaint, as in this passage from a letter to John Newton written in September, 1783:

I have indeed been lately more dejected and more distressed than usual; more harassed by dreams in the night, and more deeply poisoned by them in the following day. I know not what is portended by an alteration for the worse after eleven years of misery,[2] but firmly believe that it is not designed as the introduction of a change for the better. . . . I now see a long winter before me, and am to get through it as I can. I know the ground before I tread upon it; it is hollow, it is agitated, it suffers shocks in every direction; it is like the soil of Calabria, all whirlpool and undulation; but I must reel through it,—at least if I be not swallowed up by the way. (II, 98-99)

In the final decade of his life his despair deepened and in his letters—especially those to Samuel Teedon, self-proclaimed mediator between Cowper and God—the mood of dejection sharpened to a cry of anguish:

Friday, Nov. 16.—I have had a terrible night—such a one as I believe I may say God knows no man ever had. Dreamed that in a state of the most insupportable misery I looked through the window of a strange room being all alone, and saw preparations making for my execution. That it was but about four days distant, and that then I was destined to suffer everlasting martyrdom in the fire, my body being prepared for the purpose and my dissolution made a thing impossible. Rose overwhelmed with infinite despair, and came down into the study, execrating the day when I was born with inexpressible bitterness. And while I write this, I repeat those execrations, in my very soul persuaded that I shall perish miserably and as no man ever did. Every thing is, and for twenty years has been, lawful to the enemy against *me*. (IV, 324-325)

In 1794 Cowper lapsed into a state of overwhelming depression from which he never recovered. The letters of this period are filled with fear of impending death and grim forebodings of what awaits him in the world to come: "The most forlorn of beings, I tread a shore under the burthen of infinite despair, that I once trod all cheerfulness and joy. I view every vessel that approaches the coast with an eye of jealousy and fear, lest it arrive with a commission to seize me" (IV, 489). These were not the ships of men that Cowper feared but demon ships come for him out of the depths of hell. A few months later he again wrote to his cousin: "You know my story far better than I am able to relate it. Infinite despair is a sad prompter. I expect that in six days' time, at the latest, I shall no longer foresee, but feel the accomplishment of all my fears. Oh, lot of unexampled misery incurred in a moment! Oh wretch! to whom death and life are alike impossible! Most miserable at present in this, that being thus miserable I have my senses continued to me, only that I may look forward to the worst" (IV, 497).

A shy man, unable to compete in a world which trampled shy men underfoot, he abandoned before his thirtieth year whatever ambition he may once have had for an active public life. Responsibility for his own livelihood he abdicated in favor of those who could contend where he had failed. His financial needs fell to his family and friends; his domestic needs to Mrs. Unwin. Beset with feelings of personal insecurity, Cowper's entire mature life was overshadowed by fears of public or private disapproval which led him to withdraw from active participation in affairs outside his circle of immediate acquaintances. Entirely unsuited for the practice of law, for which he had studied, he had momentarily considered taking orders, "but," as he wrote to Mrs. Cowper, "it has pleased God, by means which there is no need to particularise, to give me full satisfaction as to the propriety of declining it; indeed, they who have the least idea of what I have suffered from the dread of public exhibitions, will readily excuse my never attempting them hereafter" (I, 81). When Cowper did submit himself again to public exhibition it was in print and not in person—but the nagging fears and doubts were still there.

In 1782 he wrote to Newton: "I sometimes feel such a perfect indifference with respect to the public opinion of my book, that I am ready to flatter myself no censure of reviewers, or other critical readers, would occasion me the smallest disturbance. But not feeling myself constantly possessed of this desirable apathy, I am sometimes apt to suspect that it is not altogether sincere, or at least that I may lose it just in the moment when I may happen most to want it" (I, 439). Cowper's letters of the next six months record his reactions to the varying assessments of his verse. He is elated when his friends praise him, dejected (though feigning indifference) when Lord Thurlow ignores the copy Cowper sent him; elated when he hears that Benjamin Franklin commended his verse, dejected when censured by the *Critical Review*. In June he wrote to Unwin expressing his gratification at the approval with which his book had met but could not help concluding with a remark that "the *Monthly Review,* the most formidable of all my judges, is still behind" (I, 483). It was characteristic of Cowper's personality that even his most optimistic statements ended on a note of doubt.

All this could not help coloring his personal relationships. He felt himself a unique case singled out by God for punishment unexampled in the experience of mankind. Accordingly, his fellow-men could not appreciate his miseries: he was cut off from them, a castaway adrift upon an endless sea. This attitude on Cowper's part, and the consciousness of others that they had to deal with a man subject to such delusions, put a double barrier between Cowper and his friends and made impossible the sort of friendship which exists between equals. The ingredients of mutual confidence and respect, as well as of a balanced give-and-take, were wanting.

There is always a certain awkwardness in the relationship between dependent and benefactor. The continual need of asking favors and acknowledging kindness establishes a feeling of subordination antagonistic to the very foundations on which friendships rest. On the surface Cowper seems to have accepted his position of dependency as a matter of course and, while not losing his sense of appreciation for past favors, exhibited a most matter-of-fact manner in asking new ones. This is especially noticeable in his dealings with William Unwin, with whom his ties were those of friendship, not of family.

Yet he seems to have taken Unwin's contributions toward his support quite for granted. "Your mother," Cowper writes, "wishes you to buy for her ten yards and a half of yard-wide Irish, from two shillings to two shillings and sixpence per yard; and my head will be equally obliged to you for a hat, of which I enclose a string that gives you the circumference" (II, 181). Or, "Thanks for the fish, with its companion a lobster, which we mean to eat to-morrow. We want four Chinese tooth-brushes: they cost a shilling each: the harder the better" (II, 194). To these frequent requests on behalf of Mrs. Unwin, Cowper regarded it as quite natural that he should append his own wants. But if Cowper came to expect such favors as a matter of course he never was ungrateful for the attentions, large or small, showed him by his friends.

When he received his desk sent by Lady Hesketh on be-half of "dear anonymous"[3] he wrote, "Oh that this letter had wings, that it might fly to tell you that my desk, the most ele-gant, the compactest, the most commodious desk in the world, and of all desks that ever were or ever shall be, the desk that I love the most is safe arrived" (II, 403). To Mrs. Newton he wrote upon receiving a gift of some seafood, "When I write to Mr. Newton, he answers me by letter; when I write to you, you answer me in fish. I return you many thanks for the mack-erel and lobster. They assure me in terms as intelligible as pen and ink could have spoken, that you still remember Or-chardside;[4] and though they never spoke in their lives, and it was still less to be expected from them that they should speak, being dead, they gave us an assurance of your affection that corresponds exactly with that which Mr. Newton expresses to-wards us in all his letters" (I, 194). Such acknowledgments reveal that unbounded warmth of heart which drew to him the loyal circle of friends who stood by him through the most trying periods of his life. Yet one never has the feeling that these are friendships between equals: Mary Unwin, Lady Austen, and Lady Hesketh all try in their own ways to mother Cowper; Newton does the same in a spiritual sense; and even

Cowper's relationships with Hayley and Johnny Johnson rest on a similar basis. The two friendships (with Newton and Lady Austen) which terminate in a rupture do so when Cowper asserts his independence.

If a strong focus on the inner and personal affairs of life is one characteristic that sets Cowper's letters apart from those of his contemporaries, yet another is occasioned by the physical surroundings in which they are written. Unlike the other major letter-writers of the eighteenth century Cowper was not a member of a circle abounding with great names. Living among the rolling hills of Buckinghamshire, first at Olney and later at Weston, he had virtually no contact with London life. While others wrote of court and society and chronicled the gossip of the fashionable world, Cowper wrote of a smaller world, one circumscribed within a radius of a morning's walk from Olney and focused largely on his garden and cottage parlor. A miniaturist in a miniature world, he took great delight in presenting its smallest details. He wrote of the singing of the birds, the braying of an ass, the gamboling of his hares, of his cucumbers or his flowers, of a door that would stick or a piece of furniture he had made; nothing was without significance, nothing unworthy of his attention. Much of the charm which the modern reader finds in the letters derives from the vivacity with which he depicts such commonplace things.

To Cowper these were matters of momentary interest, current topics on which he conversed with his correspondents, and certainly not intended for publication. Unlike Pope or Walpole he did not write letters with one eye on his correspondent and the other on posterity. After he achieved fame as a poet the idea must have occurred to him that his letters might find their way into print and, if we may judge from his comments on this possibility in a letter to the Rev. Matthew Powley, he would gladly have prevented it. Because the passage is illustrative as well of some of Cowper's other views on letter-writing, I quote it at length:

It is very possible that I might misstate a circumstance which happened so long ago as last March twelve-month, for I keep no letters, except such as are recommended for preservation by the importance of their contents, and consequently had none to refer to. By *important contents,* I mean what is commonly called *business* of some sort or other. In the destruction of all other epistles I consult the good of my friends; for I account it a point of delicacy not to leave behind me, when I die, such bundles of their communications as I otherwise should, for the inspection of I know not whom; and as I deal with theirs, for the very same reason, I most heartily wish them all to deal with mine. In fact, there seems to be no more reason for perpetuating or preserving what passes the pen in the course of a common correspondence, than what passes the lips in every day's conversation. A thousand folios of the latter are forgotten without any regret; and octavos, at least, of the former are frequently treasured till death, for no use whatever either to ourselves or others. They then, perhaps, go to the grocer's, and serve to amuse such of his customers as can read *written hand,* as they call it; or now and then, which is fifty times worse, they find their way to the press; a misfortune which never, at least seldom, fails to happen, if the deceased has been so unfortunate as to leave behind him a friend more affectionate to his memory than discreet in his choice of means to honour it. (II, 423-424)

The dearth of letters to Cowper attests to his own adherence to these principles. To him letter-writing was a thing of the moment designed to meet transient needs, not to make permanent records.

In so far as Cowper may be said to have had a model for his letters the model was polite conversation. The rules which governed the one governed the other. Thus, if an affected manner was considered bad taste in the drawing room, it was no less so at the writing table. "Affectation of every sort is odious," he wrote to Newton (II, 63). He admired, he went on to say, a style that while "plain and neat" was also proper; that could be "understood by rustics" without offending "academical ears"—in short, a style that was natural without being vulgar.[5]

It is this natural style modeled on conversation that is dominant in Cowper's letters. He departs from it markedly only when writing of his spiritual torments, at which times his prose, like the soil of Calabria, is "all whirlpool and undulation." It is even theatrical, as in the already quoted line: "The most forlorn of beings I tread a shore under the burthen of infinite despair, that once I trod all cheerfulness and joy." But on any other subject Cowper's language is that of the parlor, not of the stage. It is playful rather than heroic and in tone conversational rather than oratorical or consciously literary.

A conversational style—a style based on the spoken rather than the written language—is a great asset to the anecdotist, for it allows him to blend his own personality into the telling of his story, giving free play to his wit as he moves the action forward. The success of the story depends on the balance struck between the narrator and the tale, a balance which Cowper struck very well. Equipped with this sense and a resourceful imagination Cowper was able to turn a commonplace occurrence into a memorable event. One such occurrence he immortalized in his ballad "John Gilpin." Two years before the composition of "Gilpin" he had used another story of a runaway horse as material for a delightful sketch included in a letter to Mrs. Newton:

You have never yet perhaps been made acquainted with the unfortunate Tom Freeman's misadventure. He and his wife returning from Hanslope fair, were coming down Weston Lane; to wit, themselves, their horse, and their great wooden panniers, at ten o'clock at night. The horse having a lively imagination, and very weak nerves, fancied he either saw or heard something, but has never been able to say what. A sudden fright will impart activity, and a momentary vigour, even to lameness itself. Accordingly, he started, and sprung from the middle of the road to the side of it with such surprising alacrity, that he dismounted the gingerbread baker and his gingerbread wife in a moment. Not contented with this effort, nor thinking himself yet out of danger, he proceeded as fast as he could to a full gallop, rushed against the gate at the bottom of the lane, and opened it for himself, without perceiving that there was any gate there. Still he galloped, and with a velocity and momentum continually increasing, till he arrived in Olney. I had been in bed about ten minutes, when I heard the most uncommon and unaccountable noise that can be imagined. It was, in fact, occasioned by the clattering of tin pattypans and a Dutch-oven against the sides of the panniers. Much gingerbread was picked up in the street, and Mr. Lucy's windows were broken all to pieces. Had this been all, it would have been a comedy, but we learned the next morning that the poor woman's collar-bone was broken, and she has hardly been able to resume her occupation since. (I, 194-195)

This is Cowper's narrative technique at its best. The focus is on the horse as we follow him on his course into town. There Cowper shifts the point of view momentarily to present us with a picture of himself startled out of bed by the noise of the oncoming horse and wagon. With expectation we await the climactic crash—but Cowper, having built the story to its climax, leaps past it to the next morning: "Much gingerbread was picked up in the street. . . ." The climax is left to the reader's imagination. Only then, in a dénouement, is our attention turned to the "gingerbread wife's" injury.

Outside the narrative, the conversational style is equally dominant. To Lady Hesketh, Cowper once commented, "When I read your letters I hear you talk, and I love talking letters dearly . . ." (III, 21). The description fits his own style very neatly. He wrote talking letters in which we not only hear him talk but are aware that he is talking to a particular person. Conversation is not soliloquy and a letter can be either, depending largely on the understanding between writer and reader. Except, once again, when on the subject of his relations with God, the bond between Cowper and his reader is strong. He wrote not only of his subject but also to his correspondent.

This is no doubt facilitated by the type of subjects he chose —largely trivial matters better suited to small talk than to discourse. Though he occasionally commented on the more momentous problems of his time, on the whole he avoided them as too depressing. As he wrote to the Rev. Walter Bagot explaining why he had declined to write anti-slavery poetry: ". . . I felt myself so much hurt in my spirits the moment I entered on the contemplation of it, that I have at last determined absolutely to have nothing more to do with it" (III, 282). He touches only briefly on such matters as slavery, the war in America, or London politics and prefers the surer ground of trivia and commonplace matters. What Cowper sought in writing was escape, not involvement.

For Cowper writing was a form of therapy through which he escaped the phantoms of his mind. One of his very real problems was a want of meaningful employment. In his continual fight to maintain mental stability it was essential that he keep his mind actively engaged to avoid slipping into a fatal state of depression. To this end he turned to poetry and prose. When a suitable subject was at hand to challenge his creative ability and give exercise to his imagination he seized upon it eagerly, sometimes treating it in both prose and verse. More often than not, however, he felt the lack of material. "I assure you faithfully," he wrote to Unwin, "that I do not find the soil of Olney prolific in the growth of such articles as make letter-writing a desirable employment. No place contributes less to the catalogue of incidents, or is more scantily supplied with anecdotes worth notice" (II, 139-140). To Mrs. Cowper he wrote: "I am fond of writing as an amusement, but do not always find it one. Being rather scantily furnished with subjects that are good for any thing, and corresponding only with those who have no relish for such as are good for nothing, I often find myself reduced to the necessity, the disagreeable necessity, of writing about myself" (I, 217). In practice, though he lamented the lack of amusing topics on which to write, their absence did not stem the flow of his letters. Instead, he set pen to paper and wrote the first thoughts which came to mind: ". . . not that I have anything to say, but because I can say any thing, therefore I seize the present opportunity to address you. Some subject will be sure to present itself, and the first that offers shall be welcome" (I, 454). In spite of the cloak of wit Cowper is serious. The absence of subject matter did not remove his need to seek mental relief through writing. "Such nights as I frequently spend are but a miserable prelude to the succeeding day, and indispose me, above all things, to the business of writing. Yet with a pen in my hand, if I am able to write at all, I find myself gradually relieved . . ." (I, 214).

The winter months were always the most dangerous for Cowper. When the weather was too harsh for his long walks abroad and his garden lay dormant under the oppressive grey sky which chilled his spirit, despair returned with renewed emphasis. Then it became especially necessary to find occupation for his mind. It was during these months that he wrote most of his poetry or worked at his translation of Homer. In the autumn of 1785 his renewed correspondence with his cousin Harriet, Lady Hesketh, assumed a growing importance in his writing schedule. In a letter to her dated December 7, 1785, he comments: "At this time last night I was writing to you, and now I am writing to you again. Had our correspondence been renewed a year ago, it is possible that, having found a more agreeable employment, it might never have occurred to me to translate Homer for my amusement" (II, 399).

Lady Hesketh's proposal that she take a house at Olney to be nearer her "dear cousin" threw Cowper into a state of ecstatic joy. He turned with great energy to readying everything for her stay and for a time, between the preparations and anticipations, he was busy enough to forget his troubles. His letters to her are filled with plans and expectations and with agony at each delay. In one letter, after describing some arrangements he had made for her, he writes: "The whole affair is thus commodiously adjusted; and now I have nothing to do but to wish for June; and June, my cousin, was never so wished for since June was made" (II, 469).

Here was the sort of therapy Cowper needed. For once he became so immersed in his plans and activities that he seems to have been genuinely happy. Now when looking out the window on a winter day his thoughts turned to summer and its awaited pleasures, not to such dreary matters as his damnation and the horrors of eternal punishment. "As I sat by the fireside this day after dinner," he wrote to Lady Hesketh in February of 1786, "I saw your chamber windows[6] coated over with snow, so that the glass was hardly visible. This circumstance naturally suggested the thought that it will be otherwise when you come. Then the roses will begin to blow, and perhaps the heat will be as troublesome as the cold is now" (II, 472).

His days were spent in plans and preparations and his evenings in composing reports to Lady Hesketh. Every moment was lived through in advance, every detail relished with new joy.

And I will tell you what you shall find at your first entrance. *Imprimis,* as soon as you have entered the vestibule, if you cast a look on either side of you, you shall see on the right hand a box of my making. It is the box in which have been lodged all my hares, and in which lodges Puss at present: but he, poor fellow, is worn out with age, and promises to die before you can see him. On the right hand stands a cupboard, the work of the same author; it was once a dove-cage, but I transformed it. Opposite to you stands a table, which I also made: but a merciless servant having scrubbed it until it became paralytic, it serves no purpose now but of ornament; and all my clean shoes stand under it. On the left hand, at the further end of this superb vestibule, you will find the door of the parlour, into which I will conduct you, and where I will introduce you to Mrs. Unwin, unless we should meet her before, and where we will be as happy as the day is long. (II, 461-462)

Of all Cowper's letters this series to Lady Hesketh has perhaps the greatest appeal for the common reader. They have both continuity given by their common theme of the impending visit and a contagious enthusiasm which makes them a delight to read even for those otherwise unacquainted with the writer.

We are this moment returned from the house above mentioned. The parlour is small and neat, not a mere cupboard, but very passable: the chamber is better, and quite smart. There is a little room close to your own for Mrs. Eaton, and there is a room for Cookee and Samuel. The terms are half a guinea a week; but it seems as if we were never to take a step without a stumble. The kitchen is bad,—it has, indeed, never been used except as a wash-house; for people at Olney do not eat and drink as they do in other places. I do not mean, my dear, that they quaff nectar or feed on ambrosia, but *tout au contraire.* So what must be done about this abominable kitchen? It is out of doors: that is not amiss. It has neither range nor jack: that is terrible. But then range and jack are not unattainables; they may be easily supplied. And if it were not—abominable kitchen that it is, no bigger than half an egg-shell, shift might be made. The good woman is content that your servants should eat and drink in her parlour, but expects that they shall disperse themselves when they have done. But whither, who can say? unless into the arbour in the garden, for that they should solace themselves in said kitchen were hardly to be expected. While I write this, Mrs. U. is gone to attempt a treaty with the linendraper over the way, which, if she succeeds, will be best of all, because the rooms are better, and it is just at hand. I must halt till she returns. —She returns;—nothing done. She is gone again to another place. Once more I halt. Again she returns and opens the parlour door with these tidings: —'I have succeeded beyond my utmost hopes. I went to Maurice Smith's' (he, you must know, my dear, is a Jack-of-all-trades); 'I said, do you know if Mr. Brightman could and would let lodgings ready furnished to a lady with three servants?' Maurice's wife calls out (she is a Quaker), 'Why dost thee not take the vicarage?' I replied, There is no furniture. 'Pshaw!' quoth Maurice's wife; 'we will furnish it for thee, and at the lowest rate; from a bed to a platter we will find all.' —And what do you intend now? said I to Mrs. Unwin. 'Why now,' quoth she, 'I am going to the curate to hear what *he* says.' So away she goes, and in about twenty minutes returns.— 'Well, now it is all settled. Lady H. is to have all the vicarage, ex-cept two rooms, at the rate of ten guineas a year; and Maurice will furnish it for five guineas from June to November, inclusive.' So, my dear, you and your train are provided for to my heart's content. (III, 14-16)

Cowper did not regard his letters as literature or letter-writing in general as a literary art. Rather he looked on them in the same light he looked on conversation, as spontaneous communications between individuals. Yet it is but natural that his skill as a literary craftsman should be evident in his private as well as his public writing. He saw with the eye of an artist, an eye which perceived the balance and tempo of good narrative technique, a perception which manifests itself in his letters as well as in his poetry. In the introduction to his collection of the letters Mark Van Doren has remarked that "doubtless there is no art of spontaneity, but if there be one, Cowper is its master."[7] The truth is that in the artist art and spontaneity—the natural and the contrived—are blended. It is a mark of Cowper's mastery of his craft that the two are blended so well.

Indiana University Library

EDWARD GIBBON:
THE MAN IN HIS LETTERS

Patricia Craddock

Edward Gibbon, if we are to believe his own testimony, was a miserable letter-writer. Infrequent, belated, and often short, most of his letters display art only in their attention to the pleasure and the interests of the recipient. Gibbon certainly had no thought of being represented to posterity by his letters. In fact, he found them unhelpful even as sources for the memoirs which were to serve that purpose: "Mrs Moss delivered the letters into my hands but I doubt whether they will be of much service to me" (III, 264).[1] Among his 878 extant letters there are, of course, some which are clearly formal or studied: public letters (in Latin as well as English and French), conventional social notes, business correspondence, and letters to unsympathetic but important relatives, notably his wealthy aunt Hester Gibbon and, at times, his father. But his letters to his friends, to his sympathetic relatives (including his stepmother), and, in happy times, to his father seem as open, hasty, informal, and unartificial as his habitual apologies imply.

The most prominent quality of these letters is gaiety, and the pleasant variety in their frankness and playfulness can be exemplified by the very passages in which he apologizes for his faults as a correspondent. To his best friend, Lord Sheffield, for instance, he writes, "Most certainly I am a puppy for not having wrote to you sooner; it is equally certain that you are an ass if you expected it" (I, 173). To his stepmother, "You will think me the most impudent fellow alive: but I am really angry with *you* for not being angry with *me* on account of my long and shameful silence" (II, 175). To his friend Victor de Saussure: "On ne doit imputer mon silence ni à la mort ni à l'insensibilité. Je vis, je me porte bien, je vous aime toujours. Croyez-moi, mon cher ami, il n'en faut accuser que la paresse, monstre effroyable que l'enfer a vomi pour être le fléau de la raison, du devoir, et de l'amitié" (I, 205-206). And to Lord Sheffield again, "I beg ten thousand pardons for not being dead as I certainly ought to be" (I, 372).

It is not surprising that Gibbon's friends complained about his sloth, for they must have awaited eagerly letters which confirmed for them, and preserved for us, qualities easily overlooked by those who know only the "historian of the Roman Empire." The perspective, the acumen, and the devastating irony which are the merits of the history, the "solemn sneer" and humorless orotundity which sometimes mar it, are not absent from the letters. But the affection, the tact, the frank and generous observation of others, the wit, perception, and occasional pathos in observation of himself, and, above all, the playfulness, of the letters make them uniquely valuable for those who would know the man Gibbon. The letters have the additional virtue, for readers of the *Autobiography* and of the *Decline and Fall*, of indicating the genesis of phrases and positions of the one, and of providing insight into the evolution and demands of the other.

Because Gibbon was a Member of Parliament during the American Revolution, an inhabitant of Switzerland during the French Revolution, and an historian and "Citizen of the World" at all times, one might expect him to have devoted most of his letters to politics and public affairs. The contrary is true; he explicitly tells his friend: "As business thickens, and you may expect me to write sometimes, I shall lay down one rule: totally to avoid political argument, conjecture, lamentation declamation &c which would fill pages not to say volumes, and to confine myself to short authentic pieces of intelligence for which I may be able to afford moments and lines" (II, 178). His excuse for this decision was that "you may find them laid open in every news-paper" (II, 157). That this excuse was not merely another disguise for the demon Laziness is clear both from Gibbon's allowing the same excuse to his friends during his sojourn in Switzerland and from its use by that indefatigable correspondent Walpole (e.g., in the letter of April 3, 1777, to Sir Horace Mann). But Walpole excused his writing nothing new, rather than his not writing about public matters, and in truth Gibbon seems usually to have avoided the effort of transcribing rival arguments, describing actions, and repeating conversations and anecdotes which would have been required for illuminating comments on public affairs. His seat in Parliament became instead an excuse for not discussing politics on paper: "Sometimes people do not write because they are too idle, and sometimes because they are too busy. The former was usually my case, but at present it is the latter. The fate of Europe and America seems fully sufficient to take up the time of one Man and especially of a Man who gives up a great deal of time for the purpose of public and private information. I think I have sucked Mauduit and Hutcheson [experts on American affairs] very dry, and if my confidence was equal to my eloquence and my eloquence to my knowledge, perhaps I might make no very intolerable Speaker" (II, 57).

Gibbon's departure from public life perhaps helped to give him the perspective which an historian hopes to have before commenting on events, for he expresses opinions on public matters rather more freely and fervently in Lausanne than in London. During his extended foreign tour as a young man Gibbon had remarked such a tendency in himself: "I cannot say whether you will find me improved in any thing else, but at least I think I am become a better Englishman, and that without adopting the honest prejudices of a Hampshire farmer, I am reconciled to my own Country that I see many of it's advantages better than I did, and that a more enlarged view has corrected many errors of my praemature and partial observation" (I, 191). This comment on his youth is not disinterested; to continue his travels he had to represent their fruit favorably; but his increased comments, his requests for newspaper clippings, and even explicit admissions after his removal to Lausanne in 1783 confirm the impression that Gibbon preferred distant rather than immediate political topics.

The French Revolution, which he did not personally experience but by the excesses of which he was clearly, if remotely, threatened, was the greatest stimulus to his public spirit. At first his comments are aloof, even naïve in their offhandedness ("Are you not amazed at the French revolution. They have the power, will they have the moderation to establish a good constitution?" [III, 161]). Later he is still calm, but begins to disapprove:

What would you have me say of the affairs of France? We are too near and too remote to form an accurate judgment of that wonderful scene. The abuses of the court and government called aloud for reformation and it has happened as it will always happen, that an innocent well-disposed prince pays the forfeit of the sins of his predecessors, of the ambition of Lewis XIV, of the profusion of Lewis XV. The French nation had a glorious opportunity, but they have abused and may lose their advantages. If they had been content with a liberal translation of our system, if they had respected the prerogatives of the crown and the privileges of the Nobles, they might have raised a solid fabric on the only true foundation the natural Aristocracy of a great Country. How different is the prospect! . . . How many years must elapse before France can recover any vigour, or resume her station among the powers of Europe? As yet there is no symptom of a great man a Richelieu or a Cromwell arising either to restore the Monarchy or to lead the Commonwealth. (III, 183-184)

Eventually, even remote political questions which might tend to spread what Gibbon calls the "French disease" bring agitation: "Do not, I beseech you tamper with Parliamentary representation. The present house of Commons forms in *practise* a body of Gentlemen who must always sympathize with the interest and opinions of the people, and the slightest innovation launches you without rudder or compass on a dark and dangerous ocean of Theoretical experiment. . . . So much for politics which till now never had such possession of my mind" (III, 308). Finally, Gibbon achieves a kind of resignation, and writes to Wilhelm de Sévery, "Dans ce siecle on ne peut rien prevoir, mais je cheris l'esperance et meme l'opinion, que l'Angleterre, et la Suisse surnageront dans le deluge universel" (III, 361).

The penetrating irony, given emphasis by rhetoric, which delights Gibbon's admirers and annoys his enemies, is occasionally to be observed in the references to public affairs in his letters: "In a night or two, we shall be in a blaze of illumination from the zeal of Naval Heroes, Land Patriots, and Tallow-Chandlers, the last are not the least sincere" (II, 206); "As the latter, though less numerous, are more violent and absurd than their adversaries it is highly probable they will succeed" (III, 307) ; "Lord C's funeral was meanly attended, and Government ingeniously contrived to secure the double odium of suffering the thing to be done and of doing it with an ill grace" (II, 184). Each of these examples is characteristic of Gibbon's manner. The first illustrates his use of unexpected combinations and anticlimax, and the second his cynical response to zeal. The rhetoric of the third example will readily be recognized by those familiar with Gibbon's memoirs as similar to that of the reference to the University of Oxford, "our venerable mother," who "had contrived to unite the opposite extremes of bigotry and indifference."[2]

A number of the ironic passages in the letters either echo or are echoed in Gibbon's history and his autobiography. An obvious example of his incorporating successful phrases from the letters in the *Memoirs* is the following: "Burke's book is a most admirable medicine against the French disease, which has made too much progress even in this happy country. I admire his eloquence, I approve his politics, I adore his chivalry, and I can even forgive his superstition" (III, 216). These sentences were written February 5, 1791. In a note added after March 2, 1791, to draft E of the *Memoirs,* Gibbon wrote: "I beg leave to subscribe my assent to Mr. Burke's creed on the revolution of France. I admire his eloquence; I approve his politics; I adore his chivalry; and I can almost excuse his reverence for church establishments."[3] Similarly, his letter (January 28, 1783) to Joseph Priestley anticipates the scourging irony which that gentleman receives in the *Autobiography.*

More subtly, some topics seem to demand irony from Gibbon: "Moi-meme j'ai eté assez mal avisé pour encourir la haine d'un ordre [the clergy] puissant et nombreux qui a toujours consideré le pardon des injures comme un dogme plutot qu'un precepte" (II, 263). When Lord Sheffield zealously refused to consider the American Revolution a lost cause, Gibbon remarked, "I congratulate your noble firmness, as I suppose it must arise from the knowledge of some hidden resources which will enable us to open the next Campaign with new armies of 50 or 60000 men" (II, 168). And to William Robertson, a fellow historian and fellow sufferer from critical ignorance, "I have been lately much flattered by the praise of Dr Blair and the censure of the Abbé de Mably" (II, 360). Even in the letters, then, the coldly ironic, analytical observation of the historical scene, the grasp of the broad range of events, and the distaste for "enthusiasm" are apparent. But in his letters, Gibbon was likely to say, "From yourself and politics I now return to my private concerns" (III, 195), and the man revealed in such passages has many amiable attributes —for example, a capacity for love.

Almost everyone knows of Gibbon's love for Suzanne Curchod, which flourished in Lausanne and was thwarted by the opposition of his father. The formality and objectivity of Gibbon's report of this episode in his memoirs has led some to believe him cold and insensitive, to "congratulate Mademoiselle Curchod on her escape."[4] Lord Sheffield's expurgations may have helped to prevent some readers from responding to the emotion concealed by dignity and distance within Gibbon's account of this love. D. M. Low, however, who for the first time considered all the available evidence, including the letters between Gibbon and Suzanne, reaches the just conclusions about their relationship:

> What might strike a modern lover in these letters is the lack of intimacy displayed on both sides. The feeling is undoubted, but the approach sometimes makes one imagine that the letters were exchanged by sympathetic attorneys to the Court of Love rather than by the principals. . . .
>
> It does not seem that Mlle Curchod ever doubted the sincerity and even fervour of Gibbon's attachment. . . .
>
> Great heat and great pressure are said to go to the making of crystals, and such was the process through which Gibbon passed before this tale of youthful ardour and helplessness crystallised into the immortal 'I sighed as a lover, I obeyed as a son'.[5]

Less celebrated but more enduring affections are apparent in these letters, in the ease with which Gibbon conducts the epistolary conversation, in the concern which his friends' troubles arouse in him, in the efforts which he will always make to help them, and particularly in his expressions of grief when death overcomes his ordinary aversion to passionate statement. He genuinely loved his "Aunt Kitty" and also, but much more mildly, his stepmother. He had an avuncular affection for Maria Holroyd, and a father's for Wilhelm de Sévery. He felt himself a brother to Mme. de Sévery and to Lady Sheffield, and the love for the latter is unmistakable in his correspondence. Finally, there was his constant attachment to two steadfast friends, George Deyverdun in Switzerland and John Holroyd, Lord Sheffield, in England.

His affection for his aunt Catherine Porten was the result of gratitude. His earliest extant letter (December 31, 1750) was written to her, it was to her that he appealed in his youthful troubles (gaming debts and his father's unannounced re-marriage), and when she died his grief and self-reproach were clear:

> . . . all these reflections will not dispell a thousand sad and tender remembrances that rush upon my mind. To her care I am in-debted in earliest infancy for the preservation of my life, and health. . . . As I grew up, an intercourse of thirty years endeared her to me as the faithful friend and the agreable companion; you have seen with what freedom and confidence we lived together, and have often admired her character and conversation which could alike please the young and the old. All this is now lost, finally irrecoverably lost! I will agree with Mylady that the im-mortality of the soul is, on some occasions a very comfortable doc-trine. A thousand thanks to her for her constant kind attention to that poor woman who is no more. I wish I had as much to applaud and as little to reproach in my own behaviour towards Mrs P since I left England and when I reflect that my letters would [have] soothed and comforted her decline, I feel more deeply than I can express the real neglect, and seeming indifference of my silence. (III, 45-46)

In his maturity letters and visits to Aunt Kitty had been prompted by duty rather than merely by his own pleasure, but his real attachment is evident.

His visits to Mrs. Gibbon (his stepmother) in Bath were almost entirely the effect of duty, but even duty might not carry every fat man with gout on a hundred-mile journey by carriage for a week of daily seven-hour tête-à-têtes with his aging stepmother. Gibbon's fairly frequent performance of this duty and his good humor are a credit both to him and to Mrs. Gibbon. "Here I am," he writes typically, "in close at-tendance of my Mamma, who is better in health spirits &c than I have known her for some years. Had I attempted an Easter excuse it would have been very ill received. I am vastly complaisant, *amuse* myself in Routes and private parties and play shilling Whist with the most edifying resignation" (II, 181). Though their mutual financial affairs were in Gibbon's hands after his father's death, and though Mrs. Gibbon had no financial advantage to offer Gibbon, he wished to cater not only to her rights but to her whims in his management of the property: "I think she cannot last very long but I should be hurt if her last days were embittered by any fears or scruples . . ." (III, 161). A letter Gibbon wrote only three months before he died aptly summarizes his attitude towards Mrs. Gibbon: "I passed the day with Mrs G yesterday. In mind and conversation she is just the same as twenty years ago; she has spirits, appetite, legs, eyes, and talks of living till ninety. I can say from my heart Amen" (III, 353).

Younger ladies also enjoyed Gibbon's favor. He teased and praised Maria Holroyd from her earliest youth, and admired and encouraged her developing intelligence. Perhaps the best testimony of this attitude is that in letters to others, for he thought Maria's fault was a tendency to pride, and therefore tempered his praise with sage advice when he wrote to her. When she first entered society, he wrote affectionately to her mother, "You will admire the triumphant Maria, and your observation will soon discern whether it will be easy to brush the powder out of her hair, and the world out of her heart or to shut her eyes after they have been once opened to the light of pleasure" (III, 89). He described her more formally and thoroughly to Madame de Sévery: "La demoiselle en question vient d'entrer dans sa dix-huitieme année, mais en cultivant ses talens avec soin, on l'[a] eloigné si parfaitement du monde, qu'elle [a] conservé jusqu'a cet age la simplicité et l'innocence d'un enfant. Sans etre belle, l'ensemble de sa figure est très bien, elle est honnete, raissonnable et un peu de fierté qu'elle tient de son caractere et de sa situation ne la rendra que plus attentive aux conseils d'une personne dont elle sentira à tous egards la superiorité" (III, 93). One might contrast his description of the daughter of another old friend (Suzanne Curchod, now Madame Necker): "Mademoiselle Necker one of the greatest heiresses in Europe is now about eighteen wild, vain but goodnatured and with a much larger provision of wit than beauty" (III, 11). Since the Sheffields had no sons, and Gibbon no intention of bringing Mlle. Necker to Sheffield Place, this description, addressed to Lady Sheffield, could be much more flippant than that addressed to Madame de Sévery, but the affectionate bias in favor of Maria is quite clear. To Maria herself, Gibbon writes with a rather sententious mixture of praise and blame appropriate to a quasi-parental role (one may compare Richardson's attitude towards his "daughters"). Speaking first of, and then to, Maria, Gibbon praises her letters to him, and adds:

That amiable author I have known and loved from the first dawning of her life and *coquetry* to the present maturity of her talents, and as long as I remain on this planet I shall pursue with the same tender and even anxious concern the future steps of her establishment and life. That establishment must be splendid that life must be happy if she will condescend to apply her good sense to restrain some sallies of imagination, to soften some energies of character which are the sources of our virtues and talents, but which may sometimes betray us into error and mischance. She is endowed with every gift of Nature and fortune, but the advantage which she will derive from them depends almost entirely on herself. You must not, you shall not, think yourself unworthy to write to any man: there is none whom your correspondence would not amuse and satisfy. (III, 294)

Gibbon was usually content, on the whole, with wifelessness, but his letters to and about Maria are not the only evidence that he sometimes regretted his consequent childlessness. After Sir Stanier Porten, Gibbon's uncle, died, Gibbon wrote to Lord Sheffield about the older Porten child. "Charlotte is about Louisa's [Lord Sheffield's younger daughter's] age, and one of the most amiable sensible young creatures I ever saw. I have conceived a romantic idea of educating and adopting her; as we descend into the vale of years, our infirmities require some domestic female society: Charlotte would be the comfort of my age and I could reward her care and tenderness with a decent fortune" (III, 164-165). Those who, oblivious of the self-depreciatory epithet "romantic," condemn this pathetic scheme as cold and egotistical may be comforted to know that although Charlotte's mother would not part with her, Gibbon left the bulk of his estate to Charlotte and her brother. His other major bequest was to Wilhelm de Sévery.[6]

Though Gibbon's acts are the strongest evidence of his regard for Wilhelm—he brought him to England, acted as his banker, introduced him to society, and left him more than £3000—that regard is also clear in Gibbon's letters. To Wilhelm's mother Gibbon wrote, "J'espere que vous conservez toujours, M de Severy et vous, l'intention favourable de m'envoyer notre fils si vous voulez bien me permettre de lui donner ce nom" (III, 73). While Wilhelm was in England, Gibbon felt so paternal that he could scold the young man affectionately: "Mechant petit Garçon [,] Nous sommes tous très mecontens de votre silence depuis la lettre du 29 Juin qui nous communiqua la premiere nouvelle de votre indisposition" (III, 119). Six months later, the affection is undiminished: "Adieu mon ami, mon fils, puisque vous le voulez bien. En prenant le nom de père ce n'est pas une vaine formule dont je me sers" (III, 250). Perhaps Gibbon's not claiming honorary fatherhood when Wilhelm's real father was dying is an even clearer evidence of sensitive regard, for Gibbon recognized the depth of Wilhelm's grief for M. de Sévery. He wrote to Lord Sheffield, "Wilhelm is much more deeply wounded than I could imagine, or than he expected himself: nor have I ever seen the affliction of a son and *heir* more lively and sincere" (III, 317).

Gibbon had been impressed before by a son whose grief for his father could be unambiguous. Less than four years after his own father's death, Gibbon had written revealingly to Lord Sheffield, "If my esteem and friendship for Godfrey had been capable of any addition, it would have been very much encreased by the manner in which he felt and lamented his father's death: incredible as it sounds to the generality of sons, and as it ought to sound to most fathers, he considered the old Gentleman as a friend" (II, 12). Gibbon had not even pretended to be inconsolable when his father died; his account to Deyverdun seems an honest reflection of at least his conscious attitude: "Pour abreger un recit qui doit vous affliger mon pere est mort il y a environ trois semaines. Dans toute sa maladie, je ne me suis jamais absente de Beriton un seul jour, à peine ai je quittè sa Chambre un seul instant: tout, jusqu'à mes lectures, a etè interrompû, et je goutte la triste consolation d'avoir rempli mes devoirs de fils, jusqu'au moment où ils ont cessè. Il me reste, je le sai, bien d'autres motifs de consolation. Je les vois, mais pour les sentir, j'ai besoin que le tems ajoute ses forces à celles de la raison" (I, 267). Gibbon's mother had died when he was young, and he remembered her as having little time or interest for him; his father had grieved violently, with little attention to the boy, had exiled him in his youth, and had jeopardized his financial security by life-long extravagance. It is not surprising, then, that Gibbon sought and found familial warmth by adoption.

Although Gibbon paid extravagant compliments to Lady Elizabeth Foster (". . . to take tea with three women, the most amiable in Europe [I speak with the religious accuracy of an historian] is the perfection of human society. . . . Adieu, Vale, Goodnight! but I do not dare tell you how much I love you" [III, 267]) and Suzanne Curchod Necker ("Non, Madame, je n'oublierai jamais les momens les plus chers de ma jeunesse, et ce souvenir pur mais indelibile se confond avec l'amitié la plus vraie et la plus inalterable" [II, 262]), the most important woman in his maturity seems to have been his "sister," Lady Sheffield. He explicitly says as much: "I could never forgive myself were I capable of writing by the same post a political Epistle to the father, and a friendly letter to the daughter, without sending any token of remembrance to the respectable Matron, my dearest Mylady whom I have now loved as a sister for something better or worse than twenty years. No indeed, the historian may be careless, he may be indolent, he may always intend and never execute, but he is neither a monster nor a statue: he has a memory, a conscience, a heart, and that heart is sincerely devoted to Lady S" (III, 296).

By now it should be abundantly clear that the historian had a heart, and even a conscience; but the correspondence with Lady Sheffield, like that with her husband, also demonstrates that the historian had a sense of humor. To her he could say impudently, "As I have now spent a month at Lausanne you will enquire with much curiosity, more kindness, and some mixture of spite and malignity, how far the place has answered my expectations, and whether I do not repent of a resolution which has appeared so rash and ridiculous to my ambitious friends" (II, 375-376). For once not delinquent in a correspondence, he could condemn her and praise himself with playful hyperbole which even the grimmest critic must recognize: "Is she satisfied with her own behaviour her unpardonable silence to one of the prettiest most obliging, most entertaining, most &c Epistles that ever was penned since the Epistles of Paul of Tarsus" (III, 34). Perhaps it was her example which confirmed him in his regret for his own sister, "whose life was somewhat prolonged, and whom I remember to have been an amiable infant. The relation of a brother and a sister, especially if they do not marry, appears to me of a very singular nature. It is a familiar and tender friendship with a female much about our own age, an affection perhaps softened by the secret influence of sex, but pure from any mixture of sensual desire, the sole species of platonic love that can be indulged with truth, and without danger."[7] One wonders whether either truth or safety was jeopardized by his regard for Lady Sheffield. Perhaps his strongest expressions of grief were occasioned by her death, but it is noteworthy that he grieves more for the bereaved family than for himself. He wrote to Lord Sheffield:

My Dearest Friend, for such you most truly are, nor does there exist the person, who obtains or shall ever obtain a superior place in my esteem and affection!

After too long a silence I was sitting down to write, when only yesterday morning . . . I was suddenly struck, indeed struck to the heart by the fatal intelligence. . . . Alas what is life and what are all our hopes and projects! When I embraced her at your departure from Lausanne, could I imagine that it was for the last time? When I postponed to another summer my journey to England, could I apprehend that I never, never should see her again . . . . But she is now at rest, and if there be a future state her mild virtues have surely entitled her to the reward of pure and perfect felicity. It is for you that I feel, and I can judge of your sentiments by comparing them with my own. I have lost it is true an amiable and affectionate friend whom I had known and loved above three and twenty years, and whom I often styled by the endearing name of sister. But you are deprived of the companion of your life, the wife of your choice, and the mother of your children; poor children! the energy of Maria, and the softness of Louisa render them almost equally the objects of my tenderest compassion. I do not wish to aggravate your grief, but in the sincerity of friendship I cannot hold a different language. I know the impotence of reason, and I much fear that the strength of your character will serve to make a sharper and more lasting impression.

The only consolation, in these melancholy tryals to which human life is exposed, the only one at least in which I have any confidence, is the presence of a real friend, and of that as far as it depends on myself you shall not be destitute. (III, 327-328)

As the power of Gibbon's regard for Lord Sheffield is strikingly demonstrated in his coming to comfort him in his grief, a journey by no means easy for Gibbon, with war on the Continent, an infirm body, and the habit of procrastination, so his affection for George Deyverdun is clearest in his lasting grief after Deyverdun's death, a grief so great, a loss so much felt, that he contemplated even marriage—"Some expedient, even the most desperate must be embraced to secure . . . domestic society" (III, 191). There is pathos in his enumeration of his sources of happiness in those years "alone in Paradise": "An excellent house, a good table a pleasant garden are no contemptible ingredients in human happiness" (III, 12); "Je doute que jamais homme de lettres ait eté mieux logé . . ."

(III, 174). These attitudes, when contrasted with his great content during the Lausanne years while Deyverdun lived, show how much his friend contributed to his felicity. The long, happy letters Gibbon wrote to Deyverdun after their menage at Lausanne had been decided upon express this friendship: "Je serai donc charmé et content de votre societé, et j'aurois pu dire en deux mots, ce que j'ai bavardé en deux pages mais il y a tant de plaisir à bavarder avec un ami: car enfin je possede à Lausanne un veritable ami, et les simples connoissances remplaceront sans beaucoup de peine tout ce qui s'appelle liaison et meme amitié dans ce vaste desert de Londres" (II, 334). "Tant de plaisir à bavarder" in letters—from Gibbon it is a remarkable tribute.

Gibbon's friendship with Deyverdun was, however, equaled or surpassed by that with Lord Sheffield. More of Gibbon's extant letters are addressed to Lord Sheffield than to any other person; it is therefore fortunate that their friendship permitted Gibbon to say almost anything, and that the result of such freedom is still entertaining. The range of tone and topic in the letters to Lord Sheffield includes everything from robust gossip to serious advice about attempting to gain a seat in Parliament. Their relationship is an unexpected one. Lord Sheffield was active, impetuous, extroverted, business-like, and far from bookish (though the success of his services to his friend as literary executor is evidence that he recognized and valued literary achievement). Gibbon, inactive (almost inert), zealously unenthusiastic, somewhat introspective if not introverted, who disliked business and found in studies "le charme de [sa] vie" (II, 263), himself commented on the oddity of their friendship: "I have sometimes wondered how two men so opposite in their tempers and pursuits should have imbibed so long and lively a propensity for each other" (III, 164). They had become friends during Gibbon's second stay at Lausanne (1763-64), their "mutual attachment was renewed and fortified in the subsequent stages of [their] Italian journey,"[8] and it hardly ended with Gibbon's death. By the time they had parted in their Continental journeyings, their intimacy and understanding were so great that Gibbon could joke about his old love, Suzanne, in a letter to his new friend. "Dear Leger, Why I did not leave a letter for you at Marseilles? For a very plain reason: Because I did not go to Marseilles. But as you have most judiciously added, why did not I send one? Humph. I own that non-plusses me a little. However hearken to my history. . . . The Curchod (Madame Necker) I saw at Paris. She was very fond of me and the husband particularly civil. . . . Could they insult me more cruelly. Ask me every evening to [supper],[9] go to bed and leave me alone with his wife; what an impertinent security. It is making an old lover of mighty little consequence" (I, 199-201).

The friendship was firm by then, and it certainly could not suffer from Lord Sheffield's kind attention to Gibbon. He took care of Gibbon's financial problems for more than twenty years and always welcomed him into his home; he took care of "Aunt Kitty" for Gibbon's sake, and in general proved his loyalty by his services. As for Gibbon's contribution, though it included every service of advice and even action which he could perform for Lord Sheffield, it was probably less tangible. That Lord Sheffield valued Gibbon's letters enough to keep them even at a relatively early stage of their acquaintance suggests that Gibbon's conversation, his wit, intelligence, and playfulness, endeared him to Lord Sheffield. When Gibbon became famous (and Lord Sheffield knew more of the progress of the *Decline and Fall* than any other of Gibbon's correspondents), it must have pleased him to know that to him alone Gibbon spoke with complete freedom. Most people would not recognize the historian as the narrator of the following piece of gossip: "The same Lady [Mrs. Horneck] who at public dinners appeared to have the most delicate Appetite, was accustomed in her own Apartment to feast on pork steaks and sausages and to swill Porter till she was dead drunk. Horneck is abused by the Albemarle family [,] has been bullied by Storer, and can prove himself a Cornuto to the satisfaction of

every one but of a Court of Justice. O Rare Matrimony!"
(II, 7). Pope's portrait of Philomedé seems to have been developed here, not by abstraction or generalization, but by further coarse concrete images—and only Lord Sheffield really knew *this* Gibbon.

Lord Sheffield was among the few people with whom Gibbon could laugh at himself, and perhaps the only person to whom he could express his small miseries. Before Gibbon's period in Parliament, he spent some time trying to set his estates in order, which involved him in unaccustomed and rather ludicrous activity:

> I set down to answer your Epistle, after taking a very pleasant ride—*A Ride! and upon what?*—upon a horse—*You lye*—I do'nt—I have got a droll little Poney, and intend to renew the long-forgotten practice of Equitation as it was known in the World before the 2d of June, of the year of our Lord, one thousand seven hundred and sixty three;[10] As I used to reason against riding, so I can now argue for it; and indeed the principal use, I know in human reason is, when called upon, to furnish arguments for what we have an inclination to do. . . . What do you mean by presuming to affirm, that I am of no use here? Farmer Gibbon of no use? *Last weak* I sold all my Hops, and I believe well, at nine Guineas a hundred to a very responsible Man. . . . *This week* I let a little Farm in Petersfield by auction, and propose raising it from £25, to 35 pr annum. and Farmer Gibbon of no use? (I, 294-295)

When an English paper prematurely (September 5, 1785) announced a report of the death of "the celebrated Mr. Gibbon," Gibbon delightedly used the best historical methods to conclude, in a letter to Lord Sheffield, that the report was probably correct!

> The hope of the Newswriter [that the report was "without foundation"] is very handsome and obliging to the historian yet there are several weighty reasons which would incline me to believe that the intelligence may be true. *primo* It must one day be true, and therefore may very probably be so at present. *secundo.* We may always depend on the impartiality accuracy and veracity of an English newspaper. *Tertio,* which is indeed the strongest

argument, we are credibly informed that for a long time past, the said celebrated historian has not written to any of his friends in England and as that respectable personnage had always the reputation of a most exact and regular correspondent it may be fairly concluded from his silence that he either is or ought to be dead. The only objection I can foresee is the assurance that Mr G himself read the article as he was eating his breakfast, and laughed very heartily at the mistake of his brother historian; but as he might be desirous of concealing that unpleasant event, we shall not insist on his apparent health and spirits which might be affected by that subtle politician. (III, 30-31)

The historian's whole arsenal of argument is there: the criterion of inherent probability, the authority of the source, the interpretation of supporting circumstantial evidence, the allowance of evidence to the contrary, and the discrediting of that evidence because of the bias of the source. Perhaps only to Lord Sheffield could such a subject (Gibbon's death) have been treated in such a manner. To Dorothea Gibbon, on the same occasion, Gibbon wrote, "I must seriously beg that you would never allow yourself to be made uneasy by any flying reports, or newspaper. Be assured that if any untoward accident should stop my breath, or disable my hand my friend M. Deyverdun will send the early and authentic Gazette to Sheffield Place . . ." (III, 42). He could play at paradoxes with Mrs. Gibbon, but he could not make use of sustained parody, especially on a possibly serious topic, and he could not expect her to enjoy or appreciate his mocking of his own art. The contrast is obvious: "Miss Holroyd who arrived here yesterday informed me that you were certain that I could not be at S P as you had not received any letter from [me]. This throws me under some difficulty as I must either set aside your authority, or distrust the evidence of my senses which seems to tell me that I am actually at [Sheffield Place]" (II, 187). As in the encounter with "the Curchod" and her husband, Gibbon seems to have found Lord Sheffield, and only Lord Sheffield, sufficiently congenial and understanding to share jests about important things.

Perhaps Lord Sheffield alone was sufficiently close to Gibbon to be told of his irrational hurts, fears, and desires; "I feel and confess," Gibbon complains to his friend, "the true friendship which breathes through the apparent *harshness* of your style but is that harshness absolutely necessary? it can give you no pleasure and it sometimes gives me pain" (III, 140). Gibbon never made a speech during his term in Parliament, and Lord Sheffield knew why: "I am still a Mute, it is more tremendous than I imagined; the great speakers fill me with despair, the bad ones with terror" (II, 61). With others Gibbon concealed such ingenuousness, as he did the wistful tenderness apparent in a second letter written between the death of Lady Sheffield and his own arrival in England: "Adieu. If there be any invisible guardians may they watch over you and yours. Adieu" (III, 331).

The task of letter-writing was redeemed for Gibbon by the frankness it permitted intimates to enjoy about themselves and each other. "I have often wondered why we are not fonder of letter-writing: we all delight to talk of ourselves and it is only in letters, in writing to a friend that we can enjoy that conversation not only without reproach or interruption, but with the highest propriety and mutual satisfaction, sure that the person whom we address, feels an equal or at least a strong and lively interest in the consideration of the pleasing subject" (II, 409-410). This view of letter-writing was not assumed or temporary, for Gibbon warned Lord Sheffield not to allow others to see his letters: "Do not be fond of shewing my letter. The playful effusions of friendship, would be construed by strangers as gross vanity" (II, 151). The letter, then, was usually intimate, personal, and conversational. Such letters had several functions, none of which were public. For Gibbon as for his contemporaries, letters were like conversation: they refreshed friendship, provided gossip and information, and passed time in an agreeable companionship; but, says Gibbon, "at any time, I had rather talk an hour than write a page" (II, 1). Letters also had special functions: they reassured the absent about the health and safety of friends, and they were appropriate for cool and dispassionate consideration of difficult questions, such as allowances and alliances. Gibbon confessed that he too often failed to feel the weight or exercise the possibilities of these functions: "I begin to discover that if I wait till I could atchieve a just and satisfactory Epistle equally pleasant and instructive, you would have a poor chance of hearing from me" (III, 64) . For a time, the *Decline and Fall* was an excuse to use to Lord Sheffield: "When I am writing a page, I not only think it a sufficient reason of delay, but even consider myself as writing to you, and that much more to the purpose than if I were sending you the tittle tattle of the town, of which indeed there is none stirring" (II, 14). The lameness of the excuse Gibbon admits with some charm: "Will you excuse my present litterary business as an excuse for my not writing? I think you will be in the wrong if you do; since I was just as idle before" (II, 84).

He had other, better excuses, and his correspondents forgave him. When he did write, his letters were worth receiving; he was conscientious about the kind of note which allays anxiety; he was not very much less reliable than most of his correspondents, and he justly claimed that when a letter was really needed, he would not fail to write it: "Pour le bavardage savans ou meme amical je suis de tous les hommes le plus paresseux, mais dès qu'il s'agit d'un objet réel d'un service essentiel, le premier courier emporte toujours ma reponse" (II, 330). "I compare friendship," he said, "to charity and letters to alms, the last signifies nothing without the first, and very often the first is very strong, altho it does not show itself by the other" (I, 35). He said this to excuse, not his own silence, but his correspondent's. Yet if we amend the metaphor to allow for the man of charity who is not conscious of his considerable alms-giving, we come very close to the relationship between Gibbon's letters and the man—the friend—they reveal.

Connecticut College

James Boswell [signature]

JAMES BOSWELL'S
PERSONAL CORRESPONDENCE:
THE DRAMATIZED QUEST FOR IDENTITY

Rufus Reiberg

I

EARLY IN HIS YOUNG MANHOOD James Boswell had identified what for him was the topic of greatest interest above all other topics in the world. Sitting in his London chambers on July 26, 1763, he wrote to his close friend, William Johnson Temple, of his preparations for the forthcoming journey to Holland, where he was to study law: "I have this night received a large packet from my father with my letter of credit, and several letters of recommendation to different people in Holland. The letters have been sent open, for me to seal, so I have been amused to see the different modes of treating that favourite subject, Myself."[1] The tone may seem playful, but let us never doubt that Boswell means what he says. Two days later he was to record in his journal that after Johnson and he had talked awhile of Swift and Addison: "We then talked of Me."[2] It is clear that Johnson was willing to discuss Boswell and his concerns often and at length, but the young man's unrelenting assiduity in his quest to know himself by writing and talking about himself (and having himself written and talked about) could, on occasion, break the bounds of Johnson's patience with dramatic sharpness: "Sir, you have but two topicks, yourself and me. I am sick of both."[3]

Johnson's irritated exaggeration of the narrowness of Boswell's range of subjects stemmed from his sense that the proper dimensions of good conversation were not being observed.[4] In any event, the reader of much of Boswell's personal correspondence is likely to feel that Boswell's favorite topic tends to become his only topic; for, to a greater degree than is true of any of the other prominent eighteenth-century letter-writers, Boswell was both the perceiving subject and the perceived object of his truly personal correspondence. Yet to some extent his very defects become his virtues. If many of his letters lack the satisfying proportions, the controlled perspective, and *beau monde* air of those written by a Walpole or a Madame de Sévigné, the best of them engage our attention and concern with immediacy and vitality, and collectively they afford a record unmatched in the completeness and literary quality with which both the internal and external elements of a human life are revealed.

At this point, to be sure, it can be argued that letters which are widely recognized as models of epistolary art are precisely those which have the qualities of Walpole's or Madame de Sévigné's letters. Without joining the issue here we can keep in mind these writers as representing a normative form and style of letter which Boswell himself thought highly of but never achieved. (We think of Boswell's eager praise: "My Lord, hers are very fine." And we cannot avoid hearing Lord Eglinton's response: "Yes, a few at the beginning; but when you read on, you think her a d—nd tiresome bitch."[5])

Boswell's personal letters may be thought of as comprising three broad categories: the social letter, which usually relates events in a chronological and unforced way and observes the amenities of a comfortable relationship; the highly contrived, or artificial, letter; and the relatively spontaneous, or organically shaped, letter. The first two groups have aspects of form and style which bring most of them fairly close to certain generalized modes for such correspondence during the eighteenth century. The last type, written more nearly under the immediate pressures of states of feeling and sent to those persons with whom he communicated intimately, is more significantly self-revealing by far than the others and of greater general interest. Beyond a brief discussion of the first two types and considerable emphasis on the last, some aspects of the letters-journal relationship and elements of style and theme which vitalize the form will be touched upon. The general thesis developed is that the bulk of Boswell's personal letters constitute a series of actions in what is essentially the dramatic mode. The actions reflect Boswell's various roles as actor, stage manager, and critic and are, in their totality, his attempt to establish the identity of "that favourite subject, Myself" as a recognizable and recognized Great Person.

II

The social letter which keeps friends and family informed of one's activities, thoughts, and plans during the period since the last meeting or exchange of messages may well be the commonest kind of personal letter. It serves to keep friendships alive and sensitive, and its tone ranges from matter-of-fact to concerned, its pace from slow to sprightly, its mood from reflectively serious to quietly mirthful. It avoids the extremes of the emotional spectrum, it develops its rhythms and moods in the middle ranges, and in the hands of a master like Cowper it is a literary delight. Many of Boswell's letters to friends and acquaintances are fashioned essentially in this mode. They are good letters of their kind, mildly interesting, certainly not déshabillé, and certainly lacking the hallmarks of what we consider a distinctive Boswellian style.

A fair number of his letters sustain this mode from beginning to end; there are also many which begin in this vein and then shift to an intensity which breaks through the limits suggested as typical. For example, a letter to Temple opens on a variation of the I-regret-I-did-not-write-sooner theme, mentions a few events in journal fashion, and then, at the end of the fourth sentence, becomes sharply emotional: "I am in that dissipated state of mind that I absolutely cannot write. I at least imagine so. But while I glow with gayety, I feel friendship for you, nay admiration of some of your qualities, as strong as you could wish. My excellent friend! let us ever cultivate that mutual regard which, as it has lasted till now, will, I trust, never fail."[6]

The comparatively neutral coloration of earlier sentences activated by *am, is, delightful, came, return, go, dine, hope,* and *elegant,* changes suddenly under the impact of *dissipated, absolutely cannot, glow, gayety, admiration, strong, ever cultivate,* and *never fail.* Boswell's heightened feelings find words and phrases which in their contexts of statement we recognize as marking certain elements of a Boswellian manner, a thrusting forward of an emotion-laden ego. The basic structure of the letter has been briefly suspended by such a shift in tone, and the texture has been altered to such an extent that for a moment or two our perception of the sentences immediately following is affected even though the language shifts back to the original coloration: "Worthy Claxton had not taken my neglect amiss. He has been in a hurry when I imagined him not satisfied with me. I eat bread and cheese and drank negus with him at his chambers on Sunday evening. . . ." Bread and cheese tread so closely on the heels of glowing gayety that we may for a second have difficulty keeping the images in their separate stations.

At times Boswell opens on a reasonably calm note which seems to promise a comfortable letter, but under the pressure of his feelings he begins to soar rhetorically, so that the heightened tone dominates the letter almost completely. Expressing his pleasure at Johnson's last letter and mentioning the compliments in it which so pleased him, he breaks out after one brief paragraph into:

But how can you bid me 'empty my head of Corsica'? My noble-minded friend, do you not feel for an oppressed nation bravely struggling to be free? Consider fairly what is the case. The Corsicans never received any kindness from the Genoese. They never agreed to be subject to them. They owe them nothing; and when reduced to an abject state of slavery, by force, shall they not rise in the great cause of liberty, and break the galling yoke? And shall not every liberal soul be warm for them? Empty my head of Corsica! Empty it of honour, empty it of humanity, empty it of friendship, empty it of piety. No! while I live, Corsica and the cause of the brave islanders shall ever employ much of my attention, shall ever interest me in the sincerest manner. . . .[7]

Such power as the passage has comes from the rhythmical thrusts of the phrases as well as from the force of the statements as statements. At the last Boswell's emotion has become entangled in his self-conscious posturings and perhaps unconscious comic echoes (we hear Falstaff: "No, my good lord. Banish Peto, banish Bardolph, banish Poins . . ."). It still derives from his genuine concern for the Corsican cause, but it tends to generate the image of the Corsican patriot as stage hero.

III

The highly contrived literary letter so much in vogue during the eighteenth century came to Boswell's attention early in his career. He was aware of the completely artificial type, the calculated commentary or essay on men and manners cast in the form of a personal letter and epitomized by Montesquieu's *Les Lettres Persanes* and Goldsmith's *Citizen of the World* (the "Chinese" letters). He was equally aware of the deceptively artless but nonetheless real letter, which, when published, could win praise as a superb vehicle for elegance and wit (Madame de Sévigné's letters concerning the court of Louis XIV). As an ebullient young man about London in 1763 he delighted himself with the notion that he might gain distinction as a Man of Letters by publishing a correspondence between himself and his friend, Andrew Erskine. The notion resulted in *Letters Between the Honourable Andrew Erskine and James Boswell, Esq.*[8]

In this correspondence Boswell did not assume the role of a Chinese or Persian but rather that of Laurence Sterne, whose acquaintance he had made in London in 1760 and whose influence was strong at this time upon both Erskine and him. The Shandean pose was one of the more enthusiastic poses assumed by the young Boswell as he wrote for publication and searched for an appropriate character in which to appear. Illustrative of the quality of the collection is this passage: ". . . the death of your kittens, my dear Erskine! affected me very much. I could wish that you would form it into a tragedy, as the story is extremely pathetic, and could not fail greatly to interest the tender passions. If you have any doubts as to the propriety of their being three in number, I beg it of you to reflect, that the immortal Shakespeare has introduced three daughters into his tragedy of King Lear, which has often drawn tears from the eyes of multitudes. The same author has likewise begun his tragedy of Macbeth with three witches. . . ."[9]

In his journal for 17 February 1766 Boswell wrote: "Read *Erskine's and Boswell's Letters;* could not bear your own except for one or two. In general mere forced extravagance and no real humour."[10] His estimate is a good one. The Shandean role was not one he could play effectively.

The artificial letter was among other things a literary device for displaying the graces and skills of the writer in the whole range of social postures and gestures attendant upon the functioning of a tightly structured, keenly self-conscious society which placed a high value upon proper form. The forms for ordinary social intercourse in such matters as introductions, invitations, acceptances, and regrets were fairly well stylized; but in such matters as requesting favors the writer had a wider range in which to exercise his contriving powers. In a letter to Lady Northumberland, Boswell, seeking support for a commission in the guards, attempts to be ingratiating while asserting what he takes to be an admirable spirit of independence ("I think a Welsh rabbit and porter with freedom of spirit better than ortolans and burgundy with servility. I will by no means cringe, not even to the ancient and honourable family of Northumberland. As a family I revere it. But I revere my own mind more . . .").[11]

The letter in its entirety shows that Boswell has tried to estimate the proper mixture and sequence of elements necessary to enlist the support of the Countess: a need for sympathy coupled with an assertion of his cheerful mood, a compliment that links the two of them in spirit, a reminder that he is not asking for a favor (followed at once by the request for a favor), and an assertion of his bold independence ("I will by no means cringe . . ." is surely gratuitous). He concludes the letter with an appreciation for past favors, and an appeal to friendship and the spirit of *noblesse oblige*. Along with considerable compositional skill the letter shows Boswell's bent for introducing gratuitously into a rather formal situation certain elements of his personality which, depending upon the recipient, may either amuse or irritate. (In the given circumstances, of course, no letter could have gained for Boswell what he requested; his father had seen to that.)

Among the more successful of Boswell's artificial letters are those he contrived for the purpose of getting materials for the biography of Johnson: "My dear Madam, from the day that I first had the pleasure to meet you, when I jumpt into your coach, not I hope from impudence, but from that agreeable kind of attraction which makes one forget ceremony, I have invariably thought of you with admiration and gratitude. . . . May I presume still more upon your kindness . . . ? . . . you write so easily that you might by a small expence of time give me much pleasure. Anecdotes of our literary or gay friends, but particularly of our illustrious Imlac, would delight me."[12] Impudence, or lack of ceremony, has been transformed into epistolary ceremony of a flattering kind. The flattery is obvious and so is its aim, but flattery so individually fashioned (". . . when I jumpt into your coach . . .") is likely to achieve its aim from the admiration it wins for its form. By the time she came to "you write so easily," Mrs. Thrale must have, at the very least, smiled complacently.

Boswell had considerable success in contriving still another type of request letter. His passion for attracting the notice of the great and the celebrated resulted in a number of epistles designed to elicit brilliant responses which could then be displayed in his cabinet at Auchinleck as evidence of his intimacy with the Great and the Celebrated. And he may well have had plans for publishing such correspondence. Perhaps the finest example of this type is his letter to Goldsmith of 29 March 1773 with its famous postscript: "Pray write directly. Write as if in repartee."[13] The delightful direction to Goldsmith at the end makes it clear that Boswell wanted and expected the best from the recipients of what he took to be his own gay and brilliant letters. (Some years earlier he had twice pleaded with the undeniably gay and brilliant John Wilkes to be sure to send him complete and unmarred letters: "I have two favours to beg of you; one that your letters may be signed John Wilkes; another, that they may be sealed in such a manner that I may not tear a word in opening them"; and "P.S. I beg you may put John Wilkes at the end of your letters, that they may not look like unsigned title-deeds.")[14]

Besides the artfulness of linking the birth of his daughter with the birth of Goldsmith's play, other touches are noted by Wimsatt and Pottle, who also discuss the "innocently unscrupulous tactics" of a letter written to Garrick on the same day for the same purpose: getting a sparkling response from a celebrity.[15] What is most obvious about the use of the language of personal relationships in the letters to Mrs. Thrale and Goldsmith is that it serves ends other than those of personal communication. In this sense both letters are equally insincere; but the one to Goldsmith is much more artfully formed than the other. The oft-mentioned postscript is, in effect, a stage direction put there to make sure that the other actor on stage says his lines properly. Boswell, the producer-actor, wants a response that will demonstrate to viewers of the cabinet at

Auchinleck not merely that he is on intimate terms with Goldsmith, but that Goldsmith considers him of sufficient importance to take the trouble to create some brilliant lines.[16]

Boswell's flattering contrivances for getting himself into the circles of the great were at times most ingenuous. Having heard that Pitt (Lord Chatham) had spoken favorably of him, he requested the favor of a letter now and then, suggesting that "to correspond with a Paoli and with a Chatham is enough to keep a young man ever ardent in the pursuit of virtuous fame."[17]

IV

When we read the letters having to do with problems and interests, often extremely intimate, that Boswell needed to share with a few others, we sense a new form and function of the personal letter. In the often excited yet always controlled outpourings to William Johnson Temple especially, but also to others, the personal letter becomes a psychological, historical, and literary document of an almost unique kind. (Certain portions of Boswell's journal may be considered another form of the intimate personal letter.) It is an honest and highly dramatized record of a mind conscious of its constantly shifting states of feeling as they relate to an external world which is apprehended with a distinct sense of solid form, and as they evaluate and react to that world according to the pressures of the inner modes of being. It is different from almost anything else in eighteenth-century letters, and only in our own time perhaps, when all aspects of the psyche are serious and accepted concerns of philosophy, criticism, psychology, and the arts, has it been possible for Boswell's recorded perception of himself and the world to be given a more broadly sympathetic, if at times smiling, recognition of significance. Current interest in various aspects of the Absurd, in the Clown figure, for example, makes it possible for our generation of readers to accept Boswell as Boswell much more readily than could most persons of earlier generations.

Boswell's highly developed sense of the theatrical leads him to define himself in his letters as an actor playing various roles on a stage that he himself sets variously for rhapsodic declamation, for pastoral romance, for comedy of manners, and for heroic drama. Some letters contain elements of several of these modes of the dramatic. In full effulgence after meeting with Rousseau, Boswell declaims his account of the experience from such an exalted peak that he presents the world and himself transfigured into glory, and he seems barely able to touch earth long enough to sign the letter:

My dear Johnston,—Art thou alive, O my friend? Or has thy spirit quitted its earthly habitation? To hear of thy death would not now distress me. I would glory to think of thy exaltation.

Johnston, I am in the village which contains Rousseau. These three days I have visited that sublime sage. He has enlightened my mind. He has kindled my soul. Yes, we are immortal. Yes, Jesus has given us a revelation. I feel an enthusiasm beyond expression. Good heaven! Am I so elevated? Where is gloom? Where is discontent? Where are all the little vexations of the world? O Johnston! Wert thou but here! I am in a beautiful wild valley surrounded by immense mountains. I am just setting out for Neuchâtel. But I return to Rousseau.

I am to be alone on horseback in a dark winter night, while the earth is covered with snow. My present sentiments give me a force and a vigour like the lion in the desert.

Farewell, my dear friend.[18]

In one of his longest and most fascinating letters, sent to Temple from Ferney on 28 December 1764, he opens on a disarming note of declamation to explain why he must use an elevated style: ". . . I must pour forth the exultation of a heart swelling with joy. Call me bombast. Call me what you please. Thus will I talk. No other style can give the most distant expression of the feelings of Boswell. If I appear ridiculous, it is because our language is deficient."[19] It seems clear that Boswell was continually aware of the esthetics of language as an expression of feeling and that for him certain language was fitting despite its inappropriateness for others. After commenting on his visits to the German courts and describing (less intensely than to John Johnston) his meeting with Rousseau, he recounts in highly dramatic narrative style his first meeting with Voltaire:

I returned yesterday to this enchanted castle. The magician appeared a very little before dinner. But in the evening he came into the drawing-room in great spirits. I placed myself by him. I touched the keys in unison with his imagination. I wish you had heard the music. He was all brilliance. He gave me continued flashes of wit. I got him to speak English, which he does in a degree that made me now and then start up and cry, 'Upon my soul this is astonishing!' When he talked our language he was animated with the soul of a Briton. He had bold flights. He had humour. He had an extravagance; he had a forcible oddity of style that the most comical of our *dramatis personae* could not have exceeded. He swore bloodily, as was the fashion when he was in England. He hummed a ballad; he repeated nonsense. Then he talked of our Constitution with a noble enthusiasm. I was proud to hear this from the mouth of an illustrious Frenchman. At last we came upon religion. Then did he rage. The company went to supper. Monsieur de Voltaire and I remained in the drawing-room with a great Bible before us; and if ever two mortal men disputed with vehemence, we did. Yes, upon that occasion he was one individual and I another. For a certain portion of time there was a fair opposition between Voltaire and Boswell. The daring bursts of his ridicule confounded my understanding. He stood like an orator of ancient Rome. Tully was never more agitated than he was. He went too far. His aged frame trembled beneath him. He cried, 'Oh, I am very sick; my head turns round,' and he let himself gently fall upon an easy chair. He recovered. I resumed our conversation, but changed the tone. I talked to him serious and earnest. I demanded of him an honest confession of his real sentiments. He gave it me with candour and with a mild eloquence which touched my heart. I did not believe him capable of thinking in the manner that he declared to me was 'from the bottom of his heart.' He expressed his veneration—his love—of the Supreme Being, and his entire resignation to the will of Him who is All-wise. He expressed his desire to resemble the Author of Goodness by being good himself. His sentiments go no farther. He does not inflame his mind with grand hopes of the immortality of the soul. He says it may be, but he knows nothing of it. And his mind is in perfect tranquillity. I was moved; I was sorry. I doubted his sincerity. I called to him with emotion, 'Are you sincere? are you really sincere?' He answered, 'Before God, I am.' Then with the fire of him whose tragedies have so often shone on the theatre of Paris, he said, 'I suffer much. But I suffer with patience and resignation; not as a Christian—but as a man.'

Temple, was not this an interesting scene? Would a journey from Scotland to Ferney have been too much to obtain such a remarkable interview? I have given you the great lines.[20]

In this letter Boswell has hit upon a form and style calculated to give a sense of highly dramatic immediacy. He has constructed a scene whose verbal vehicle consists chiefly of a series of short declarative sentences, heavily loaded with verbs denoting action. It is presented as a confrontation of two epic-dramatic heroes with the narrator introducing sufficient comment and direction to remind us that he, one of the heroes, controls both the point of view and the development of the action ("I got him to speak English . . ."; "I demanded. . . . He gave . . ."; "I called. . . . He answered . . ."). The insistent use of *he* and *I* as sentence subjects emphasizes the dramatic opposition in a scene which shows Boswell assuming a staged equality with one of the greatest names of the age. We see again one of the characteristics which mark his use of dramatic elements. It is not that he is the only letter-writer of the century to think and write in dramatic terms (although he does so far more extensively than most of the others); it is that he tends always to set a stage on which he insistently plays a highly visible major role, if not the lead.

It is fair to say that Boswell's art is true to his knowledge of facts and to his perception of the state of his consciousness. He is concerned with an accurate presentation of both, and at times the one may conflict with the other so much that a new stage presentation is given within the same basic plot unit. For example, in the confrontation with Voltaire Boswell's emotional state is reflected in the heightening of metaphors and thrust of statement which bring us an Ajax confronting a

Hector, so to speak. And to the extent that we can suspend disbelief and accept Boswell and Voltaire as appropriately cast in the heroic mold, perhaps a difficult task for many readers, we can accept the heroics of the scene. But when Voltaire falls gently upon an easy chair, our sense of the action is drastically changed. We have, not the fall of a hero in combat, but the calculated stage faint of an old man. The heroes disappear, the stage is reduced to human dimensions, the metaphors lose some of their excitement, and we go along on a different level of presentation. Boswell does not manipulate his feelings and perceptions for preconceived ends; rather his shifting states of consciousness inform the structure that is achieved, a structure which, in other words, has been organically shaped.

Undoubtedly Boswell is intent here upon truthfully portraying the states of his consciousness rather than in realizing a pure literary form, but he assuredly is aware of his role as a producer of drama; the apostrophe to Temple makes this clear. Boswell has staged a production, cast himself in one of the leading roles, and then disengaged himself to comment on the results. In such letters his attempts to create immediacy are only a step away from the form best suited to such purposes: dramatic casting of conversation once the scene is set, with only an occasional stage direction. He had already used this form in his journal, and he was to use it in a letter to Temple concerning one stage in his pursuit of Miss Catherine Blair:

What think you, Temple, was her answer? '*No;* I really', said she, 'have no particular liking for you; I like many people as well as you.' (Temple, you must have it in the genuine dialogue.)

Boswell. Do you indeed? Well, I cannot help it. I am obliged to you for telling me so in time. I am sorry for it.

Princess. I like Jeany Maxwell (Duchess of Gordon) better than you.

B. Very well. But do you like no man better than me?

P. No. . . .

B. And if you should happen to love another, will you tell me immediatly, and help me to make myself easy?

P. Yes, I will.

B. Well, you are very good (often squeezing and kissing her fine hand, while she looked at me with those beautiful black eyes).[21]

The direct presentation of experience through dramatic casting of conversation testifies further to Boswell's impulse to see himself and the world in theatrical terms, and, of course, many notable passages in the *Life of Johnson* are presented in the form used in this letter. We might say that Boswell's true genius lay in this mode of apprehension, whether or not expressed overtly through formal *dramatis personae* (dozens, perhaps hundreds, of the people in his journal could be properly cast by a director from the brief and telling descriptions of them). Consider the characters and the absurdly delicious stage action, combining elements of farce and romance, in Boswell's account of an infatuation with a gardener's daughter:

> In short, Sir, the gardener's daughter . . . is so very pretty that I am entirely captivated by her. . . . Only think of the proud Boswell, with all that you know of him, the fervent adorer of a country girl of three and twenty. I rave about her. . . . My fancy is quite inflamed. It riots in extravagance. . . .
>
> I take every opportunity of being with her when she is putting on fires or dressing a room. She appears more graceful with her besom than ever shepherdess did with a crook. I pretend great earnestness to have the library in good order and assist her to dust it. I cut my gloves that she may mend them. I kiss her hand. I tell her what a beauty I think her. . . . That we may not be too often seen together, she and I write notes to each other, which we lay under the cloth which covers my table. . . .
>
> Good heavens! what am I about? It would kill my father. Have I returned safe from London, from Italy, and from France to throw myself away on a servant maid? . . .
>
> I have got a lock of her hair which I dote upon. She allowed me to cut it off. . . . Surely I have the genuine soul of love. When dusting the rooms with my charmer, am I not like Agamemnon amongst the Thracian girls?[22]

As we have seen, in letters reflecting moments of greatest excitement, Boswell's narrative style tends to form itself in short, sharp statements of action and emotion, as if he were in haste to set down each momentary state of perception and feeling as it occurred. In some letters his mood and, to a lesser degree, his style change several times during the course of the writing, and we find several actors on the stage, as it were. In an extended missive to Belle de Zuylen (Zélide), for example, Boswell gives us aspects of the man of principle and strong will, the disarmingly candid self-appraiser, the anxious and beseeching friend, the patronizing male, the exhorting mentor, the domestic tyrant in a moment of apology, the smugly rational moralist, and the self-conscious writer of letters, all embodied in Boswell the perplexed lover. The opening of this letter is interesting for the way in which Boswell sees himself as two persons playing roles: "You know I am a man of form, a man who says to himself, Thus will I act, and acts accordingly. In short, a man subjected to discipline, who has his *orders* for his conduct during the day with as much exactness as any soldier in any service. And who gives these orders? I give them. Boswell when cool and sedate fixes rules for Boswell to live by in the common course of life, when perhaps Boswell might be dissipated and forget the distinctions between right and wrong, between propriety and impropriety. . . ."[23]

Boswell's projection of himself in the third person in such statements as "Boswell when cool and sedate fixes rules for Boswell to live by . . ." is characteristic of one who tends to see events, even mental events, as dramatic experiences. The duality of consciousness implied was well put by Boswell himself in an essay, "On the Profession of a Player," in the *London Magazine* for September 1770: "If I may be allowed to conjecture what is the nature of that mysterious power by which a player really is the character which he represents, my notion is that he must have a kind of double feeling. He must assume in a strong degree the character which he represents, while he at the same time retains the consciousness of his own character. The feelings and passions of the character which he represents must take full possession as it were of the antechamber of his mind, while his own character remains in the innermost recess."[24]

To be sure, Boswell's presentation of Boswell giving orders to Boswell is not the same thing as a player attempting to represent another person. But in either case a kind of "double feeling" exists. In Boswell it may take the form of an objectification of himself as two separate persons, or it may take the form of different states of perception of a developing, changing action (conversation), as in the scene with Voltaire. Or it may manifest itself in a tension between different states of perception involving an event which calls for a conventional response. In a letter describing the funeral of his wife we find such a tension, a pull of opposites. Especially characteristic of Boswell is the way in which he resolves the situation by taking the front center position on the stage:

> But alas to see my excellent wife, and the mother of my children, and that most sensible lively woman, lying cold and pale and insensible was very shocking to me. I could not help doubting it was a deception. I could hardly bring myself to agree that the body should be removed, for it was still a consolation to me to go and kneel by it, and talk to my dear dear Peggie. She was much respected by all who knew her, so that her funeral was remarkably well attended. There were nineteen carriages followed the hearse, and a large body of horsemen and the tenants of all my lands. It is not customary in Scotland for a husband to attend his wife's funeral. But I resolved, if I possibly could, to do her the last honours myself, and I *was* able to go through with it very decently. I privately read the funeral service over her coffin, in presence of my sons, and was relieved by that ceremony a good deal.[25]

Here is a juxtaposition of recollected anguish at the death of his wife and prideful satisfaction at the size of her funeral cortege. The anguish and pride are resolved into an asserted feeling of relief, and what emerges from the language is a sense of Boswell as a self-satisfied intruder at his wife's funeral. It may be that no one in the *actual* situation viewed him in this light. But the *recorded* situation, which he has staged and developed in relation to his own feelings and actions, emphasizes the attention-getting thrust of his ego into a pattern of established social behavior. And it is intrusiveness of some kind that marks so much of this self-recorded life. In this passage his feeling of relief owes as much to his own sense of self-assertion (". . . and I *was* able . . .") in the violation of custom as it does to his awareness of a ritual "decently" conducted. Certainly the tone and action pull first one way and then another in the given situation. To the observer on the outside Boswell lets himself appear not as one displaying a consistent and appropriate emotion or range of emotions but rather as an object (faintly ludicrous?) caught in the middle of a psychic game of tug-of-war. On the one hand, the attachment to his wife which seems to be the reason for his disrupting the customary pattern tempts the romantics among us to do him honor; on the other hand, the almost complacent tone about his handling of the service, as well as the pride in the funeral attendance, tempts us to see staginess and romantic posturing in the whole affair.

A Hogarth may sketch an opposing pair—industrious and idle apprentices—and if there is amusement on our part, it does not involve Hogarth, because he has not formally involved himself. But Boswell both *portrays* and *is* the two, so to speak. Subject becomes its own enveloping object; the artist's conflicting emotions become a formal part of *one* artifact; the producer becomes the actor on the stage. The result may be an art, or craft, of personal truth, but its aesthetic unity approaches that of the dancer and the dance. If Boswell hoped that he would be distinguished from his performance (as well as by it), he was to learn that the more effectively he revealed the complex workings of general human nature as manifested in and around him, the more he was likely to be considered the simple embodiment of the less desirable characteristics he displayed in his revelation. Mixed and opposing discriminations of the psyche may, to some, indicate not the complexity of reality but lack of taste or even of value. Forceful, and occasionally absurd, intrusions of the ego, whether in life or letters, may be

260

all very well with Temple and Erskine and Johnston, perhaps with Rousseau, but not with the Earl of Chatham or the King of Prussia—and certainly not with Lord Auchinleck, one's classically stern and disapproving father.

V

In considering briefly the relation between Boswell's letters and his journal, we may begin by repeating what was said earlier: some parts of the journal may be thought of as intimate personal correspondence. This is true especially of the journal before his marriage in 1769. Indeed, the 1762-63 portion of the journal was sent weekly in packets to his close friend, John Johnston of Grange, and on some occasions he read sections to friends. But though he wrote chiefly for himself and in part for one or two choice spirits, he was aware that in certain circumstances he might be indiscreet enough to reveal intimacies to those who ordinarily would not be privy to them: ". . . another shocking fault which I have is my sacrificing almost anything to a laugh, even myself; in so much that it is possible if one of these my companions should come in this moment, I might show them as matter of jocularity the preceding three or four pages, which contain the most sincere sentiments of my heart; and at these would we laugh most immoderately. This is indeed a fault in the highest degree to be lamented and to be guarded against."[26]

That there is a close biographical relationship between the letters and the journal is indicated by the success the editors of the McGraw-Hill "reading" editions of Boswell's selected writings have had in using letters to integrate the record where portions of the journal are missing, or to illuminate episodes or concerns not thoroughly or significantly covered in the journal, or to reveal the state of Boswell's mind in relation to certain events. That there is a literary relationship between the two is made clear by the manner that is unmistakably Boswellian in each and both: the pervasiveness of his ego, the rapid changes of moods and postures, the naïveté and confusion about his status in the world, the romantic enthusiasms and black despondencies, the exact sense of significant detail, the theatricality of perception. Yet there are some obvious differences in form and content that should be touched upon.

The journal, as one would expect, is a regular chronological record according to calendar sequence by days, and it is usually but by no means always a chronological sequence of events within a given day. It is one of the prominent patterns of regularity in Boswell's activities with, to be sure, many lapses and much unevenness as a record. In his journal Boswell enters numerous details of daily activity not found typically in the letters: what he ate for meals and where, what he paid for clothes and lodging, who called upon him, where he went calling, what books he read, what plays and concerts and lectures and balls he attended, how he had his hair dressed, what sermons he heard in what churches, what anecdotes and neighborhood news came his way. And he may include comments, sometimes extended ones, indicating the state of his mind in relation to the events recorded. "The state of my mind," he wrote in his journal on 9 July 1774, "must be gathered from the little circumstances inserted in my Journal. The life of every man, take it day by day, is pretty much a series of uniformity; at least a series of repeated alternations. It is like a journal of the weather: rainy—fair—fair—rainy, etc. It is seldom that a great storm or an abundant harvest occurs in the life of man or in the progress of years."[27]

But when the great storms, or even high winds, did occur —certain love affairs, Corsica, the Douglas cause, John Reid, Mrs. Rudd, for example; or when the harvest did prove abundant—fine conversation with Johnson and the members of the Club—Boswell expanded his journal to pages that are literature. Indeed, many such pages served as printer's copy for the *Life of Johnson* in some of its most brilliant portions. The total expanded journal gives Boswell a firm place as a literary artist independently of those works published in his lifetime.

VI

A good part of the attractiveness of Boswell's intimate letters comes from his complete responsiveness to events both
outside and inside himself. His range of sensitivity was great
and the relation between his physical well-being and psychical
well-being was extremely close. An ingrown toenail could
cause almost as much distress as the humiliation forced upon
him by Lord Lonsdale, at least in its immediate expression. Of
the one he writes: "So trifling a matter as letting the nails of
my great toes grow into the flesh, particularly in one foot, produced so much pain and inflammation and lameness and apprehension that I was confined to bed, and my spirits sank to
dreary dejection."[28] And of the other: "I am alone at an inn,
in wretched spirits, and ashamed and sunk on account of the
disappointment of hopes which led me to endure such grievances. I deserve all that I suffer."[29]

He can glow romantically at the thought of marrying
Zélide and living "in supreme happiness with a handsome and
most accomplished lady," especially since he would at once
have an independent fortune of a thousand pounds a year.
But he considers her bent for mathematics and philosophy, her
lack of prudence, decides she would make a husband miserable
within a year, and questions rhetorically: "Should I not curse
myself for having married a Dutchwoman?"[30] It is this skip-
ping from one end of the emotional spectrum to the other
in short spaces of time that gives Boswell a liveliness hard to
match. It also, and obviously, calls his maturity into question.

Some years ago W. H. Auden suggested that the reason
each of us confronts himself, especially the self of his youth, in
reading Boswell is that in all other respects than being a skill-
ful observer and writer Boswell is "such a thoroughly ordinary
man." As Auden sees the matter, the tension that characterizes Boswell's personal writing results on the one hand from
his ordinary and desperate desire to become a conventional
man and on the other from an extraordinary inability to "lose

his humanity and become a mechanical doll" because "his childlike appetite for the immediate moment is too strong."[31] There is nothing startling about Auden's perception; it seems clearly true but not exclusively true, and it can be related to the notion of Boswell's dramatized quest for identity.

"Yet the delusion of Westminster Hall, of brilliant reputation and splendid fortune as a barrister, still weighs upon my imagination. I must be *seen* in the courts. . . . The Chancellor, as you observe, has not done as I expected. . . . Could I be satisfied with being Baron Auchinleck, with a good income for a gentleman in Scotland, I might no doubt be independent. But what can be done to deaden the ambition which has ever raged in my veins like a fever?"[32] Ambition such as this is perhaps ordinary enough, and the intensity of its metaphorical expression testifies to a desperation that might be called blood-brother to that of Hamlet's uncle ("For like the hectic in my blood he rages"). Boswell of course would not have seen his idealized image as anything ordinary but rather something greatly distinctive (a characteristic which may put another stamp on his ordinariness). For us, what is relevant is that he has in stock a good many trite phrases, allusions, echoes, and images from the classics, the novel, and the drama which, along with his use of exclamation, apostrophe, and rhetorical question, help to project a sense of the dramatic, even the theatrical. It might be too much to say that his frequent theatricality is for him always unconscious, or at most self-conscious, and therefore natural; but undoubtedly it would be too much to insist that such perception and expression on his part are always the result of an ego-consciousness that is imposed upon self-consciousness. There is considerable testimony to the effect that Boswell's personal writings convey transparency of statement, and so we conclude that his theatricality as such is essentially artless.

But not always. Consider Boswell writing in 1793: "The choice of a minister to a worthy parish is a matter of very great importance; and I cannot be sure of the real wishes of the people without being present. Only think, Temple, how serious a duty I am about to discharge. *I James Boswell, Esq!*"[38] Here he is not only self-conscious but ego-conscious, and all of us— Temple, Boswell, and ourselves—know that an attempt is being made to puff a role into greater importance than would ordinarily be associated with it in the eyes of the world. The man who had said three years earlier that he could not be satisfied in the role of the Laird of Auchinleck tries now (as on other occasions) to convince his audience and chiefly himself that the role he has been forced to play is of vast importance indeed.

A survey of the progress of this drama over the years shows us how Boswell came to change the relation of his life to roles in which he projected himself. In the early years the images of the Great Persons were outside himself, embodied in others or in idealized abstractions. And his letters show how he attempted to establish his identity by relating it to these images: by imitation (Sterne), by association (Johnson, Goldsmith, Voltaire) , by recognition conferred upon him (the Countess of Northumberland, Lord Chatham), and by half-serious, half-playful assertion ("Surely I am a man of genius";[34] "I am really the *Great Man* now"[35]).

As the years went by and his station in life appeared more and more to be that suggested by the actual life he led, he tried at times to view such a life as being important enough to make his station that of a Great Person. He did not convince himself completely or for long. Given his particular sensitivities it may have been impossible for him to do so, for his view of himself and his experiences at any one time depended for the most part upon the state of his feelings and not upon a rational judgment: "When I recal the infinite variety of scenes through which I have passed, in my moments of sound sensation, I am elated; but, in moments of depression, I either forget them all or they seem indifferent."[36] But whether in depression or elation, Boswell kept the letters going and saw that they were preserved and returned as part of his total record of revelation, a record which could later be re-lived and examined with perhaps a better perspective for evaluation.

VII

During one frantic period of his life Boswell so dreaded the thought of unprivileged persons seeing the extent to which he revealed himself in a letter to George Dempster that he concluded with the direction, "Burn me as I burn you." But on the next day at the close of another letter beseeching Dempster's advice Boswell reversed himself with "O Dempster, write to me without delay, and instead of burning those frantic pages return them, that I may read them calmly. Pray do."[37] We feel sure that he would have found it impossible to consider for very long the notion of having his letters burned. Or anything he wrote. He needed to have his outpourings to others collected and returned as a permanent part of his record for himself. It is true that in large part he sought his identity in the images reflected by others ("You told me I was 'the most liberal man you have ever met with, a citizen of the world. . . .' . . . you said I looked as if I had a thousand men at my back. . . . But I set a higher value on your parting words . . . 'I shall never forget your civilitys to me. You are engraven upon my heart.' Was you realy in earnest?"[38]), but he sought also to evaluate himself as seen in the record and measured against firmly held principles and ideas of morality, religion, feudality, and ceremony. And so his letters (and journal) were a part of him in a way that goes beyond the notion of creative expression being a part of the creator. Beyond a sense of possessiveness about his artistry, beyond his need (a very real one) to objectify and complete his experiences by recording them, beyond any thought of what materials might be useful to future publishing schemes, beyond gratification at the immense amount and great variety of experience recorded, the reassurance of their sheer physical presence was important for his psychological survival.

Aside from the artistry of the writer it is the completeness and honesty of the self-revelation that are perhaps most impressive. Had Boswell had more of a sense of the *beau monde,* he would not have thrust his ego so forcefully into certain epistolary situations. Had he been conventionally selective, he would have omitted much personal detail that now delights us. Had he been gifted with a sense of irony, he would have avoided certain excesses and juxtapositions which made him laughable to others. Had he been dishonest, he might have made himself appear to better advantage in much of what he wrote. And yet he was by no means blind to the dangers involved in exercising talents such as he knew were his. In the year before he died, he wrote (with a touch of smugness and moralizing that may be forgiven) to his son Alexander, who seemed to be developing a talent like his father's for the delineation of personality:

Your last letters have afforded me a most satisfactory entertainment; and you may make yourself quite easy, for they are faithfully committed to the flames according to your desire. It pleases me to observe your attention to *character* and *manners* and the shrewdness of your remarks. But as you yourself suggest, you may write in that free manner confidentially to me, and I desire you may continue so to do. But you must be very cautious of letting other people know that you are such an *Observer* and such a *censor morum,* as they may be apt to misunderstand and form a wrong notion of you. I speak from experience, because I am certain that there is not in reality a more benevolent man than myself in the World; and yet, from my having indulged myself without reserve in discriminating delineations of a variety of people, I know I am thought by many to be ill natured; nay, from the specimens which I have given the World of my uncommon recollection of conversations, many foolish persons have been afraid to meet me, vainly apprehending that *their* conversation would be *recorded.* No study, however, is more improving than the study of *Man;* and my friend Courtenay pays me the compliment of having "imbibed" from Dr. Johnson

That great art, the art to know Mankind.[39]

It may not be too much to assert that to the extent that Boswell learned to know Mankind he did so as a corollary of his earnest efforts to know himself. And surely Courtenay is wrong, and surely Boswell underestimates himself. He would have come to know Mankind and to write about it in the Boswellian manner had he never met Dr. Johnson.

And knowing this, we know too that Boswell's dramatized quest for identity could never have been realized in the way in which he had hoped—general recognition and acceptance of himself as a Great Person. The quality of his personal and literary intrusiveness could never square with all the demands of his society's norms for both acceptability and distinction. As for the collective presence of the letters (and journal), although it did indeed offer the psychological assurance of a wonderfully complete life record by which he could measure and compare himself with himself and with many others, this same collective presence offered finally too much and too convincing evidence of who and what he was. As Boswell read over, especially in later years, the vast accumulation, he came to see ever more clearly and painfully what we perceive much more casually about him. The years of trying various roles, of establishing hundreds of dramatic situations for himself, of conscientiously furnishing the stage with multitudinous and accurate details, of serving as critic and commentator for his own performances, of soliciting the opinions of others about the performances, all came to one simple truth for him: he was what he was; he was not something else. For him it was not a happy truth. For us the total performance is a memorable one.

Indiana University

THE FAMILIAR LETTER
IN THE EIGHTEENTH CENTURY:
SOME GENERALIZATIONS

HOWARD ANDERSON AND IRVIN EHRENPREIS

I

BEFORE PUTTING TOGETHER some tentative conclusions implied by the other essays in this collection, we might speculate as to how the eighteenth century happened to become the great age of the personal letter. A literary form seems to flourish when its powers are just being realized, when the removal of obstacles or a freeing of resources makes gifted writers turn to it as an unworked mine, and test its strength through experimentation. One could say that several resources employed by the great letter-writers were made peculiarly available toward the end of the seventeenth century, and that the development of their art resulted, to a degree at least, from these conditions.

For instance, the composition of informal letters depends on the possibility of a frequent, candid exchange between writers who trust each other. Replies may not always be sent, but the likely chance of an early reply seems a necessary ingredient in the attitude of the true epistolary author. Yet while persons of wealth and power have always had messengers to carry their scrawls, it took the development of a convenient, reliable postal service to provide less exalted correspondents with an equivalent amenity. Only after the Glorious Revolution did the English post office give that kind of service. Then, however, business increased so rapidly that by 1704 the post office was receiving 75 percent more money per year than in 1688;[1] and in spite of the immense burden of pensions placed upon these revenues, enough profits remained for the service to be improved radically through the proliferation of cross posts (directly linking towns on separate main highways) and by posts (linking small towns and villages to larger centers) . Although there was always the danger that letters of interest to the government might be opened in London, this practice did not affect ordinary correspondence; and the easing of restrictions on speech and printing following the Revolution promoted a general freedom of expression. After the postal services of England, Scotland, and Ireland were merged in 1711, there was a fresh increase in efficiency; and Ralph Allen's near-half-century as a benevolent entrepreneur, systematically expanding the by- and cross-deliveries, made a daily post normal in scores of places from Truro to Haddington. Thus letter-writers in every part of the British Isles could experiment with some certainty that their labors would not go unseen. They were perhaps the more likely to take care that their letters should be long and worth reading because throughout the century the recipient had to pay the post, and might be inclined to judge rather critically what he had paid for.[2]

Luckily, the growth of these advantages followed an appropriate evolution in prose style. By this we mean not simply the emergence, during the Restoration, of the general features associated with a flexible, "natural," modern prose but also a smaller trend relating to letters as such, and based on an accumulation of published specimens, particularly French and Latin. Whereas the French models served mainly to provoke emulation, the Latin were commonplaces for critical theory. It may be significant that several volumes of French letters appeared in translation as our epoch was getting under way. Guez de Balzac had been available in English since the Commonwealth, but Dennis' and Dryden's *Voiture* appeared in

1696; Boyer's collection of *Letters of Wit* (including Bussy Rabutin) five years later; and Madame de Sévigné a couple of decades still later. Although English writers capable of imitating such works were hardly in need of translations, the appetite of less cultivated readers suggests that a new vogue was making its influence felt.

For the elegant analysis and judgment of that vogue, ancient example was important.[3] While critical dogma had not yet congealed around epistolary art, the amateur had some fairly distinct expectations, one of them being that precisely the modern, "natural" prose was the correct medium for the familiar letter. (Letters of "business," according to men of taste, had to be still less artful than personal letters; and Chesterfield blamed Temple's diplomatic correspondence as being too "affected," although "very pleasing.")

If the French exemplars mainly influenced practice, it was Cicero, Pliny, and Seneca who operated as the classic sources of theory. While these three do not represent the same tradition, they share a common element that seems more significant than any differences: from Cicero on, the whole genre may be viewed as an escape from formality, a release from the sort of rules associated with "higher" kinds of literature. Cicero himself reserved for his letters not only an informal subject matter but informal diction as well. The genre seems to start out (if we omit fabrications and pastiches like Phalaris and Lucian) as a vehicle for remarks too light or limited to deserve solemn publication; and the style, in Cicero, follows the matter in being unpretentious. Seneca disagreed with Cicero about what a letter should say, and censured him for having told Atticus to deliver whatever thoughts occurred to him. But though Seneca wished letters to be more profound, even he believed the profundities should be understated, alluded to—above all, not set forth as philosophical expositions in full dress.

Though Pliny is often taken as mediating between the practice of the other two, it seems more pertinent to observe that when the controversy about epistolary style was revived in the seventeenth century, it became part of the large argument over naturalness in prose. The issue was not whether letters should be more or less formal; neither the Ciceronians nor the Senecans had any doubt on that score. Rather, it concerned how best to achieve informality—with the Senecans objecting to the lucid but artificial organization of their opponents' work, and the Ciceronians replying that the figures and allusions in the Senecan letter were artificially abstruse, overwrought. The disagreement continues in the eighteenth century, when good and bad examples of both kinds abound. At its best, the ordinary style of a writer like Burke, logically but unobtrusively organized, seems natural enough; and if the allusive, metaphorical, associative style of Sterne may seem so too, the "nature" is certainly not the same. The whole disagreement may be seen as part of that other, still larger one concerning the proper functions of reason and imagination, with everyone agreed that each had its place but not on what the place was.

II

The best familiar letters of the eighteenth century seem distinguishable from those of earlier and later masters in that the writer revealed his own character through candid accounts of matters other than simply himself. The hallmark of candor was taken to be spontaneity. Writers so very dissimilar as Swift and Cowper, Sterne and Burke, claim along with Pope that their letters convey "thoughts just warm from the brain without any polishing or dress." Throughout the century, epistolary theory subordinated "art" to "nature," the composed to the unplanned, with an enthusiasm scarcely looked for in an age celebrated for its decorum. Johnson meant to ridicule the code when he wrote to Mrs. Thrale,

In a man's letters you know, madam, his soul lies naked, his letters are only the mirrour of his breast, whatever passes within him is shown undisguised in its natural process. Nothing is inverted, nothing distorted, you see systems in their elements, you discover actions in their motives.

Of this great truth sounded by the knowing to the ignorant, and so echoed by the ignorant to the knowing, what evidence have you now before you. Is not my soul laid open in these veracious pages? do not you see me reduced to my first principles? This is the pleasure of corresponding with a friend, where doubt and distrust have no place, and everything is said as it is thought. (27 October 1777)

But even he censured Pope for sounding "studied and artificial." The range of subscribers to the code is impressive. That Walpole, with his dilettantish leanings, should "persist in saying whatever comes uppermost" (8 October 1777) is perhaps less significant than that he echoes the great professional, Pope, who claims that his letters are "scribbled with all the carelessness and inattention imaginable" (19 November 1712).

Whatever so many writers may have meant by insisting on the spontaneous, they could not have meant the same thing. We can, of course, say that they intended nothing more than conventional acquiescence in a myth of graceful ease, or *sprezzatura,* left over from the Renaissance; and such an explanation does in fact shed some light on the apparent agreement between Walpole and Pope. But this is to say little more than that both of these writers were aware of a paradox obvious to far less perceptive men, that the effect of spontaneity is not easily achieved. Indeed, the letters that the eighteenth century judged its best are not thoughtless outpourings; their charm and their power, as well as their very appearance of spontaneity, are the result of considerable, if varied, art. And our own age, while it has wider grounds for valuing thoughtless outpourings, largely agrees with the eighteenth century that they are not good *letters.*

To appreciate the candor of the best correspondents of the period, one need only recall the immense tradition of rhetorical or pedantic epistles to be found in the literature they knew. Even limiting ourselves to the familiar letter, and setting aside epistolary travel diaries, petitions to patrons, and other articles which could be entered mechanically under the heading of *epistolae,* there remain the powerful examples of Renaissance humanists and the wit-laden efforts of their successors, where refinement of style often overpowers the revelation of self. Almost invariably the manner of such belletristic letter-writers is less expressive of a real than a deliberately shaped character, altered in accordance with a literary ideal or a didactic purpose. Sometimes a would-be domestic message consists of a brief communication embedded in a large dry ground of formulas. Sometimes an air of bright, anecdotal good nature is only the calculated mode of a request for preferment. Often the phrasing and vocabulary are carefully chosen from Ciceronian examples and intended to serve as a model for the recipient in turn to preserve, display, and imitate. A Harvey or even an Erasmus is aware that his letter will come under stylistic scrutiny, and adapts his opinions and his expression to the requirements of the style he recommends. It is striking how often the humanists' letters are either self-consciously precious or else concerned explicitly with problems of style.

Reacting against such patterns, the eighteenth-century writer liked to compare his letters with polite conversation. Only speech and gesture are more direct modes of communication than the letter. But the kind of speaking which writers of the period had in mind, when they compared their own compositions with talking to a friend, was an informed, entertaining exchange carried on between persons belonging to a circle of familiar acquaintances, who shared a common knowledge of literature, history, and what we might clumsily call social institutions. What Robert Hall said of Cowper's letters can be said with equal justice of Swift's, Lady Mary's, Gray's, Walpole's, and Chesterfield's: "To an air of inimitable ease and carelessness, they unite a high degree of correctness, such as could result only from the clearest intellect, combined with the most finished taste."[4] Discounting the hyperbole of this judgment, one accepts the analysis. If a good letter-writer had to appear candid and spontaneous, if he had to reveal his character in his manner, he was nevertheless expected to supply a substitute for the courtesy of visible gesture through the courtesy of his style, where finished periods and coherent paragraphs indicated to the recipient that the author had been at some pains to make him comfortable. Consequently, any allusiveness which implied that both persons of a correspondence were members of a select group was balanced by a degree of refinement sufficient to indicate that no undue advantage was being taken of this creditable fact. By further implication, if the carefulness of one's style suggested a proper balance between service and respect, too much casualness would have suggested some measure of insolence.

The "natural" conversation recommended as a model is therefore that of people who take particular care to speak well. Their talk makes incomparably better use of language than does that of the uncultivated. However natural it may be, it remains a social art, different from written literature but allied to it. In fact, the stress laid upon the link between familiar letters and conversation indicates as much about the artful nature of the latter as the spontaneity of the former.

Steele's letters to Prue, his wife, lie outside this definition and are close to the typical twentieth-century letter: "Sober or not, I am / Ever Yours," Steele writes in the shortest of these notes (16 February 1717)—suggesting that other means of communication had an easy priority over the one at hand, that meetings would provide the real exchange of information and argument, that the message was a gap-bridger, that in any emergency the writer could quickly appear in person before the recipient. In the course of another letter to Prue, Steele says, "Your son at the present writing is mighty well employed in tumbling on the floor of the room and sweeping the sand with a feather" (16 March 1717), an observation of the least possible interest to anyone besides the correspondents and of only transient interest to them. If Steele and Prue had been in a room together, he might have made either of these com-

cause he acts so directly himself, so regardless of the reader. One feels drawn into a vortex. One does not read because Lawrence has anecdotes and descriptions to give, but because the personality is extraordinary and is embodied in the expression. Even with his beloved Cynthia Asquith, who was sufficiently remote, in class and manners, to induce some degree of self-transcendence in Lawrence, he could rise no nearer to a comprehensive view of himself, his reader, and the emotions moving between them, than a remark like this: "Because I feel frightfully disagreeable, and not fit to consecrate myself to novels or to short stories, I'll write a letter. I like to write when I feel spiteful; it's like having a good sneeze. Don't mind, will you?"—or else this offhand dismissal of her troubles in order to get back on the track of his own: "I'm sorry you've got a cold. But what do you expect, after purpling in Venice— Frieda's been in bed . . ." (25 November 1913) .

IV

In the handling of the *tertium quid*—not self, not subject, but reader—the eighteenth-century letter-writer is perhaps most remarkable. Unlike Lawrence, his aim is not merely the incarnation of his sensibility in immediately apprehensible terms but the expressing of the self to others. A common way of marking limits is to say that the letter is bounded on one side by the essay—in which the substantive element takes over— and on the other by the confession, in which awareness of the reader is subordinated to preoccupation with self. It is of course such awareness that saves even the most personal letters of the eighteenth century from being sheer confession. Some of Cowper's letters, and parts of Sterne's *Journal to Eliza,* tend to lose this awareness, not because they fail to communicate the very real sufferings of the two men but because our insight into their suffering is not shared with them. If the intention is to communicate, the writer must lead his reader to share a point of view—he must devise a means of at least seeming to look at himself objectively.

278

Several admired letter-writers of the nineteenth century, even figures apparently so distinct from one another as Jane Welsh Carlyle and William James, seem, in their excess of responsiveness, their almost frantic exuberance (suggesting a flight from nervous depression), to blot out the recipient of the letter, making him an absorptive pad for their intellectual perspirations; a fever of observation, reaction, and self-analysis in them seems to underlie even their best anecdotes. When the ailing Mrs. Carlyle says (28 November 1856) that Geraldine Jewsbury, "if I asked for a glass of water, would spill half of it by the way, and in compensation would *drop tears on my hand* and answer me that I was 'sure to die'! and then fall to kissing me wildly (when I was, perhaps, in an interval of retching and perfectly *hating* to be kissed!) and bursting out into passionate sobs! (which of course did not prevent her from going out into company half an hour after, and being the life of it!)," one feels as uneasy about the invalid's hysteria as the nurse's. Similarly, when James, who once said he "held a descriptive letter in abhorrence" (25 August 1891), reported his visit to the Grand Canyon in an account that never leaves his own sensibility to supply a visual detail of the phenomenon (3 January 1906), his reader may have suspected that James was more interested in exploring his own consciousness than in writing to him.

Compare this manner with the various ways used by eighteenth-century letter-writers to show their awareness of their readers. Swift, for example, in writing to Stella and Rebecca Dingley, teasingly remembers the peculiarities of the way each of them walks; but in teasing he also pays pleasant attention to the unique qualities of each woman. More subtly, most of the writers of the period pay their readers the compliment of assuming that literary allusions will be recognized; thus the frequent quotations and allusions imply an awareness of reading—even of a culture—shared. In quite another way, Mme. de Sévigné leaves no doubt of the depth of her feeling upon hearing the news of her daughter's recent illness: "Il m'est impossible de me représenter l'état où vous avez été, ma bonne, sans une extrême émotion; et quoique je sache que vous en êtes quitte, Dieu merci, je ne puis tourner les yeux sur le passé sans une horreur qui me trouble" (20 June 1672). The attempt to make her emotion a thing observable by both writer and reader, an object rather than a fleeting aspect of her sensibility, is characteristic of the era. Intimate though the two women are, the letter is no mere servant of that intimacy; it is an occasion for making something independent out of it, indeed of establishing it. Her awareness of her reader dominates the letter.

Some of the methods used by the writer of the familiar letter to achieve the effect of distance from himself can be described in terms of other genres. Like several nondramatic forms, the letter borrows constantly from the drama: the writer arranges, if he can, a scene revealing the oppositions inherent in the actors as well as the reason for them. Thus the letter can take on the fascination of the theater; but this is not the only effect. The writer's very ability to present his own experience successfully in this way customarily implies an understanding of it, a perspective which the reader can accept as his own. Swift's power in the *Journal to Stella* is very remarkable. Here he is, on the verge of his great career as a political polemicist in England, dining with a cousin who has no idea of his genius or his pride:

I dined to-day with Patty Rolt at my cousin Leach's, with a pox, in the city: he is a printer, and prints the *Postman,* oh, ho, and is my cousin, God knows how, and he married Mrs. Baby Aires of Leicester; and my cousin Thomson was with us: and my cousin Leach offers to bring me acquainted with the author of the *Postman;* and says, he does not doubt but the gentleman will be glad of my acquaintance, and that he is a very ingenious man, and a great scholar, and has been beyond sea. But I was modest, and said, May be the gentleman was shy, and not fond of new acquaintance; and so put it off: and I wish you could hear me repeating all I have said of this in its proper tone, just as I am writing it. 'Tis all with the same cadence with oh hoo, or as when little girls say, I have got an apple, miss, and I won't give you some. (26 October 1710)

As this instance suggests, the drama of familiar letters is usually at least intended to be comic, because humor is the simplest way for a man to suggest that he stands outside himself. Thus the dramatic dialogue which Boswell and Sterne use so profusely in their letters presents them as heroes, more often than not, *manqués*. It is normal for the letter-writer to smile at his own mistakes.

So it is with the letter's use of epic material. Whether it is Boswell again, in the role of a fallen idol, or Walpole and Gray borrowing Miltonic language to describe the indescribable Alps, they make fun of themselves and their epic through similes that show them as conscious of their pose as we are. If Swift can achieve the grand manner and sustain it, the reason is probably his knack for disguising letters of business as familiar letters, pretending to address a lord lieutenant as a friend but really seeking preferment for a favorite; and even Swift tends to undercut himself down to size.

Certainly, the leaning of the familiar letter is toward "realism," in a sense proper to the novel of the period. As has been remarked in an earlier chapter, the letters share with the novels a detailed concern with the analysis of human character and problems of social life. It is to be expected that Richardson's personal letters would include some revelations of the dangers and difficulties of social situations for which his novels are celebrated, but what is true of his letters is more brilliantly typical of those of Lady Mary, of Walpole and of Chesterfield. Most notably, the letters of Lady Mary and her sister share the overriding concern with courtship and marriage that has dominated the novel from the eighteenth century to the twentieth. Further, the tendency of epistolary anecdote, as of the novel, is to expose the diminishing fact behind the public façade. Again Lady Mary's gossip-filled letters to Lady Mar, with their revelation of the sordid truth about elegant society, are only the best among many examples. In a different way, Johnson's extremely mundane concerns in some of his letters to his intimate friends allow the reader to glimpse a side of the great man which he would never expose in public. In yet another way, Burke's "political chat" raises gossip from the individual or merely social to the larger field of politics, but again with the frequent effect of revealing the less than noble motives and attitudes that occupy so large a place in that milieu as in others. In telling such stories, and producing the hidden motives that impelled the visible actions, the letter-writer implicitly grants himself the kind of understanding and acceptance of genuine human nature that makes his candor welcome to the reader. It is this candor, this note of spontaneous veracity—and not merely the advantage of a consistent point of view—that led the epistolary novelist to base his structure on the familiar letter.

For all its appearance of being on the edge of eighteenth-century art, without the theoretical apparatus or the prestige of established genres, the familiar letter is nevertheless accountable as the exemplary form of the period. A large claim. All that is really necessary is to recognize that the letter tried to handle the problem that occupied serious critics of literature from Pope to Johnson: how does art combine expression and objectivity, nature within and without? The answer of the form was provided only by instances, but they all reflect the profoundly social quality of the age; and their implied motto is, Know thyself by knowing others.

Indiana University and the University of Virginia

NOTES

The Correspondence of the Augustans

1. *The Correspondence of Jonathan Swift,* ed. Harold Williams, 5 vols. (Oxford, 1963-1965), II, 122. References to this edition will hereafter be cited in the text by volume and page.

Jonathan Swift

1. *Remarks on the Life and Writings of Dr. Jonathan Swift* (London, 1752), pp. 156, 176.

2. *The Correspondence of Jonathan Swift,* ed. F. Elrington Ball (London, 1910-14), III, 347-348. Because only three volumes of Harold Williams' edition of the *Correspondence* (Oxford, 1963) have thus far appeared, all quotations from Swift's letters are from Ball's edition. I have where possible compared Ball's and Williams' versions of letters quoted. Ball regularly modernizes spelling, capitalization, and punctuation; but there are no significant substantive differences in the two texts.

3. See, e.g., Swift's account to Stella of Guiscard's attempt on Harley's life (*Journal to Stella,* ed. Harold Williams [Oxford, 1948], I, 210-212), and cf. Swift's more formal account of the incident in a letter to Archbishop King (I, 238-242). David Nichol Smith notes that Swift is at his most unstudied in the letters to Ford (*The Letters of Jonathan Swift to Charles Ford* [Oxford, 1935], pp. xxvii-xxviii).

4. II, 53-54. Swift more than once used this device of enumerating trivia to emphasize the dullness of his circumstances (see, e.g., II, 164).

5. *The Prose Works of Jonathan Swift,* ed. Herbert Davis (Oxford, 1939–), X, 67; hereafter cited as *Works.*

6. "The Art of Story-Telling," *The Intelligencer,* 2nd ed. (London, 1730), pp. 163-165.

7. For these pamphlets, see *Works,* IX, 63-81; II, 43-63.

8. The pamphlet is in *Works,* IX, 85-94; the letter to Varina is in I, 31-35.

9. *Observations upon Lord Orrery's Remarks on the Life and Writings of Dr. Jonathan Swift* (London, 1754), p. 262.

10. *Works,* IV, 91; italics mine. The poem is "To Mr. Delany" (ll. 33-40), *The Poems of Jonathan Swift,* ed. Harold Williams, 2nd ed. (Oxford, 1958), I, 214-219.

11. III, 254-255. For an extended example of this kind of letter, see VI, 61-63.

12. III, 42. It should be noted that in this letter Swift was responding to Bolingbroke's description of his own life of philosophic calm (pp. 24-28)—a description which itself was more than slightly a pose.

13. *Poems,* II, 553-572 (ll. 89-94). In the proem to this poem there is another echo of the letter to Bolingbroke, when Swift envies Pope's metrical skill: "When he can in one Couplet fix / More Sense than I can do in Six" (ll. 49-50).

14. III, 282. Just as the letter to Bolingbroke later supplied Swift with details for his role in "Verses on the Death of Dr. Swift," so the misanthrope depicted in the letter to Pope later figured in another of Swift's poems, "The Life and Genuine Character of Dr. Swift" (II, 545-550). In this poem, a survivor says of the Dean, ". . . his only scope / Was, to be held a *Misanthrope*" (ll. 130-131).

15. *Letters Written by Sir William Temple, Bart.* (London, 1700), pp. [ii-iii].

ALEXANDER POPE

1. Swift to Pope, 26 February 1729/30, in *The Correspondence of Alexander Pope*, ed. George Sherburn (Oxford, 1956), III, 92. (Hereafter cited as *Correspondence*.)

2. Preface to the quarto edition of Pope's *Letters* (1737) in *Correspondence*, I, xxxix-xl.

3. In his introduction to the *Correspondence*, Professor Sherburn briefly relates the history of these publications; he also reprints (III, 458-467) "A Narrative of the Method . . .," the contemporary account—which he merely designates as "Pope-inspired" although most commentators attribute it to Pope himself—of the appearance of the 1735 letters.

4. R. H. Griffith, *Alexander Pope: A Bibliography* (Austin, Texas, 1922, 1927), I, part ii, xlvii.

5. With his acquisition in the mid-nineteenth century of the manuscript letters of Pope to Caryll, Charles Wentworth Dilke discovered the liberties that Pope had taken in "editing" his correspondence (*The Papers of a Critic* [London, 1875], I, 93 ff., with a detailed account of the publication of the letters beginning p. 287). To Dilke, and more particularly to the Rev. Mr. Elwin, Pope's Victorian editor, the poet seemed guilty of tampering, and the latter devoted the greater part of his introduction to the *Works* to an account of the printing of the letters (*The Works of Alexander Pope* [London, 1871-89], I, xxvi-cxlvii), seeing the complex of intrigue as further evidence of the turpitude of a man whose morals he was constantly calling into question. Recent judgment has been more objective; without attempting to whitewash Pope, modern commentators like Griffith and Sherburn have viewed the facts with an awareness of the unique problems of the Augustan author and with insight into Pope's special motivations.

6. To John Caryll, Sr., 19 November 1712, in *Correspondence*, I, 156.

7. Professor Sherburn cites a letter to Steele, misdated 18 June 1712, as probably the first one of Pope's to appear in print, in the *Spectator* for 16 June 1712 (*Correspondence*, I, 146-147). Shortly after, a letter to Steele on 15 July was published in *Guardian* No. 132, while one to him on 7 November of that year was printed in *Spectator* No. 532.

8. To Steele, 7 November 1712, in *Correspondence*, I, 150.

9. "Introduction," *Correspondence,* I, xv.

10. To Addison, 30 July 1713, in *Correspondence,* I, 183.

11. Maynard Mack, review of *Correspondence, PQ,* XXXVI (July 1957), 390.

12. To Lady Mary Wortley Montagu, 20 August [1716], in *Correspondence,* I, 355.

13. To Lady Mary Wortley Montagu, 18 August [1716], in *Correspondence,* I, 352-353.

14. To John Caryll, Sr., 8 July [1729], in *Correspondence,* III, 38.

15. In *Correspondence,* I, xxxix.

16. To Lady Mary Wortley Montagu [June 1717], in *Correspondence,* I, 405.

17. *Correspondence,* I, 105, 238, 353; III, 433.

18. To the Hon. Mrs. H[ervey], [1720], in *Correspondence,* II, 41-42.

19. *The Prose Works of Alexander Pope,* ed. Norman Ault (Oxford, 1936), pp. 289-290.

20. *Ibid.,* p. 292.

21. Joseph Spence, *Anecdotes . . .,* ed. Singer and intro. Dobrée (London, 1964), pp. 118-119.

22. To Henry Cromwell, 21 August 1710, in *Correspondence,* I, 97.

23. To Henry Cromwell, 24 June 1710, in *Correspondence,* I, 90. For a discussion of the influence of Voiture on Pope, and on Wycherley, see E. Audra, *L'Influence Française dans l'Œuvre de Pope* (Paris, 1931), pp. 315 ff.

24. Swift to Pope, 26 February 1729/30, in *Correspondence,* III, 92.

25. To William Fortescue, 17 August 1739, in *Correspondence,* IV, 193.

26. Wycherley specifically cites Voiture in two of the letters to Pope (*Correspondence,* I, 34, 53), and the influence of his contrived wit pervades all this correspondence.

27. To Wycherley, 26 October 1705, in *Correspondence,* I, 11.

28. To Swift, 28 November 1729, in *Correspondence,* III, 79.

29. See, for example, Irvin Ehrenpreis, "Personae," *Restoration and Eighteenth-Century Literature: Essays in Honor of Alan Dugald McKillop,* ed. Carroll Camden (Chicago, 1963), pp. 25-37.

30. To John Caryll, Sr., 22 June 1716, in *Correspondence,* I, 343-344.

31. As when he writes to Caryll about some poems by his grandson—"I would rather see him a good man than a good poet; and yet a good poet is no small thing, and (I believe) no small earnest to his being a good man." (*Correspondence,* III, 340.)

32. To the Earl of Marchmont, 10 October 1741, in *Correspondence,* IV, 364.

33. Maynard Mack, " 'The Shadowy Cave': Some Speculations on a Twickenham Grotto," *Restoration and Eighteenth-Century Literature,* p. 86.

34. Reuben Arthur Brower, *Alexander Pope: The Poetry of Allusion* (Oxford, 1959), pp. 164-165.

35. *Ibid.*, p. 182.

36. Swift to Pope, [June] 1737, in *Correspondence*, IV, 77.

37. Swift to Pope, 1 June 1728, in *Correspondence*, II, 497.

38. Lines 212 ff. of "Dialogue II" of the *Epilogue to the Satires* of course come to mind, but one might also cite a letter to Swift: "That I am an Author whose characters are thought of some weight, appears from the great noise and bustle that the Court and Town make about any I give: and I will not render them less important or interesting, by sparing Vice and Folly, or by betraying the cause of Truth and Virtue. I will take care they shall be such as no man can be angry at but the persons I would have angry. You are sensible with what decency and justice I paid homage to the Royal Family, at the same time that I satirized false Courtiers, and Spies, &c. about 'em. I have not the courage however to be such a Satyrist as you, but I would be as much, or more, a Philosopher. You call your satires, Libels; I would rather call my satires, Epistles: They will consist more of morality than wit, and grow graver, which you will call duller. I shall leave it to my Antagonists to be witty (if they can) and content myself to be useful, and in the right." (*Correspondence*, III, 365-366.)

39. Maynard Mack reviews some of these diatribes in "The Muse of Satire," *Yale Review*, XLI (1951), 80-92.

40. Review of *Correspondence* (see note 11 above), p. 394.

41. Swift to Pope, 31 October 1729, in *Correspondence*, III, 65.

42. There is a charming note from Bolingbroke addressed "To the three Yahoos of Twittenham," in *Correspondence*, II, 383-384.

43. To Swift, 12 October 1738, in *Correspondence*, IV, 134.

44. To Lady Mary Wortley Montagu, 20 August [1716], in *Correspondence*, I, 356-357.

45. Edward, Earl of Oxford to Pope, 25 September 1724, in *Correspondence*, II, 261.

46. *Lives of the English Poets*, ed. G. B. Hill (Oxford, 1905), III, 160.

47. Lady Mary Wortley Montagu to Pope, [September] 1718, in *Correspondence*, I, 522-524.

48. To Swift, 2 October 1727, in *Correspondence*, II, 447.

49. To Lord Bathurst, [1725?], in *Correspondence*, II, 292.

50. To Richard Nash, [? April 1739], in *Correspondence*, IV, 170.

51. To John Caryll, Sr., 19 April 1714, in *Correspondence*, I, 218-219.

52. To Martha and Teresa Blount, 17 September [1718], in *Correspondence*, I, 512.

53. To Mrs. Henrietta Howard, 20 June [1727], in *Correspondence*, II, 435.

54. To the Earl of Burlington, [?1741], in *Correspondence*, IV, 323.

55. To William Fortescue, 5 August [1727], in *Correspondence*, II, 441.

56. To Martha Blount, 4 September [1728], in *Correspondence*, II, 513-514.

57. To Jonathan Richardson, 21 November [1743], in *Correspondence,* IV, 484.

58. To Lords Marchmont and Bolingbroke, [January 1743/4], in *Correspondence,* IV, 490-491.

59. To Hugh Bethel, 20 February [1743/4], in *Correspondence,* IV, 499.

LADY MARY WORTLEY MONTAGU

1. In this slightly revised version of a paper read at the Conference on Eighteenth-Century Letter-Writers at Indiana University in 1964, all quotations from Lady Mary's letters are taken from the manuscripts, some of them previously unpublished, and are normalized. My three-volume edition of her *Complete Letters* (Clarendon Press) prints the full texts in literal transcription. Lady Mary's four correspondences previously unknown are those with Philippa Mundy, James Stuart Mackenzie, Chiara (Bragadin) Michiel, and Francesco Algarotti.

Her periodical *The Nonsense of Common-Sense* (1737-38) was edited by me in 1947. Some of her miscellaneous prose is printed in her *Letters and Works,* ed. Lord Wharncliffe and W. Moy Thomas (1861), vol. II. Other newly discovered writings are discussed in my biography *The Life of Lady Mary Wortley Montagu* (1956).

SAMUEL RICHARDSON

1. Richardson to the Reverend Johannes Stinstra, cited in Alan Dugald McKillop, *The Early Masters of English Fiction* (Lawrence, Kansas, 1956), pp. 47-51.

2. *The Correspondence of Samuel Richardson,* ed. Anna Laetitia Barbauld (London, 1804), I, xxxvii.

3. Cited by McKillop, *Early Masters,* p. 49.

4. *Ibid.,* p. 48.

5. *Correspondence,* I, clxxxi.

6. Cited by Brian W. Downs, *Richardson* (London, 1928), p. 47.

7. *Correspondence,* I, iii-iv.

8. *Ibid.,* VI, 24.

9. *Ibid.,* IV, 21-22.

10. Leslie Stephen, "Richardson's Novels," in *Hours in a Library* (New York, 1904), I, 88.

11. *The Rice Institute Pamphlet,* XXXVIII (April 1951), 36-54.

12. *Correspondence,* IV, 121-122.

13. *Ibid.,* III, 245.

14. Everyman Edition, II, 431.

15. *Correspondence,* VI, 187.

16. In *The Providence of Wit in the English Letter Writers* (Durham, N.C., 1955), William Henry Irving devotes less than two pages to Richardson

and observes that in his letters to his friends "he is straightforward in style and a bit dull" (p. 271).

17. *Correspondence,* II, 245.

18. *Ibid.,* I, 165.

19. *Ibid.,* II, 223-224.

20. *Ibid.,* II, 199.

21. *Ibid.,* II, 220-221.

22. *Ibid.,* II, 203-204.

23. *Ibid.,* II, 237-238.

24. *Ibid.,* IV, 141.

25. *Ibid.,* III, 299-300.

26. *Ibid.,* IV, 110-111.

27. *Ibid.,* I, cl-clii. The relevant passages in Lady Bradshaigh's letter appear in VI, 281-282.

28. *Ibid.,* II, 206.

29. *Ibid.,* IV, 181.

30. *Ibid.,* IV, 182.

31. *Ibid.,* IV, 200-201.

32 *Samuel Richardson, Printer and Novelist* (Chapel Hill, N.C., 1936), p. 203.

33. *Ibid.,* p. 203.

34. *Correspondence,* I, ccviii.

35. *Ibid.,* IV, 342-343.

36. *Ibid.,* IV, 378.

37. *Ibid.,* V, 30.

38. *Ibid.,* VI, 23. The portrait is reproduced as the frontispiece to Paul Dottin's *Samuel Richardson* (Paris, 1931).

THE EARL OF CHESTERFIELD

For convenience of reference, Bonamy Dobrée's standard edition of *The Letters of Philip Dormer Stanhope, 4th Earl of Chesterfield* (London, 1932, 6 vols.) is mentioned below as *Letters.* To aid readers who possess other editions, the dates of letters are also given.

1. *Letters to his Son,* 9th ed. (London, 1787), I, 33 (4 October 1738).

2. *Ibid.,* I, 109 (Isleworth, July). Cf. John Tavernier, *The Newest and Most Compleat Polite Familiar Letter Writer,* 4th ed. (Berwick, 1768), p. 3: "Letter writing is but a sort of literary conversation, and that you are to write to the person absent, in the manner you would speak to him, if present."

3. *Ibid.*

4. *Letters,* p. 1799 (19 December O.S. 1751).

5. See note 1.

6. *Letters,* p. 968 (20 July O.S. 1747).

7. *Letters,* p. 2104 (26 March 1754).

8. *Letters*, pp. 1233-1234 (27 September O.S. 1748).

9. Mcrcdith Read, *Historic Studies in Vaud, Berne, and Savoy* (London, 1897), I, 400-401. For comment, see C. Price, "Some New Light on Chesterfield," *Neuphilologische Mitteilungen*, LIV (1953), 279.

10. *Letters*, p. 732 (18 February 1746).

11. *Letters*, p. 2022 (25 May 1753).

12. *Letters*, p. 2529 (12 August 1763).

13. *Letters*, p. 2575 (31 December 1763).

14. *Letters*, p. 2058 (16 November 1753).

15. *Letters*, p. 1492 (18 January N.S. 1750).

16. *Letters*, p. 2910 (30 January 1770).

17. *Letters*, p. 290 (2 November 1734).

18. A. M. Broadley, *Chats on Autographs* (London, 1910), p. 183.

19. *Letters*, p. 2880 (16 March 1769).

20. *The Life and Times of Selina, Countess of Huntingdon* (London, 1839), II, 379. For comment, see C. Price, "Further Chesterfield Gleanings," *Neuphilologische Mitteilungen*, LVI (1955), 116-118.

21. *Letters*, p. 1581 (24 September O.S. 1750).

22. *Letters*, p. 771 (23 September 1746).

23. *Letters*, p. 1545 (24 May O.S. 1750).

24. *Letters*, pp. 1066-1067 (11 December O.S. 1747).

25. *Letters*, p. 2091 (26 February 1754).

26. *Letters*, p. 504 (28 June 1742).

27. *Letters*, p. 1617 (15 November O.S. 1750).

28. *Letters*, p. 890 (27 March O.S. 1747).

29. For text and comment, see C. Price, "One of Chesterfield's Letters to his Son," *TLS*, 1 July 1955, p. 572.

30. *Letters*, pp. 442-443 (Sunday); pp. 435-436 *(Jeudi soir)*.

31. 1688. Printed in his *Miscellanies* (1704), pp. 1-84.

32. *Miscellanies*, p. 2.

33. *Ibid.*, p. 6.

34. *Ibid.*, pp. 67, 64.

35. *Letters*, p. 1799 (19 December O.S. 1751).

36. *Ibid.*

37. *Letters*, p. 2070 (1 January 1754).

38. *Private Correspondence of Chesterfield and Newcastle, 1744-1746*, ed. R. Lodge (London, 1930), p. v.

39. *Letters*, pp. 589-590 (30 March N.S. 1745).

40. *Letters*, p. 572 (12 March N.S. 1745).

41. *Letters*, p. 2383 (26 October 1761).

42. C. Price, "Five Unpublished Letters of Lord Chesterfield," *Life and Letters*, LIX (1948), No. 134, p. 6.

43. *Letters*, p. 771 (23 September 1746).

44. S. L. Gulick, Jr., *A Chesterfield Bibliography to 1800* (Chicago, 1935), pp. 4-7.

45. See the unpublished dissertation (Chicago, 1925) by Virgil B. Heltzel, "Chesterfield and the Tradition of the Ideal Gentleman," *passim*.

46. Quoted from Cibber's *Apology*, ed. Lowe (London, 1889), I, 14-15, by R. Coxon, *Chesterfield and his Critics* (London, 1925), p. 181.

47. *Letters*, p. 1442 (24 November O.S. 1749).

48. *Letters*, p. 1468 (19 December O.S. 1749).

49. *Letters*, p. 1457 (9 December O.S. 1749).

50. *Letters*, p. 1400 (22 September O.S. 1749).

51. *The London Packet*, 17-20 February 1775.

52. *Letters*, p. 1680 (11 February O.S. 1751).

53. *Letters*, p. 1245 (19 October O.S. 1748).

54. *Letters*, p. 1599 (1 November O.S. 1750).

55. *Letters*, p. 1381 (10 August O.S. 1749).

56. *Letters*, p. 1745 (6 June O.S. 1751).

57. *Letters*, p. 2221 (28 February 1757).

58. *Letters*, pp. 2067-2068 (29 December 1753).

59. Dryden, *All for Love*, IV, i.; *Letters*, p. 1209 (5 September O.S. 1748).

60. John Boyle, 5th Earl of Orrery, *Orrery Papers* (London, 1903), II, 178-179.

61. *Letters*, pp. 1457-1458 (9 December O.S. 1749).

SAMUEL JOHNSON

1. Sir Walter Raleigh, ed., *Johnson on Shakespeare* (Oxford, 1908; reprinted 1931), Preface, pp. xxix, xxxi.

2. R. W. Chapman, ed., *The Letters of Samuel Johnson* (Oxford, 1952). Throughout this paper I shall cite the letters by giving Chapman's reference numbers in parentheses in my text.

3. *Boswell's Life of Johnson*, ed. G. B. Hill, rev. L. F. Powell (Oxford, 1934-50), II, 474.

4. Boswell's *Life*, III, 181.

5. Katharine C. Balderston, "Johnson's Vile Melancholy," *The Age of Johnson* (New Haven, 1949), pp. 3-14.

LAURENCE STERNE

1. *Letters of Laurence Sterne*, ed. Lewis P. Curtis (Oxford, 1935), p. 117. Citations from Sterne's letters are to this edition, and will hereafter be noted parenthetically in the text. (Some important recently discovered letters are printed in *TLS*, April 8, 1965, p. 284. And see *TLS*, May 6, 1965, p. 356.)

2. Ed. James A. Work (New York, 1940), p. 540. Citations from *Tristram Shandy* are to this edition.

3. Sterne's habit of re-using his own phrases makes hazardous Professor Curtis's reliance upon "quotation" as a means of detecting forgeries. See his essay, "Forged Letters of Laurence Sterne," *PMLA*, L (1935), 1076-1106.

4. See for instance: repetition, Curtis, pp. 117 and 120, 329 and 342; factual distortion, pp. 81 and 87; a letter which he improves before sending, p. 99.

5. While my emphasis in this paper is on the novelty of Sterne's style in contrast with that of many other eighteenth-century writers, his methods owe a great deal to such anti-Ciceronians as Montaigne, Browne, and Burton. Like these earlier writers, and the Latin anti-Ciceronians from whom they in turn derive, Sterne used one rhetoric to show that another kind misrepresented human experience.

6. Henri Fluchère, *Laurence Sterne, de l'homme à l'œuvre* (Paris, 1961), p. 214.

7. See Lydia's letter to Mrs. Montagu: Curtis, p. 434.

8. It would be particularly interesting to see more of his letters to Hall-Stevenson, of which Sterne remarked, "He has recᵈ hundreds, they have been wrote most of 'em in too careless a way" (p. 407).

9. See note 3.

10. It is worth noting that just before writing two letters aping the "John-Trot-Style" Sterne had received condescending epistles from Bishop Warburton, both of which begin with the formula Sterne mocks. See Curtis, pp. 112, 118.

11. On this subject, see particularly John Traugott, *Tristram Shandy's World: A Study of Sterne's Philosophical Rhetoric* (Berkeley and Los Angeles, 1954).

12. "Sterne Épistolier," *Revue Anglo-Américaine*, XIII (1936), 299.

13. For contrasting interpretations (which stress the conscious and artful elements) of the *Journal to Eliza,* see especially Rufus Putney, "Laurence Sterne, Apostle of Laughter," in *The Age of Johnson: Essays Presented to Chauncey Brewster Tinker* (New Haven, 1949), pp. 159-170; A. D. McKillop, *The Early Masters of English Fiction* (Lawrence, Kansas, 1956); and see the remarks of Richard Griffith on the "Platonic" nature of Sterne's affair with Eliza (cited in Curtis, p. 306, n. 2).

HORACE WALPOLE

1. R. W. Ketton-Cremer, *Horace Walpole: A Biography,* 2nd ed. (London, 1946), pp. 113-120.

2. I have used *The Yale Edition of Horace Walpole's Correspondence* (New Haven, 1937–) wherever possible. For a thorough study of Walpole one must still refer to the Toynbee edition, which is not as fully annotated and does not contain letters from the correspondents to Walpole.

3. *Essay on Criticism,* II, 362-363.

291

4. John Pinkerton, ed., *Walpoliana,* 2nd ed. (London, 1804), I, i-ix.

5. *Ibid.,* pp. i-ii.

6. To West, 28 September 1739 N.S.

7. To his Mother, 13 October 1739 N.S.; To West, 16 November 1739 N.S.

8. To Chute, 20 August 1743 O.S.

9. To Montagu, 13 November 1760.

10. To Mann, 21 August 1746 O.S.

11. To Mann, 20 March 1747 O.S.

12. To Montagu, 28 January 1760.

13. To Mann, 2 April 1750 O.S.

14. To Montagu, 2 February 1762.

15. To Robertson, 4 February 1759.

16. To Montagu, 8 December 1761.

17. To Montagu, 28 January 1760.

18. To Lincoln, 5 September 1744 O.S.

EDMUND BURKE

A four-volume selection of Burke's letters was published in 1844, under the title *The Correspondence of Edmund Burke,* by Earl Fitzwilliam and Sir Richard Bourke. A new and complete edition (with the same title) is being prepared under the general editorship of Thomas W. Copeland. Of the projected ten volumes five have appeared (Cambridge University Press and University of Chicago Press, 1958-65, containing letters for the years 1744-89. Whenever possible, this edition has been used. In the notes below, the 1844 selection is referred to as "F. & B.," the modern edition as "TWC."

1. *Letters of William Cowper,* ed. J. G. Frazer (London, 1912), I, 81.

2. TWC, I, 39.

3. *Ibid.,* I, 101.

4. *Ibid.,* I, 22.

5. *Ibid.,* I, 111.

6. *Ibid.,* I, 354-355.

7. *Ibid.,* I, 356.

8. *The Letters of David Garrick,* ed. David M. Little and George M. Kahrl (Cambridge, Mass., 1963), II, 702-703.

9. TWC, I, 171-172.

10. *Letters,* I, 332.

11. *The Works of Edmund Burke* (Bohn, London, 1854-89), II, 279— hereafter cited as *Works.*

12. TWC, I, 108.

13. *Boswell's Life of Samuel Johnson,* ed. G. B. Hill; rev. L. F. Powell (Oxford, 1934), IV, 276.

14. F. & B., III, 480.

15. *Ibid.*, III, 133.

16. *Johnsonian Miscellanies,* ed. G. Birkbeck Hill (London, 1897), I, 426.

17. *The Memoirs of the Life of Edward Gibbon,* ed. G. Birkbeck Hill (London, 1900), p. 201.

18. F. & B., IV, 199.

19. TWC, II, 371.

20. *Ibid.,* I, 285.

21. *The Correspondence of Alexander Pope,* ed. George Sherburn (Oxford, 1956), I, 160.

22. TWC, II, 5.

23. *Ibid.,* III, 389.

24. *Ibid.,* III, 388-389.

25. *Ibid.,* II, 82.

26. *Ibid.,* II, 155.

27. *Correspondence,* I, 155.

28. *Works,* I, 378-379.

29. TWC, IV, 140.

30. *Letters,* I, 216.

31. TWC, IV, 448.

32. *Works,* I, 372.

33. TWC, IV, 261.

34. *Works,* I, 375.

35. F. & B., III, 149.

36. *Ibid.,* III, 173.

37. TWC, III, 457.

38. *Ibid.,* II, 253.

39. *Ibid.,* II, 255.

40. *Ibid.,* II, 257.

41. *Ibid.,* II, 128.

42. *Ibid.,* II, 258.

43. *Ibid.,* II, 281-282.

44. F. & B., IV, 149.

45. TWC, IV, 405-418.

46. F. & B., III, 137-138.

47. *Ibid.,* III, 108 ff.

48. TWC, III, 431-436; IV, 83-88.

49. *Ibid.,* IV, 70.

50. *Ibid.,* III, 89; IV, 79-80.

51. *Ibid.,* II, 491.

52. F. & B., III, 82.

53. For a rare example see F. & B., III, 358: "I know nothing of the pamphlet of the— (hang it, I forget his name) on a counter-revolution."

54. TWC, II, 286, 316, 336; III, 67-68, 196.

55. See James T. Boulton, *The Language of Politics in the Age of Wilkes and Burke* (London, 1963), pp. 125-126. (It is worth noting that the Popeian misquotation—"But soft—by regular degrees, not yet"—in the *Reflections* is anticipated by an allusion in a letter of 1779: ". . . fair and softly, and by degrees," TWC, IV, 76.)

56. TWC, II, 377. (For an explanation of Burke's reference to the "Rolls Chappel" see the earlier letter, TWC, II, 224.)

57. *Ibid.,* II, 43.

58. *Works,* II, 334.

59. TWC, III, 434.

60. *Ibid.,* III, 281.

61. *Ibid.,* IV, 197.

62. *Ibid.,* III, 40.

63. *Ibid.,* IV, 296.

64. F. & B., III, 510.

65. *Ibid.,* IV, 276.

66. TWC, I, 318.

67. *Ibid.,* IV, 295.

68. F. & B., IV, 433.

69. *Works,* II, 473.

70. *Ibid.,* II, 549.

71. TWC, IV, 234.

WILLIAM COWPER

1. William Cowper, *The Correspondence of William Cowper,* ed. Thomas Wright (London, 1904). Subsequent references to this work are indicated in the text by volume and page number enclosed in parentheses.

2. Since his third mental collapse in January, 1773.

3. Theodora Cowper, Lady Hesketh's sister, with whom Cowper had been in love in his youth.

4. Cowper's house at Olney.

5. Cowper was referring to style in writing sermons when he made these observations, but the inference beyond the specific seems clearly justified. He adhered to the "plain and neat" style in his own letter-writing and gives affectation as his reason for his dislike of Pope's letters.

6. The windows of the draper's house where it was originally proposed Lady Hesketh should stay.

7. *Selected Letters of William Cowper,* ed. Mark Van Doren (New York, 1951), p. 16.

EDWARD GIBBON

1. All references to the letters will be indicated by volume and page of *The Letters of Edward Gibbon,* ed. J. E. Norton (New York, 1956).

2. *The Autobiography of Edward Gibbon,* ed. Dero A. Saunders (New York, 1961), p. 82.

3. *The Autobiographies of Edward Gibbon,* ed. John Murray (London, 1896), p. 342. The date of the note can be established as follows. Gibbon dated draft E at the end, March 2, 1791. But the MS shows extensive additions made at a different time from the original draft of the passages concerned. The notes, including the notes for such additions, are numbered and added consecutively. Therefore the notes were written after the additions, which were written after the draft was completed.

4. Anna Robeson Burr, *The Autobiography* (Boston, 1909), p. 312.

5. *Edward Gibbon 1737-1794* (London, 1937), pp. 90-91.

6. Low, p. 349.

7. *Autobiography,* p. 49.

8. *Autobiography,* p. 149.

9. "summer" in MS.

10. Miss Norton explains that Gibbon's refusal to ride had prevented his accompanying his friends on excursions while visiting Lausanne.

JAMES BOSWELL

Abbreviated titles have been used for works referred to more than twice:
Boswell for the Defence
> *Boswell for the Defence, 1769-1774.* Edited by William K. Wimsatt, Jr. and Frederick A. Pottle, New York: McGraw-Hill Book Company, Inc., 1960.

Germany and Switzerland
> *Boswell on the Grand Tour: Germany and Switzerland, 1764.* Edited by Frederick A. Pottle, New York: McGraw-Hill Book Company, Inc., 1953.

Letters
> *Letters of James Boswell.* Collected and edited by Chauncey Brewster Tinker, 2 vols., Oxford: The Clarendon Press, 1924.

London Journal
> *Boswell's London Journal, 1762-1763.* Edited by Frederick A. Pottle, New York: McGraw-Hill Book Company, Inc., 1950.

1. *Letters,* I, 32.

2. *London Journal* (copyright 1950 by McGraw-Hill Book Company; this and following quotations by special permission), p. 326.

3. *Boswell's Life of Johnson,* ed. George Birkbeck Hill and rev. L. F. Powell (Oxford, 1934-1950), III, 57, and n. 3.

4. Insofar as letters were considered written conversation, they too might be considered subject to rules of proportion. Boswell thought it absurd to stand upon ceremony in correspondence with close friends and wrote to Temple: "When we are together we never think of parcelling out our sentences in a reciprocal proportion. At least I dare say that in general I speak three

sentences for one of yours. Why then should I think that written conversation should be managed so very differently?" (*Letters*, I, 26-27.)

5. *London Journal,* p. 241 n. 1.

6. *Letters,* I, 223.

7. *Letters,* I, 155.

8. Letters/ Between/ the Honourable/ Andrew Erskine,/ and/ James Boswell, Esq;/London:/ Printed by Samuel Chandler,/ For W. Flexney, near Gray's-Inn-Gate, Holborn./ MDCCLXIII. The letters were actually written in 1761 and 1762.

9. *Ibid.,* p. 132.

10. *Boswell on the Grand Tour: Italy, Corsica, and France, 1765-1766,* ed. Frank Brady and Frederick A. Pottle (New York: McGraw-Hill Book Company, Inc., 1955), p. 288. Quoted by permission of the publisher.

11. *London Journal,* p. 108.

12. *Letters,* II, 313.

13. *Letters,* I, 192-193.

14. *Letters,* I, 84, 90.

15. *Boswell for the Defence* (copyright 1960 by McGraw-Hill Book Company; this and following quotations by special permission), p. 151.

16. Obviously the exchange between Boswell and Goldsmith may be thought of as written conversation (see note 4), but eighteenth-century drama is replete with repartee, and Boswell's handling of group conversations in the *Life,* for example, usually suggests careful staging. The point is that Boswell sees situations like this as dramatic ones.

17. *Letters,* I, 111.

18. *Germany and Switzerland* (copyright 1953 by McGraw-Hill Book Company; this and following by special permission), p. 235.

19. *Germany and Switzerland,* p. 290.

20. *Germany and Switzerland,* pp. 293-294.

21. *Letters,* I, 139-140.

22. *Boswell in Search of a Wife, 1766-1769,* ed. Frank Brady and Frederick A. Pottle (New York: McGraw-Hill Book Company, Inc., 1956: this and following quotations by special permission), pp. 3-5.

23. *Letters,* I, 45-46.

24. Cited also in *Boswell for the Defence,* p. 17.

25. *Letters,* II, 374.

26. *London Journal,* p. 192.

27. *Boswell for the Defence,* p. 222.

28. *Letters,* II, 283.

29. *Letters,* II, 397.

30. *Germany and Switzerland,* p. 37.

31. W. H. Auden, "Young Boswell," *New Yorker,* XXVI (Nov. 25, 1950), 146-148.

32. *Letters,* II, 353.

33. *Letters,* II, 445.

34. *London Journal,* p. 181.

35. *Letters,* I, 160.

36. *Letters,* II, 432.

37. Brady and Pottle, *Boswell in Search of a Wife, 1766-1769,* pp. 187, 189.

38. *Letters,* I, 72.

39. *Private Papers of James Boswell from Malahide Castle in the Collection of Lt.-Col. Ralph Heyward Isham,* ed. Geoffrey Scott and Frederick A. Pottle (Mount Vernon, N. Y., 1928-34), XVIII, 318-319; used by permission of McGraw-Hill Book Company, present owners of the copyright.

THE FAMILIAR LETTER IN THE EIGHTEENTH CENTURY

1. Howard Robinson, *The British Post Office* (Princeton, N. J., 1948), p. 81.

2. R. W. Chapman, "The Course of Post in the Eighteenth Century," *Notes and Queries,* CLXXXIII (August 1, 1942), 67-69.

3. It is pleasing to observe one Latin treatise offering early homage to the greatest vernacular artist, Mme. de Sévigné, in R. P. Hervé-Claude de Montaigu's poem *Ratio conscribendae epistolae* (1713).

4. Letter of 19 August 1823, to John Johnson, in Cowper's *Private Correspondence,* ed. Johnson (London, 1824), I, xiii.

5. *The Age of Erasmus* (Oxford, 1914), p. 209.

INDEX

Addison, Joseph: Pope's fabricated letter to, 37; Walpole on, 168, 169-70, 182; mentioned, 53, 244

Algarotti, Francesco: affair with Lady Mary, 54; Lady Mary's letters to, 54-57; dialogues on *Optics* of, 57

Allen, P. S.: on Erasmus' letters, 276

Arbuthnot, John: letter-writing style of, 3, 45; and Swift, 3, 4-5, 26

Arnold, Matthew: on Gray, 149-50

Asquith, Cynthia, 278

Atterbury, Francis, Bishop of Rochester: and Pope, 44, 46

Atticus, 93, 271

Auden, W. H.: on Boswell, 263-64

Augustans, 41, 43, 110, 134; correspondence of, 1-13 *passim*

Austen, Lady, 214-15

Bagehot, Walter: on Lady Mary, 61

Bagot, the Rev. Walter, 219

Balderston, Katherine C.: on Johnson, 117

Balmerino, Lord, 179

Balzac, Guez de, 50, 270

Barbauld, Anna L. (editor of Richardson's letters), 72, 73, 86, 89

Barber, Francis, 126

Baretti, Giuseppe Marc' Antonio, 111, 122

Barry, James, 193-95, 197

Bath, 95-96

Bathurst, Lord, 20, 46

Belfour. *See* Bradshaigh, Lady

Berkeley, Countess of, 21

Berkeley, Earl of, 8

Besborough, Lady, 184

Biographers: value of letters to, 2, 148-51

Blair, Catherine, 256

Blount, Martha, 6

Bolingbroke, Lady, 5

Bolingbroke, Lord, 5, 14, 16-17, 26, 27-28, 30, 44

Bono, Signora Laura, 62-63

Bonstetten, Charles-Victor de, 153, 162-63

Boswell, James: compared with literary contemporaries, 245, 252, 255; literary letters of, 245, 248-52; social letters of, 245, 246-48; letter-journal relationship, 246, 252, 261-62; quest for identity of, 246, 265, 266, 268; imitates Sterne, 249, 265; ambition of, 251-52, 260-61, 263-66, 268; and Goldsmith, 251-52, 265, 296n*16*; correspondence with cele-brated persons, 251-52, 260-61, 265; modern readers and, 252; romantic interests of, 256-58; W. H. Auden on, 263-64; mentioned, 110, 122, 158, 163

—style of intimate letters: intrusion of self in, 244-56 *passim*, 260-61, 267, 268; as record of his psyche, 245-46, 252, 255-56, 260-61, 264-68; use of dramatic techniques in, 246, 248, 253-59 *passim*, 263-66, 268, 281, 296n*16*; changes of moods in, 247, 258-60; Boswell on, 253-54, 267, 295n*4*; sense of significant detail in, 255, 268

—subjects in intimate letters: Dr. Taylor, 112; Corsica, 247-48; Rousseau, 253, 260-61; Voltaire, 253-56, 259, 265; funeral of his wife, 259-60; Zélide, 263

—and Samuel Johnson: correspondence of, 110, 122-25, 190, 247-48; relationship, 116, 122, 123-25, 170, 244-45, 265, 267, 268; trip to Hebrides, 118-19, 122-23

—*Life of Johnson*, 109, 122, 153, 170-71, 257, 262

—correspondents: Lady Northumberland, 249-50, 265; Mrs. Thrale, 250-51; John Johnston, 253, 260-61; his son, Alexander, 267-68. *See also* Temple, William Johnson

Botham, John (Mrs. Laurence Sterne's brother-in-law), 136

Bourke, John, 207

Boyle, John. *See* Orrery, Earl of

Bradshaigh, Lady, 74, 79, 86-91

Brower, Reuben: on Pope, 42-43

Brown, James: on Gray, 149

Burke, Edmund: personal letters of, 186-88, 189, 190-91, 193-95; letters to political associates, 190-95, 196-209 *passim*; and Garrick, 187-90, 196; Johnson on, 190; his son on, 191; as "*Novus Homo*," 192-93, 201, 205-06; letters to Rockingham group, 192-207 *passim*; use of letter form in published writings, 193, 202; letters of echo philosophy, 195, 197, 201-02, 206; on disintegration of family ties, 199-200; and Junius letters, 200-02; late letters of, 203; Gibbon on, 228-29

—letter-writing style: Burke on, 186-96 *passim*, 198, 204, 209, 272; compared with other eighteenth-century writers, 186, 187-90, 191, 192, 194; seriousness of, 186-91, 195, 196-98; careful use of language, 188, 191, 194-95, 207, 272;

299